THE ROMAN IRON INDUSTRY IN BRITAIN

THE ROMAN IRON INDUSTRY IN BRITAIN

DAVID SIM

Front cover image: Pyramid balista *bolts from Vindolanda.*
Copyright The Vindolanda Trust

First published 2002
This edition published 2012

The History Press
The Mill, Brimscombe Port
Stroud, Gloucestershire, GL5 2QG
www.thehistorypress.co.uk

British Library Cataloguing in Publication Data.
A catalogue record for this book is available from the British Library.

ISBN 978 0 7524 6865 5

Typesetting and origination by The History Press
Printed in Great Britain

CONTENTS

LIST OF ILLUSTRATIONS AND TABLES

Text figures

Colour plates

Tables

ACKNOWLEDGEMENTS

Writing a book is a great undertaking, and one which could have only been achieved with the help and support of my family, friends and colleagues. I would like to extend my thanks to the following individuals and organisations for making this volume possible: Dr Henry Blythe and Dr Alan Williams; John Frew for his cheerful help with sample preparation, testing and photography over the years; Barry Winfield, Heather and Owen Hazelby, and Laura Dodd.

Alan Wilkins for his help with the classical texts; Cohort Secundo Augusta and David Richardson for their generous permission to reproduce **colour plates 10, 11, 15, 21** and **22**, The Roman Military Research Society for kindly allowing the use of **colour plates 16** and **17**; Alan Wilkins and Len Morgan for their expert advice on *ballistas*; the Trustees of the National Museums of Scotland for kindly allowing the use of figure **19**; Robin and Pat Birley and the Vindolanda Trust for generously permitting the examination of various Roman iron artefacts over the years, and for the use of **colour plates 12, 13** and **18** and figures **40** and **46**; and Dr Mike Bishop for allowing the use of his collection of museum data published in the Appendix. I would also like to acknowledge the financial support for the some of the research reported here received from the Leverhulme Trust.

There are many others who have been involved in differing ways with the preparation of this book and while it has not been possible to name them all and list their kindnesses individually, their support is also gratefully recognised.

Special acknowledgement and thanks are made to the following: Dr Jamie Kaminski for his expert knowledge of the Roman charcoal industry, who has contributed the chapter on charcoal production, and additionally assisted with the preparation of the manuscript; Professor Michael Fulford for his support and guidance; and Professor Richard Chaplin for allowing the use of the facilities in the Department of Engineering.

FOREWORD

The inspiration for this book was the desire to produce a single volume, which covered the whole Roman-iron making process, from the first stage of finding the ore right through to the completion of the artefact. Other books have been written focusing in great detail upon some aspect or another of iron production in antiquity, and these have provided valuable sources of information. In order to keep to a manageable size, I have chosen to focus on the British iron industry, although due reference is made to the influence of the rest of the Roman empire where appropriate. Similarly, I have adopted as a theme the production of the familiar arms and armour of a Roman soldier. The basic techniques used in the production of these items will however be the same for all iron artefacts.

This book does not claim to be the final word on its topic; many aspects of the Roman iron industry are the subject of current study by experimental archaeologists, archaeologists, archeometallurgists and classicists, and new information is becoming available all the time. This study probably raises as many questions as it answers. I have highlighted the huge amount that is not known, and discuss some alternative procedures to the traditionally held views of production. It is hoped that, as well as giving information and pleasure, this book may stimulate some readers to join the group who work on this fascinating subject, and so help provide answers to the many problems that remain unsolved.

It has been difficult to strike a balance between saturating the text with references, making it unreadable in the process, and giving due credit to the many other researchers. I have aimed to be thorough and comprehensive in my acknowledgement of both early and recent work in the field, but inevitably some errors or omissions may remain. For these I accept full responsibility.

David Sim
Reading
November 2011

Prologue

On a warm summer afternoon in the year AD 128, just south of the great wall built by Hadrian, a Roman blacksmith is standing outside his workshop. He has just completed a full set of arms and armour, and is making a tally to check that everything he has been asked to make is accounted for. He is a legionary and a superb fighting man, but he is also proud of his skills as a blacksmith, and the sight of the equipment that he has made is a boost to his self-esteem. He has often thought that people never seem to understand [illegible]er how much work goes into making things, or how important it is to be well-or[illegible]ed. For anything to be made, he has to make sure the iron, charcoal, tools and the other smiths are all in the same place at the same time. Nothing is left to chance; no one will ever say he forgot part of an order. On his wax tablet he marks off the following items: one helmet, one set of body armour, one shield boss, one sword, one dagger, two *pila* heads, one pick axe, total weight 20kg of iron. His gaze wanders over the camp and his eyes come to rest on the temple where the standard of the Legion is kept, and he remembers that day all those years ago when as a young man full of pride he swore his oath to the eagle of his Legion. His reverie is disturbed by the sight of several civilian men unloading from the mules the billets of iron he ordered. The billets are heavy, and most of the group can only manage to carry two or three at the most. One man calls out to him,

'Blacksmith, what's this lot for?'

And he replies: 'It's iron for the Eagles'

In this fictional account we meet the finished product of the blacksmith's art, namely the weapons and armour that will be used by the soldiers. These items represent the end of a long story that involves large amounts of both natural resources and manpower expended to transform iron ore into the arms and armour of a Roman legionary. It is the purpose of this book to reveal the complicated and fascinating processes that have to be conducted to make such iron artefacts.

Our Roman blacksmith stands at the end of a long tradition of craftsmen, whose skills go back to the very start of man's use of metal. The first metalworkers hammered the metal to change its shape. This is the process known as forging, and copper and later bronze were fashioned in the same way. For more than a thousand years before iron was discovered, the men who forged copper and bronze were highly skilled in their art; and it was these craftsmen who were the first to forge iron, once it became available in large enough quantities. The discovery of iron, and later steel, changed everything. Steel could be made harder than any other known metal, and thus could be used to cut almost every material; even very hard stone could not resist an edge made of hard steel.

By the time of the Romans, the blacksmith's tools had reached their terminal stage of development; indeed they were in every respect almost identical to those used by blacksmiths today. Even the advent of electricity in the modern era has only meant that electric rotary fans have replaced traditional hand pumped bellows.

Quite often, iron artefacts from the archaeological record are no more than a fragile mass of corrosion products (rust), and in this condition they are neither attractive nor stimulating to those who are not enthusiasts. It is likely that this unappealing appearance has led to the importance of iron being underestimated. The lack of interest has also meant that little attention has been given to how iron artefacts came into being in the first place. Little thought has gone into considering the immense technical problems that had been overcome, and the huge amount of resources in terms of materials and man power needed to obtain a piece of iron ore (**colour plate 1**) and transform it into an item such as a sword (**colour plate 2**).

This book aims to take you back into that forgotten world through the different processes involved in the vast iron industry that, as we shall see, must have employed thousands of people. Although considering examples and drawing on information from throughout the Roman Empire, this book will deal mainly with the production of iron in Britain. In later chapters discussing the manufacture of artefacts I will consider a range of items that our Roman legionary would have created. However, the basic techniques that he would have employed would be the same for military and civilian blacksmith alike.

1

AN OVERVIEW OF THE ROMAN IRON INDUSTRY

I start with a tale from blacksmithing mythology. When the temple at Jerusalem was completed, King Solomon was so pleased with the work he decided to confer the title *Father of craftsmen* on one of the artisans who had helped to build it. All the craftsmen were summoned to appear before the King and give an account of why the honour should be theirs; this meeting was to be followed by a banquet with the chosen craftsman as the guest of honour.

Accordingly each man stated his case. The stonemason said, 'If I had not cut the stone there would be no building'. The carpenter said, 'If I had not carved the wood there would be no doors or fittings or furniture'. The tiler said, 'Without me there would be no beautiful floors', and the weaver said, 'Without me there would be no wall hangings.' So each in turn spoke, until last of all they came to the blacksmith, who said, 'I am the Father of craftsmen, because I make all the tools for the others and without me none of them would be able to perform their skill'.

Solomon saw the truth of this and conferred the title *Father of craftsmen* on the blacksmith. (The King's tailor was so outraged that he crawled under the banqueting table and snipped pieces out of the blacksmith's apron with his scissors, which is why to this day all blacksmiths have a fringe at the bottom of their aprons.)

This tale helps us to understand how essential iron was to ancient societies. We will see later in this chapter both the huge variety of iron items which existed in Roman times, and which relied on the skill of the iron workers for their production, and the vast scale of the industry.

The Roman world

While it is not the place of this study to detail what life was like in the Roman world – and there are other excellent books on this very topic – it is important that the reader should have at least a general picture. In the past romantic ideals, or perhaps a wish not to cause offence, has restrained authors from portraying in lurid detail some aspects of Roman 'culture'. However, in order to gain a correct appreciation of the way in which Roman life operated, it is necessary to make some fundamental observations.

Rome existed for war; indeed it may be said that to the Romans, as to the Greeks, peace interfered with war (Hanson Davis 1989). Rome conquered with its military might and controlled its conquests with the same military machine. It was a society that was ruled by a small ruling elite, and their world was divided into two: those who lived within the empire, and the barbarians who were outside it, and therefore of no consequence.

The role of iron in the Roman world

The importance of iron in the Roman world cannot be over-emphasised. It can be equated with the dependence of the modern world on steel, and one would be hard-pressed to find any manufacturing activity in the ancient world that did not rely in some way on iron. Manning (1985), in the contents of his catalogue, classified the following iron artefacts:

Tradesmen's tools embracing:

metalworking, (blacksmithing, copper and bronze-smithing, also jewellery making (goldsmithing and silversmithing))
the timber industry: woodland management, carpentry, fine cabinet making
stone working: quarrying, stone dressing, carving and sculpting
plasterers' tools;
tools for processing wool and cloth, leather working (tanning, cobling);
agricultural tools
farriers' tools
mining

Other equipment for daily activities such as:

transport: land, river and sea
surgical instruments
domestic equipment: knives, razors and cleavers, locks and keys, *styli*, toilet implements
structural fittings for both domestic and civil buildings
armour and military equipment, weapons, shackles

This is not a complete list, but it serves to show how vital iron was to the functioning of society in the Roman world.

Overview of the technical aspects of iron making

The production of iron artefacts is a complex task, dependent upon not only the raw materials, but also the skills of the craftsmen involved in all aspects of the iron industry. Figure 1 shows schematically an overview of the iron production process. Initially the

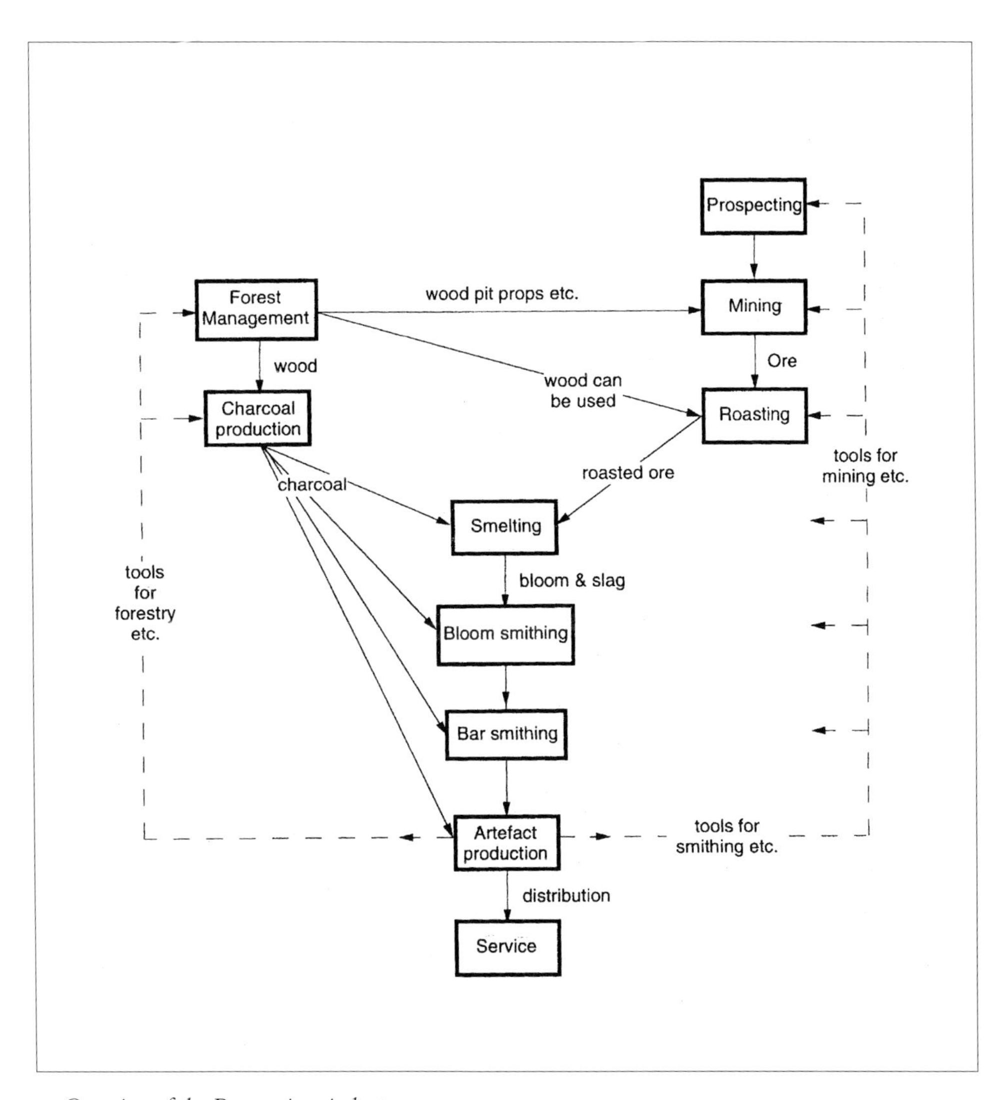

1 *Overview of the Roman iron industry*

iron ore must be found (*prospected*) and then *mined*, before being prepared for *smelting* by *roasting*. The activities of mining, roasting and smelting require considerable input from other resources: notably wood (for both fuel and structural purposes) but also manpower, with the attendant organisation. Once the ore has been mined, roasted and smelted to produce the bloom, it again requires considerable processing and support in terms of fuel and labour to refine the bloom to bar ready for the blacksmith to manufacture the final product. The various stages that are covered in detail in the following chapters in this book are identified here.

Prospecting

The first stage in the production of an iron artefact was to find a source of iron ore. The prospector relied on the surface appearance of rocks and soil to indicate the presence of mineral ores. He had to be able to recognise the visual signs, such as the type of vegetation, which could be an indicator of the kinds of minerals present. With little in the way of scientific method available, experience was the prospector's most valuable asset.

Mining

Mining, or the extraction of the ore, was a major undertaking. The Romans established a system of control on many mines to ensure that they were run for the benefit of the Empire. The simplest form of mine, open cast, was essentially a pit that was open to the elements. This type has many advantages over the more traditional image evoked (a shaft leading below ground from which various galleries and workings follow the ore seam), the most direct being the immediacy of return upon effort: the material could be dug from the ground straight away, with little or no preparation. There was also no need for lighting, ventilation, drainage and shoring (of the galleries and shafts), and it would have been easier to remove the ore from a pit.

Having said all this, the Romans did create mines accessed by shafts; but these tended to be reserved for high value (e.g. silver or gold) or high quality (yield) ores. An intermediate technique of mining was bell pitting, in which an access shaft was dug, and the seam excavated in a cylinder around the shaft until the roof became unsafe, at which point it was backfilled and another shaft dug nearby to repeat the process.

Preparation of the ore – washing and roasting

Once the ore had been removed from the ground it was first washed to remove any excess material such as clay. It was then roasted, which served several functions: it dried the ore and made it more porous, and also made it easier to break the ores into smaller pieces needed for smelting.

Fuel

The single most important fuel in the ancient world was charcoal, the residue obtained as a result of the incomplete combustion of either vegetable or animal materials, but most usually of wood. At the end of the process the material has lost both volume and weight and is almost pure carbon: for example if wood is used, the volume is reduced by one third and the weight is approximately one quarter of the original. Charcoal is capable of burning at a temperature of 900°C, but the use of an air blast will enable temperatures of 1600°C to be reached in a furnace. It was the principal fuel for the *smelting* of iron.

It should be noted that although the use of coal is recorded on many Roman sites, and was readily available in some locations, it is not suitable for *smelting* iron because the sulphur content makes the metal too brittle for forging. Coal was utilised however in other industrial processes, and certainly can be used for the *forging* of iron; as a superior fuel, there is no doubt the smiths exploited this. In fact, in most places where mineral coal outcrops it was mined by the Romans.

Smelting

Ancient iron production differs in many ways from its modern counterpart, and so the two basic processes are outlined here in order to avoid confusion between ancient and modern methods. The processes are called the *direct method*, or bloomery process, which was used in antiquity, and the modern *indirect method* employed today. The latter is a relatively modern process in which liquid iron is produced from the ore in a blast furnace at a high temperature, and then further processed into other ferrous products such as cast iron and steel. In the direct method, the ore is heated at a temperature below that at which iron melts, but high enough that the unwanted mineral content of the ore (termed *slag*) can become liquid and run out. The ore undergoes a chemical reaction with the gas produced by burning the charcoal, and this reduces the ore to iron. Thus the iron is extracted both physically and chemically, and a sponge-like bloom of iron is produced for further refining. This process was used in Europe from the time iron was first smelted until the fifteenth century.

Refining the bloom – bloomsmithing

The product of the smelting process is called a *bloom*, which is a mass of pure iron separated by slag. In this condition the iron is unworkable, and has to be refined to produce the material which can be forged into artefacts. The objective of the next stage in the cycle is therefore the removal of slag and the welding of the iron into a solid mass or billet.

For welding to occur, the surfaces to be joined must be clean and have as little oxide on them as possible; iron oxide has a higher melting point than iron and acts as a barrier between the pieces to be welded. The presence of slag between the particles of iron also prevents the iron from welding. However, the slag also binds the bloom together and keeps it as a solid mass, so needs to be removed in a way that prevents the bloom collapsing as a result. This process is called bloomsmithing – heating and hammering the bloom to expel the slag and consolidate the iron by welding the particles together.

Smithing a billet to a bar – barsmithing

A billet is often too large to be of any use for artefact production save when large objects such as hammers are to be made. For smaller items the iron billet would have been forged down to bars of various sizes and cross-sections (square, round, rectangular, etc.) depending on the type of work the smith was conducting. Semi-skilled workers or apprentices would have carried out this task, as it requires only basic skills.

The bars would have been of what is called in smithing jargon '*a handling length*' – long enough to be held comfortably while working on the heated end. A smith only uses tongs when there is no alternative and it is always preferable to work on the end of a bar.

Artefact production

The bar is now ready to be turned into an artefact and, as we have already seen, the range of iron items from the Roman era is astounding. There was hardly any activity that did not make use of iron in some part of its operation. Many artefacts could be produced by semi-skilled labourers, who might be employed in making large numbers of the same item such as nails but many other items needed the skills of an experienced blacksmith to bring them to realisation. Iron was a material that was in constant demand, not only for new objects such as weapons and tools but also to replace existing items, which will either have been lost, broken, stolen or simply worn out.

Chapter 7 describes the production of a variety of weapons and tools in common use in the Roman world. The function of these items would have been specific, but the techniques employed to produce the various forms would have been used for the full range of items discussed earlier.

The production and heat treatments of steel (the iron-carbon alloy) are discussed in chapter 8. It will be seen that the Romans made full use of the alloy and appreciated its enhanced strength and hardness.

The final chapter discusses the possibilities of the use of mechanical processing to speed up the many processes which will be described. It will be seen throughout that the Roman iron industry must have been of considerable importance and size to produce enough for everyday needs.

The size of the British iron industry

Although Britain did export some iron, most was mined for the manufacture of artefacts to be used in Britain. Davies (1935: 140) notes that there was a very good supply of iron ore in Gaul that would have been much easier to export to the rest of continental Europe should it be required. If we accept this fact, it is a great help in sizing the British iron industry as a whole. Aiano (1975: 40-1) places a 'conservative estimate' of the annual iron consumption in Roman Britain at 1.5 kg/head. This figure is based on the assumption that the need would be rather lower than the 4.5 kg/head that he quotes for the seventeenth century; and from this he goes on to project an annual output of 2250 tonnes (with an assumed population of 1.5 million).

More recent work by Millet (1990: 185) puts the population of Britain at that time at nearer 3.6 million, which would equate to 5400 tonnes per year: whichever figure is more correct, it can be seen that the volume of ferrous products used was considerable. Healy (1978: 196) estimates that the consumption of the Empire as a whole was 82,500 tonnes per annum.

The iron industry required a great deal of support and organisation. Using the figure of 5400 tonnes, we can work backwards to obtain an estimate of the mass of raw materials needed to produce this final output. It will be shown in later chapters that the extraction of iron from the ore and each stage of the subsequent processing entails loss of material, as summarised in **Table 1**.

Table 1 Efficiency of the various processes involved in iron production

Process	Yield (%)
Extraction of bloom from ore*	20
Consolidate bloom	50
Smith billet	80
Forge bar	80
Forge artefact	90

*This assumes a high-grade ore with 50% iron content

Hence a total of 5400 tonnes of finished product would require 93,750 tonnes of ore to be mined and processed, which would need 112,500 tonnes of charcoal just to smelt it (Crew 1998: 51), the equivalent of 787,500 tonnes of wood (Cleere 1976: 240). Further processing would require even more charcoal – not a trivial matter, and one discussed in chapter 3.

The volume of labour needed to support this level of production would have been high, and is very difficult to estimate accurately. Based on his experimental work, Sim (1994: 393) calculates a figure equivalent to about 50,000 men just for the smelting and bloomsmithing operations. If we treble this figure to allow for the barsmithing and artefact production, as well as mining, charcoal production and overall administration of these activities, the industry as a whole would have required at least 150,000 men, which is equivalent to 4.2% of the total population (based on Millet's figures). In addition to this direct involvement, the support industries required to feed, clothe and shelter this workforce indicate the level of organisation and importance which must have been attached to the iron industry.

2

CHARCOAL

Of all the impacts associated with iron production in pre-Industrial Revolution society, those related to the generation of the fuel have achieved the widest attention. Prior to the discovery of the conversion of coal to coke by Abraham Derby in 1709, charcoal was the only major fuel available for industrial operations such as smelting. This is because the fuel needs for the iron smelting process are highly specific. The impurities found in coal, such as sulphur, can contaminate iron smelted with it, and dry wood alone could not attain the high temperatures required for smelting. To compensate for this, wood needed to be converted to charcoal, the carbon residue created when wood is heated without sufficient air for complete combustion. Charcoalification results in the removal first of water, then the volatile compounds. Wood converted to charcoal has two functions in iron production.

Firstly, it provides an excellent source of heat for smelting. The absence of water in charcoal compared to 'dry' wood results in a hotter, more easily controlled heat; 'dry' wood produces an inconsistent temperature during combustion because of the vaporisation of internal moisture. Secondly, in the context of bloomery iron production, charcoal represents more than just a source of heat energy; it is a source of almost pure carbon, that is converted first to carbon monoxide, then to carbon dioxide. This allows the chemical reduction of the ore during smelting.

Archaeological evidence for charcoal production

There is little evidence from the archaeological record for the method of charcoal burning used in the Roman period, but classical authors writing about the Mediterranean region suggest that both charcoal kilns and pits were used. Theophrastus in his *History of Plants* (V.9.4) records the progress of a charcoal burn:

> They cut and require for the charcoal heap straight smooth billets: for they must be laid as close as possible for the smouldering process. When they have covered the kiln, they kindle the heap by degrees . . . such is the wood required for the charcoal heap.

This can be supplemented with Pliny's account in his *Natural History* (XVI.8.23) of a clay structure used as a charcoal kiln. Although evidence for pit structures is also recorded, this is predominately by Greek authors such as Theophrastus in his *History of Plants* (IX.3.1-3), and Aelian (*NA* 1.8) (Olson 1991: 414).

However, archaeological evidence for charcoal production sites from any period is rare. Tylecote (1986: 225) suggests that charring pits, or 'pit-steads', have been recovered from an Early Bronze Age context in Mildenhall, East Anglia. He also tentatively suggests that trenches found on the Roman iron production site at Wakerley could be examples of pit-steads. There is currently no archaeological evidence from the Weald or the Forest of Dean for pit kilns but a possible example of the remnants of an above-ground charcoal kiln, or clamp, has been recovered from the Weald, at the Romano-British industrial complex at Bardown (Cleere 1970: 15). Here a 3m diameter area of Ashdown Sand had been baked to a depth of 1-2cm. A little charcoal was found in association with the area, and the feature was sealed by the construction of a slag-metalled road. It is possible that the burning horizon could be the archaeological manifestation of a charcoal clamp that was originally at the periphery of the Bardown site, but later became incorporated into the industrial area. It is likely that the major form of charcoal production would have been through the utilisation of heaps and kilns.

The two methods of charcoal production each have their own advantages and disadvantages. The creation of a pit requires a significant input of labour, unless a minepit or natural hollow could be modified; however, the same pit can be reused and, if several episodes of such reuse are undertaken on a single site, the resultant baking of the pit walls would serve to prevent contamination of the charcoal. In contrast, the above-ground clamp would be destroyed after every episode of charring and the major advantage of this method derives instead from its mobility: the simplicity of clamp construction allows it to be constructed near, or at, the site of wood cutting.

The rarity of evidence for charcoal production in the archaeological record is not surprising, given that the process would have occurred in woodlands and forests often at some distance from the sites of iron production which tend to be the focus of excavation. Charcoal production is also a mobile activity, that follows the available woodland resources and is dependent on the demand from iron producers; and this mobility, in conjunction with the low weight of charcoal, is not conducive to the development of significant infrastructure, as it does not require (for example) the metalled trackways associated with other off-site activities such as iron ore mining.

Similarly, the primary components of a kiln would leave little trace in the archaeological record: when the charcoal is removed, the kiln wall is destroyed. In an ideal context the only remaining evidence for charcoal production would be the area of intensely fired earth or clay, carbon-rich soil in the immediate vicinity of the kiln and, in exceptional circumstances, burnt kiln lining and material culture. However, the absence of above-ground features means that sites only tend to be revealed when the carbon-rich soil is exposed by ploughing, which itself almost inevitably results in the degradation or destruction of the site.

It is also quite difficult to distinguish between the archaeological remains of a charcoal clamp and a bonfire; both have a similar signature of carbon rich soil. By their very nature, charcoal production sites are not associated with much diagnostic material culture due to the short periods of occupation and the mobile nature of charcoal burners, who are unlikely to travel with little more than perishable belongings. Bonfire sites are also unlikely to have much material culture, and in the absence of such evidence, the dating and interpretation of these charcoal scatters is highly problematical because the ambiguous stratigraphy of these sites, in addition to the cost, deters the use of radiocarbon determination. The major difficulties associated with the recovery of these sites therefore include the low archaeological visibility, the ambiguity of interpretation of charcoal production and bonfire sites and the problem of dating.

The production of charcoal

The production of charcoal from wood has implications for the environment. Accurate estimates of the conversion figures for wood to charcoal are notoriously variable, primarily because of the difficulties of quantifying wood in terms of volume and weight, as a result of its irregular shape and variable water content. The ratio of wood to charcoal produced therefore varies between 4:1 and 12:1: an accepted contemporary average is 7:1 (Cleere 1976: 240).

Green wood is composed of an average of 50% water; this can be reduced to 30% after seasoning. The removal of water during the process of charcoal production results in both weight loss and volumetric loss. Charcoal is more efficient to transport than dry wood: production off-site would result in a significantly lighter load, greater compaction due to the smaller size of the charcoal pieces compared to branch wood and the loss of volume due to charcoalification. This can reduce the number of journeys required by 40-50% compared to transporting dry wood.

However, the transportation of charcoal to iron production sites compared to wood would result in some fragmentation and loss of the charcoal – this could be anywhere between 5-20% depending on the length of the journey. The carriage of charcoal was limited to some extent by the inherent friability of the material, and it has been calculated that transport beyond 5-6km would degrade the charcoal sufficiently so as to make it almost valueless as a fuel (Cleere and Crossley 1985: 133, 135). However, in most cases it would be unlikely that the material would have to be transported so far; for example, in the eastern High Weald the distance between some of the largest industrial sites was as a little as 3.5km (between Beauport Park and Oaklands), or 5km (from Beauport Park to Crowhurst Park). The problems of charcoal degradation and loss during transportation does not apply in any significant degree to the smaller-scale iron production operations, where it is likely that all the elements of production would have occurred in a relatively spatially confined area, and the distinction between on-site and off-site would have become increasingly blurred as the size of exploitation decreased.

Labour

The manpower requirements of charcoal production are rarely considered in relation to the those of iron production. The production of charcoal is labour-intensive. A gauge of this can be derived from analogy with the medieval era; after the onset of the Black Death, the price of charcoal doubled to compensate for the shortage of forest workers (Cleere and Crossley 1985: 99). Further parallels can be drawn with the labour requirements of charcoal blast furnace production: a petition to the Sussex MPs in Michaelmas 1661, which notes the condition of the iron works as being 'much decayed', places a great deal of emphasis on the employment required to cut and cord the wood which was essential to sustain iron production (Fletcher 1975: 17).

Several stages are involved in the production of charcoal, not least the location of a suitable source of wood. Under ideal circumstances, a single man can cut a cord of wood a day. However, personal experience by the author suggests that this output is highly dependent on weather conditions, variable daylight hours, the nature of the tools used, the health of the workers, and the nature of the environment. Accessibility to wood sources is often hampered by the presence of scrub, brambles and other low-level vegetation.

Once the wood has been cut, it has to be transported to the site of the charcoal clamp, which would normally be only a short journey – it would be in the interest of the operator to limit the distance travelled. The clamp has to be constructed, and although in itself this does not require a great deal of time, the extraction of the turfs or sods needed does involve a significant input of labour. Once lit, the clamp has to be tended constantly to prevent accidental combustion of the charcoal. Although more than one clamp can be lit and observed at any one time, the forest worker cannot leave the immediate area.

Aside from the physical cutting of wood, the environmental impacts associated with charcoal burning are related to the construction of the clamp. Clamp construction requires some form of barrier to prevent access of air once charcoalification has commenced. A relatively airtight version could be achieved with leaves and turfs or sods, depending on the local availability of material. The creation of the clamp would therefore result in the removal of surface foliage that could result in some cases in accelerated surface runoff prior to regeneration of the vegetation. While at the level of small-scale operations this might have been minimal, the industrial-class facilities could have witnessed the removal of hectares of turves and sods to facilitate the annual needs of charcoal production.

The selection of wood fuel

There is a significant body of evidence suggesting that ancient societies were aware of the various properties of different woods. The use of wood was however determined by both its perceived viability as a fuel and its abundance in the natural environment.

The evidence derived from the Weald suggests that oak underpinned charcoal production for iron making in the Roman Weald (Kaminski 1996). However, ancient perceptions of this species as a source of charcoal were apparently negative: Homer records in the *Iliad* (IX.212) that oak and box were avoided for charcoal production. Pliny in his *Natural History* (XVI.32) notes that with the broad-leaved oak it ...

> ... only pays to use it in a copper-smith's workshop, because as soon as the bellows stop it dies down and has to be rekindled repeatedly: but it gives out showers of sparks. *A better charcoal is obtained from young trees* [author's italics].

Theophrastus in his *History of Plants* (V.9. 1-6.) records that:

> The best charcoal is made from the closest wood, such as evergreen oak, arbustus; for these are the most solid, so that they last longest and are the strongest; wherefore they are used in silver mines for the smelting of ore. Worst of the woods is oak (deciduous), since it contains the most mineral matter, and the wood of older trees is inferior to that of younger, and for the same reason the wood of really old trees is especially bad. The best charcoal comes from trees in their prime, and *especially from trees which have been topped.*

The theories of these ancient authors do not tally with the oak-dominated charcoal assemblages that have been obtained from iron production in the Weald and Forest of Dean but this discrepancy can be attributed to the dominance of oak in the natural environment.

The evidence for the use of wood fuel in metal production contexts from around the British Isles suggests that the wood types 'selected' are also predominantly based on the availability of wood in the local environment. For example, in northern England, Wales and Scotland alder has a much greater representation in the debris from iron and other metal production sites, while in southern England the genus is very poorly represented. This appears to be a function of the greater distribution of alder in northern England, which results from the higher rainfall. As a general rule the factors that govern selection are availability first and foremost, followed by real or perceived fuel quality.

There is currently no statistically valid archaeological evidence for the selection of wood for *specific processes* during iron production, such as roasting, smelting or smithing. This is simply a result of the rarity of charcoal analysis from the primary contexts of furnace structures or roasting hearths. However, Theophrastus in his *History of Plants* (V.9.1-6) indicates that selection of wood was practised in some contexts:

> Different kinds of charcoal are used for different purposes: for some uses men require it to be soft, thus in iron-mines they use that which is made of sweet chestnut when the iron has already been smelted.

This implies that there was a difference between the charcoal used for smelting the iron and that used for secondary and tertiary operations: but this cannot be confirmed from the archaeological evidence. Where detailed analysis of the wood from iron productions has been undertaken on a regional basis (such as in the Weald), there does not appear to be evidence for deliberate selection of wood (Kaminski 1996).

Management or regeneration?

Both Theophrastus (*History of Plants* V.9.6) and Pliny (*Natural History* XVI.32) suggest that the best quality of charcoal could be obtained from younger wood and regenerated wood. This certainly appears to correspond with the predominance of branch wood and young wood from the slag deposits of the High Weald.

It is impossible to determine if the deliberate utilisation of managed woodland products was practised or if regenerated wood was used; the evidence from charcoal found in slag deposits is not subtle enough to distinguish between regrowth and the utilisation of coppice or pollards. Slag deposits are not primary deposits and the wide range of sources of debris these contain, in conjunction with the enhanced attrition, also serves to conceal profiles of age and size that might give an indication of the nature of exploitation. The essential difference between the two methods of exploitation is one of perception of the woodland resources. The utilisation of regrowth is an *ad hoc* exploitation without any attempt to influence the natural processes, while the management of woodland implies a knowledge of the regenerative properties of woodlands and a commitment of labour and resources that spanned generations. The concept of management implies a different psychological awareness of the woodlands to that employed in other economic strategies.

However, the majority of the charcoalified material that has been recovered from slag deposits in the eastern High Weald derives from branch wood, rather than trunk material from mature trees. An exception to this is the early first-century site at Turners Green in the High Weald, which produced a charcoal assemblage dominated by mature oak. This also appears to differ from the data provided by Straker (1931: 110-1), which records a preponderance of larger timber on Roman sites. There is the distinct possibility, considering the dominance of branch wood recovered by the author, that selection procedures based on the size of fragments might have been introduced in earlier charcoal extraction from Roman sites. The domination of branchwood is not entirely unrealistic: the industrial complexes of the eastern High Weald were populated and producing iron prior to the invasion and after the conquest would have required substantial quantities of wood to sustain the operations. As such the woodlands would have been cut during the Late Iron Age and the early Romano-British. By the second century the majority of wood used for smelting would have been from regenerated or managed sources.

In an iron production region of any great size, such as the Weald, the Jurassic ridge in Northamptonshire, or the Forest of Dean, it is apparent that multiple strategies of woodland exploitation would have occurred simultaneously. At any one time the woodlands would therefore have been at varying stages of growth.

The probability that the major Roman industrial iron production centres were reliant on coppice management was first forwarded by Rackham (1983: 41). There are certain difficulties with the concept of widespread woodland management in the eastern High Weald. The data provided by Rackham essentially projects medieval management strategies onto the Roman Weald, with a classic short rotation coppice system; however, two factors cause concern. During the medieval era there was a significant input of time and energy into the protection of coppice woodlands from grazing animals by the construction of woodbanks. The work of Rackham has resulted in the recovery of large numbers of these structures, and at Rayleigh Hills in Essex, Rackham (1983: 41), has suggested that beneath possible Anglo-Saxon land boundaries are 'faint earthworks which probably mark a set of wood edges in Roman or earlier times.' However, despite extensive searches by the author, there is, as yet, no evidence from the Weald of any such structures that can be attributed to Roman origins. It is unlikely that the banks would have been prone to degradation in the environment of the High Weald as the region has not been subject to the same extensive agricultural activities as much of southern Britain.

Deforestation

The ancient authors of the Mediterranean region provide much literary evidence for the effects of mining and metal production on the local environments. Strabo (XIV.6.5) noted that:

> In ancient times plains of Cyprus were thickly overgrown with forests, and therefore were covered with woods and not cultivated. The mines helped a little against this since the people would cut down the trees to burn the copper and the silver and the building of the fleets helped further.

The same analogy can be attributed directly to the iron industry. The island of Elba produced some of the best ores in the Roman world, but could not produce the wood required to roast and smelt the ore; as a result, after some initial roasting, the ore had to be transported to the mainland where charcoal and wood could be obtained from the Ligurian mountains (Forbes 1958: 18). Pliny records in his *Natural History* (XXXIV.96) that 'the effect of the shortage of fuel on the roasting operation is particularly noticeable in Gaul'. He also notes that there was a similar shortage for the metallurgists in the Campanion region (XXXIV.67).

However, comparison with the Mediterranean region and southern Europe is not entirely satisfactory. The physical and vegetational environment of the Mediterranean and its borders differs considerably to that which is evident in Britain, and the climatic regime is also more extreme. It is probable that many of the factors that influenced deforestation in the Mediterranean region – for instance soil erosion – were enhanced by grazing, climate and physical relief. These considerations cannot be applied unilaterally to Britain (Mather 1990: 34).

A great deal of caution has to be expressed with the use of literary evidence and the extrapolation of this data to elucidate the nature of the Roman environment in Britain or Northern Europe. The analysis of polleniferous sediments from the vicinity of prehistoric mining sites in the British Isles has revealed a much more varied response to early mining activity. Pollen obtained from the vicinity of the Bronze Age copper mines at Mount Gabriel, County Cork, suggests that woodland clearance was on an extremely small scale during the operation of the mines, with limited changes to the *taxa* composition. Analysis of pollen derived from blanket peat near the Bronze Age copper mining facility at Copa Hill, Cwmystwyth, Wales, suggests that evidence for impact could only be discerned as intermittent percentage declines in the representation of *taxa* such as hazel and oak (Mighall and Chambers 1989). However, despite the use of wood for kindling to allow for the extraction of ore, there was little need for the production of charcoal, and as such the wood requirements of the mining sites would have been less than those of a similarly sized iron production site.

The estimation by Cleere (1976: 240-1) for the area of woodland required to provide charcoal for iron production was between 2-3.5km^2 per annum in the eastern High Weald. Cleere (1976: 241) concludes that:

> By the time iron making in the eastern Weald ceased in the mid-third century (with the possible exception of the Footlands settlement), nearly 300km^2 of forest had been cleared (or 500km^2 using the larger annual figure), and the area around Battle ... must have been devastated. Indeed the deforestation in this area may well have contributed in some measure to the Fleet's abandonment of the eastern Weald as its iron making base in the mid-third century.

It would be likely that if such hypothetical depletion of woodland resources did occur in the Battle/Hastings region then there could have been a movement into the central High Weald, which had predominantly supported small-scale bloomery production, and as a result would have theoretically been better provided with woodland resources. This did not happen in the High Weald during the mid-third century, where there is also a decline in the number of late third to fourth-century bloomery sites.

Evidence is more conclusive in the blast furnace era of production, and suggests that the Wealden iron industry collapsed prior to the depletion of either fuel or mineral resources. This indicates that natural phenomena were not the only factors to influence industrial activity (cf. Zell 1994: 235). In mid-European woodlands, *long-term* deforestation is not a function of woodcutting for industrial exploitation, unless the land is converted to a new use that prevented tree growth – for example agriculture to support iron production, or site infrastructure such as working areas or mining sites. In some contexts regeneration can also be prevented by the degradation of the soil profile, as witnessed in some sandy lithologies. Small-scale extraction sites would have been less likely to have sustained the development of large site infrastructure although, as the size of operations increased, the nature of associated infrastructure was likely to increase incrementally.

It is probable that the pre-Roman sites would have generated some long and short-term impact on the local landscape. This could be manifested in the form of some limited woodland management, necessary to sustain the iron production sites and provide for the needs of the local settlements. Alternatively, the local woodlands could have been cut, and the regrowth would have supplied later users. Only the conversion of land to arable or pasture would have had a significant impact on the arboreal communities, preventing regrowth. However, the disarticulation caused by the conquest could have had a detrimental effect on local agriculture (if only in the short term). It is possible that some sites could have accelerated degradation of the local environment but this is impossible to ascertain from the charcoal evidence alone.

In either case, at the time of the conquest certain areas (including the eastern High Weald) would already have the economic infrastructure necessary to support iron production and, more importantly, a woodland environment that was partially modified as a result of pre-conquest activity. This could form the basis of the fuel supply for the early Roman industries.

3

SMELTING

Basic principles of iron making

The modern system of iron making is called the *indirect method*, in this process iron ore together with limestone and coke are put in a furnace and heated until they all melt into a liquid. The limestone acts as a flux and serves to combine with the lighter impurities to form slag, that floats on top of the iron. This is then skimmed off, leaving relatively pure iron that can then be processed further into steels and cast iron. However, until the fifteenth century, iron was extracted from its ore by what is known as the *direct* method, which is described below.

There are several types of iron ores, which may be grouped broadly into oxides (Fe_2O_3) and carbonates ($FeCO_3$) (also sulphides but these would not have been used owing to the undesirable sulphur content). In very simple terms, the direct method of iron production involves heating the ore in an oxygen-starved atmosphere of carbon monoxide (CO), which is provided by burning the charcoal. The carbon monoxide has a strong affinity for oxygen allowing it to form carbon dioxide (CO_2) where possible, thus *reducing* (removing the oxygen from) the iron ore (Fe_2O_3) to leave iron (Fe):

$$Fe_2O_3 + 3CO \rightarrow 2Fe + 3CO_2$$

Where a carbonate ore is used, this must first be roasted to produce iron oxide, which can then be reduced to iron:

$$FeCO_3 \rightarrow FeO + CO_2 \text{ (decomposition by heating)}$$
$$\text{and } 2FeO + Qw\ O_2 \rightarrow Fe_2O_3 \text{ (ready for reduction as above)}$$

In addition to the chemical process, the iron has to physically separate from the other mineral impurities such as silica (SiO_2) and alumina (Al_2O_3), which are the basic compounds in sands and clays. As noted above, in the modern iron making process limestone is employed as a flux that will combine with these compounds to produce slag. In Roman times, this use of limestone was not known, and a portion of the iron had to be sacrificed in order to make a slag compound.

$$2FeO + SiO_2 \rightarrow Fe_2SiO_4$$

Iron oxide will reduce to iron at a temperature of 800°C, but in practice the operating temperature of a bloomery furnace is in the region of 1200°C, much lower than the melting point of iron (1540°C). The most significant factor in the process is the temperature at which the slag becomes fluid, 1150°C. At this heat, the furnace is hot enough for the slag to become a liquid and drain away from the iron, but not hot enough to turn the iron into a liquid. Thus the products of this process are a spongy mass of iron with some slag impurities in it known as the bloom (which will be further processed by *bloomsmithing*, to expel the slag and consolidate the iron), and the separated slag.

Preparation of the ore

Once the ore has been recovered from the ground, it must first be processed in order to make it suitable for smelting. As with the production of charcoal, which was carried out close to where it was needed, the ore processing was conducted near to the site of excavation in order to avoid the unnecessary transportation of ore. This point is illustrated very clearly by (amongst others) the industrial complex at Bardown.

Here, the proximity of the other major components for iron production – namely the water and furnaces – can clearly be seen.

The first step in the ore preparation process is washing, which whilst usually reserved for heavier ores (such as gold), was also used to enrich/clean iron ores disseminated in, for example, clay (Davies 1935: 41). In addition to this washing, the ore itself often contained a certain amount of water. Cleere and Crossley (1985: 35) report that the carbonate ore (siderite) in the Weald tended to '... contain a good deal of water'. Thus the next stage in the processing was *roasting* the ore, either in simple pits or purpose built ovens. Cleere and Crossley (1985: 35) describe two examples of hearths that were:

> ... indisputably used for ore roasting. These were pits approximately 2.5m long by 0.8m wide, dug into the natural soil to a depth of about 0.2m. They were lined with stones along the sides, probably originally in about four courses, giving a total depth of about 0.4-0.5m, and the walls and base were liberally coated with puddled clay.

The size of the oven would presumably vary as required from site to site, although there is a practical limit on how large they could be, and once this was reached additional ovens would have to be constructed to cope with the demand.

Although the main objective of roasting was to dry the ore, the process also produced another useful result. When driving the water off, the trapped steam caused by the heating would build up an internal pressure, which could only be released when the ore shattered, thus breaking into smaller, more manageable pieces. Roasted ore was also more porous and easy to break down further if required. Breaking the ore into smaller pieces would provide a larger surface area per unit volume of material in

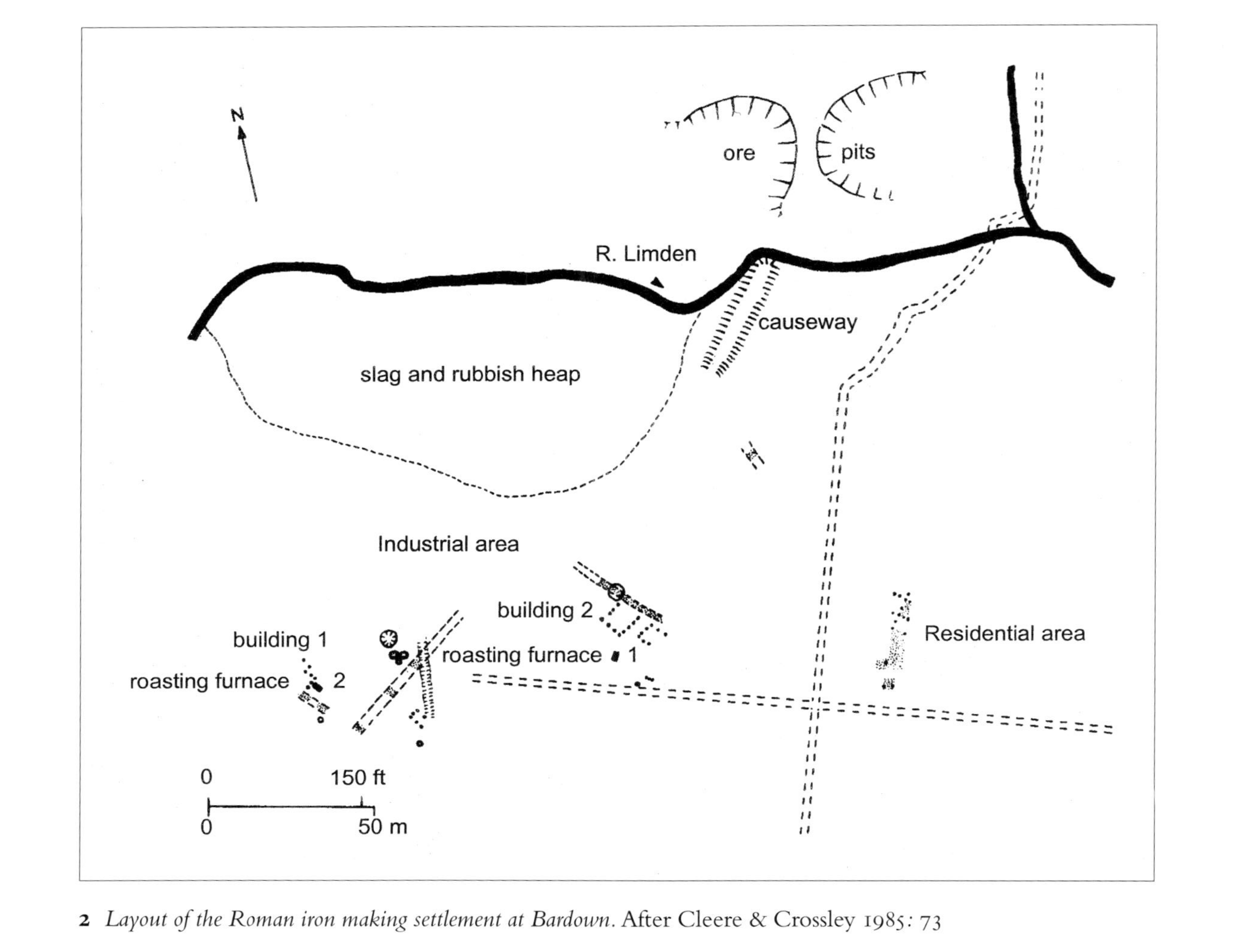

2 *Layout of the Roman iron making settlement at Bardown*. After Cleere & Crossley 1985: 73

order to progress the chemical reduction reaction. The size of ore pieces used in the furnace would vary, but typically the ore would be broken into pieces about the size of a walnut using a hammer or possibly an edge runner (**89**). Where required, the ore would be ground yet more finely into a powder, using an ore mill (**87**). An important additional function of roasting in the case of the carbonate ore, would be to drive off the carbon dioxide (CO_2) to produce the iron oxide ready for smelting.

The smelting furnace

Once the ore had been washed and roasted, it was ready for smelting, which was carried out in purpose built furnaces. The exact nature of the various types of those used in antiquity is still unclear, because few examples are found in good condition and the upper parts are usually missing, therefore the shape of the furnace above ground level is largely a matter of conjecture. While distinction between versions is not exact, the following types are well established: Coghlan (1977) distinguishes between the simple bowl, the domed or pot furnace and the shaft furnace. Cleere (1972) expanded the method of classification on the basis of the slag tapping, or lack of it (i.e. whether the slag was drained away from the furnace or collected in the bottom of it). Slag tapping has the great advantage of allowing the furnace to be reused without considerable work, since the slag is removed from the furnace during operation. Cleere's classification is as follows (**3**).

Group A non slag-tapping furnaces
Diagnostic features:
(a) No provision for tapping of molten slag.
(b) Hearth below surface of surrounding ground.
(c) Blown by forced draught.
Sub Group 1. No superstructure (bowl furnace).
Sub Group 2. Superstructure - cylinder or truncated cone.

Group B slag-tapping furnaces
Diagnostic features:
(a) Provision for tapping of molten slag.
(b) Hearth level with surface of surrounding ground.
(c) Superstructure.
Sub Group 1.i. Blown with forced draught, cylindrical superstructure.
Sub Group 1.ii. Blown with forced draught, conical or hemispherical superstructure.
Sub Group 2.i. Blown with natural draught, cylindrical superstructure.
Sub Group 2.ii. Blown with natural draught, conical or hemispherical superstructure.

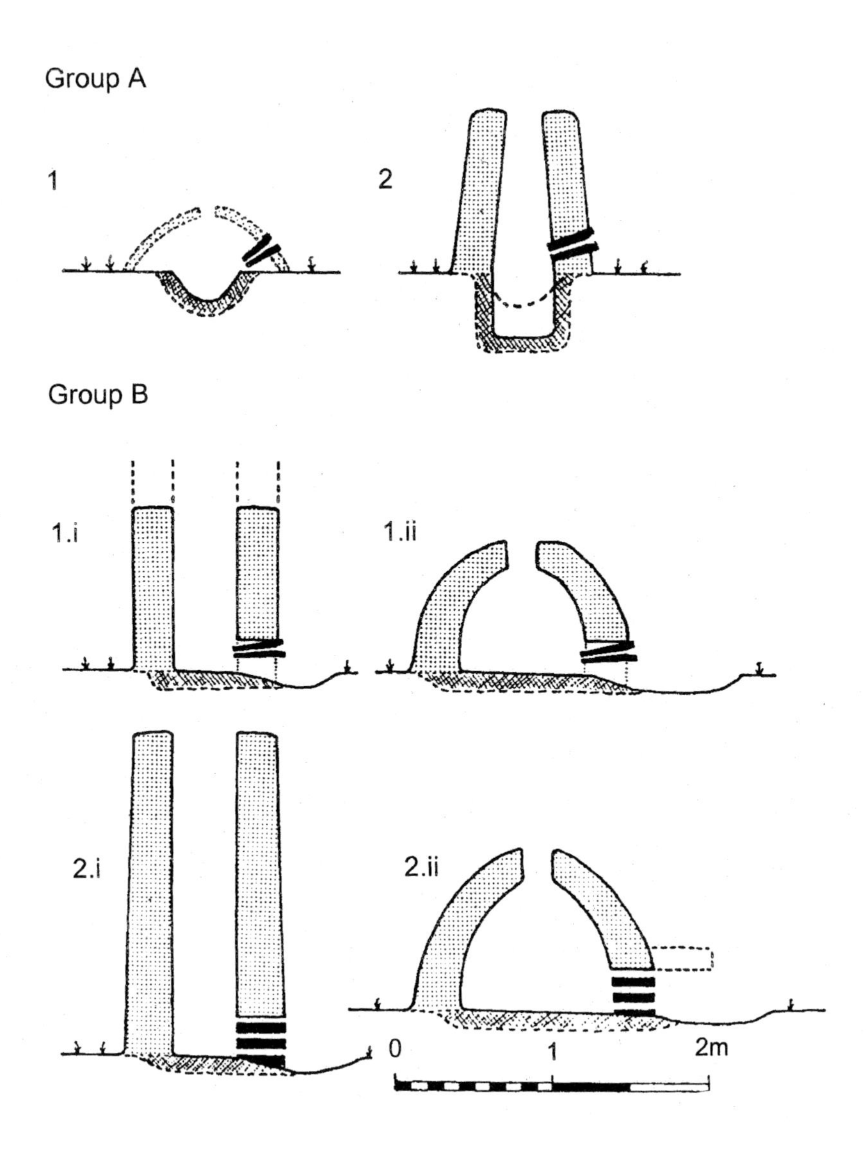

3 *Cleere's classification of early iron smelting furnaces.* From Cleere 1972, fig. 11

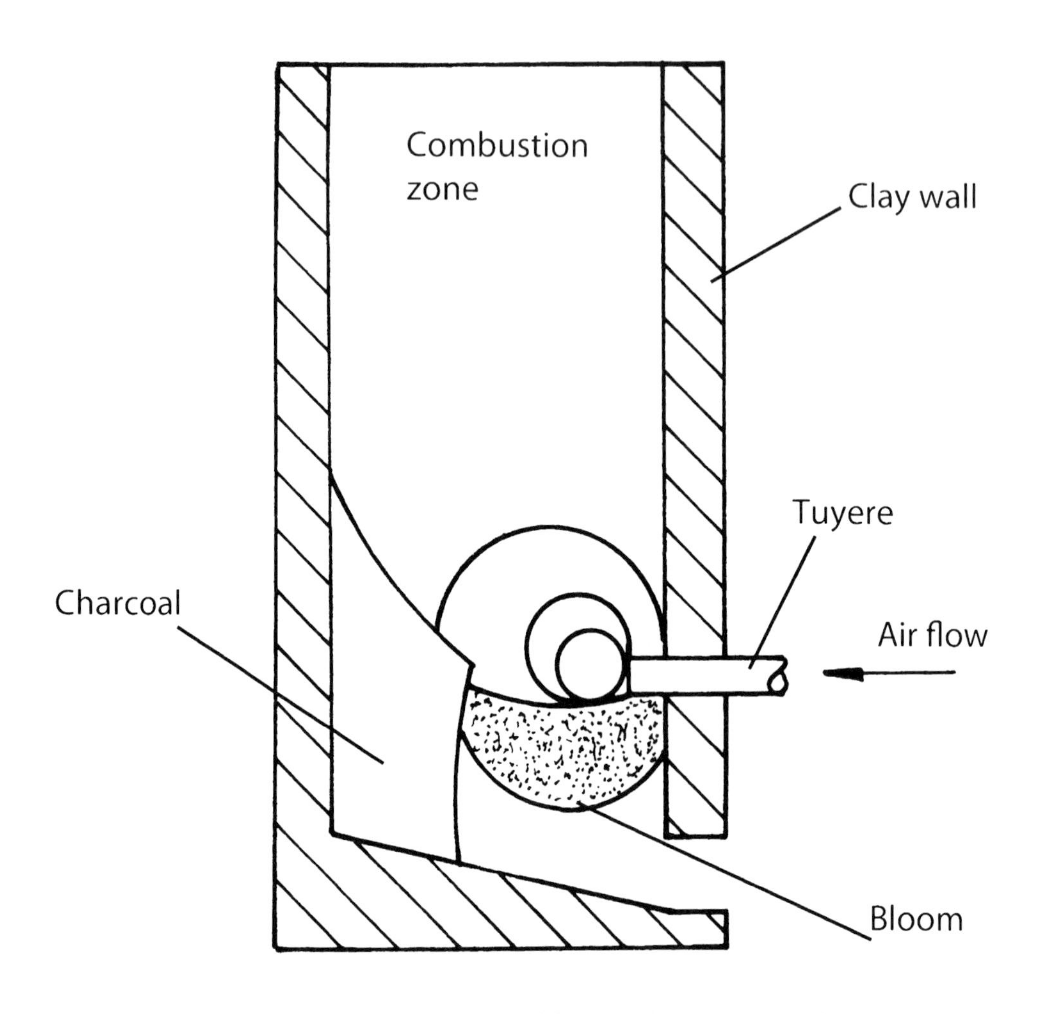

4 *Schematic diagram of a section of a shaft furnace*. After Tylecote *et al.* 1971

In order to raise the temperature in the furnace, it was necessary to create a draught through the structure. This would easily have been created by bellows, the blast pipe of which would have been protected from the heat of the furnace by means of a *tuyère*. Whilst no bellows are known to survive in the archaeological record (Cleere and Crossley 1985: 43), the more robust clay tuyères are found quite often in iron working sites. In its simplest form the tuyère is a conical tube with a hole about 25mm diameter through the middle. The taper would have produced a good fit with the hole in the furnace, ensuring that the air was directed in. More complicated, double tuyères have also been found (Cleere and Crossley 1985: 44), which would give the option to work with two pairs of bellows at once. This would increase air flow through the furnace and, if worked in anti-phase, could provide a more even, steady blast.

Tylecote *et al.* (1971) undertook an extensive investigation into the bloomery process, and report that the Romans used the more sophisticated slag tapping type furnaces (**4**). Further, Tylecote (1987: 100) states that 'The low shaft furnace is clearly the principal type of the Roman period and it appears in many varieties ...'. The slag tapping type of furnace does have several advantages over the bowl type:

1. the furnace superstructure would not have to be destroyed in order to have access to the bloom, i.e. a shaft furnace was re-usable;
2. higher temperatures were achievable;
3. more iron could be produced in one charge
4. the slag was removed.

Furnace construction materials

Cleere (1971: 209) reports that the Holbeanwood furnaces (in the Weald) were constructed entirely from local clay. In their excavated state, they were cylindrical in form, about 0.3m in internal diameter, with wall thickness of up to 0.3m and height up to 0.6m (but it is likely that the top of the structure was missing: the Ashwicken furnaces reported by Tylecote *et al.* (1971: 342) were of similar internal diameter and about 1.4m high). It was usual for this type of furnace to be built into a bank that would serve to both support and insulate the structure.

More recent work by Crew (1998) at Laxton (Northamptonshire) discusses the excavation of one of a group of large furnaces (possibly as many as 24), which display a typical internal diameter of 1.2m (**5**). The furnace is projected to stand approximately 2m high, with about an additional 1m below ground level where, as with the smaller furnaces built into the banks, it would have been supported and thermally insulated. Crew identified four stages of furnace construction, the earliest phase being a stone casing with clay lining of total thickness 0.4m. Subsequent additions of clay were made, the soft clay being fired a deep red indicating prolonged periods of considerable heat. The construction of these furnaces represents a considerable investment of time and materials, indicating the organisation and importance of iron production at that site. The subsequent clay lining provides evidence for furnace reuse and a maintenance regime.

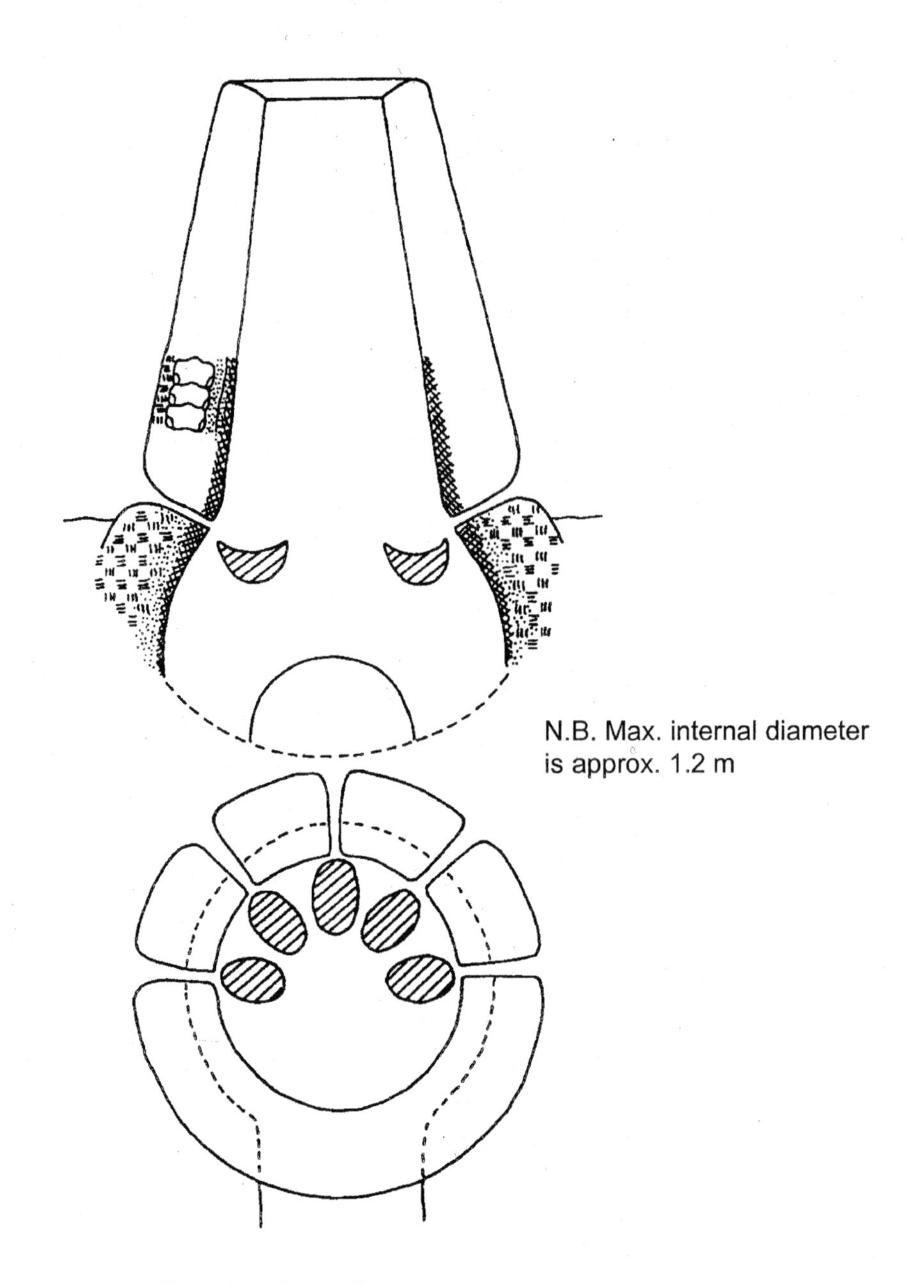

5 *Reconstruction of one of the furnaces found at Laxton.* From Crew 1998

Operation of the furnace
The furnace is charged with layers of iron ore and charcoal. Upon combustion, the charcoal produces the carbon monoxide gas required to react with the oxygen in the iron oxide. The resulting carbon dioxide escapes through the top of the furnace leaving behind iron. As the temperature in the furnace rises, the materials in the ore melt. The impurities form liquid slag at about 1135°C, which collects at the bottom of the hearth and is tapped off. As iron does not melt until 1540°C, at a temperature of 1200°C it is a semi-liquid that forms droplets which concentrate near the tuyère. This procedure is continued until the bloom which builds up below the tuyère is so large the air will not circulate and the process stops. Larger furnaces were constructed with several tuyères, which served to ensure a uniformity of flow throughout the bed, and also acted as the nucleus for several smaller and hence more manageable blooms (**5**).

The significance of the furnace material
All the materials present in a Roman iron smelting furnace will contribute to the physical nature and chemical composition of the bloom. As the intentional addition of fluxes is not attested until the Middle Ages, the materials present in Roman smelting are iron ore, fuel and the furnace lining.

Fulford and Allen (1992: 197) have shown that furnace linings were significantly consumed in the direct iron-making process, especially when rich ores were used.

The interior of furnaces were relined with clay of 10mm to 30mm thickness before re-firing. It was added to the surface of glassy, vesicular clay created during the previous smelting. The clay was altered mineralogicaly and changed physically to a glassy liquid which sloughed off the furnace wall and so could enter into and react with the charge of iron ore and charcoal. Analysis of the non-ferruginous matter in the slags shows that it was derived from the furnace lining.

They add that if clay had not been derived from the furnace walls, it would have been necessary to add it.

Shaft furnace yield

Experiments were undertaken by Tylecote *et al.* (1971) to produce bloom iron from ore using a reconstructed Roman shaft furnace based on those found at Ashwicken, Norfolk. The results showed that an 8kg bloom of iron could be produced from 50kg of partially roasted siderite (a carbonate ore) using about 40kg of charcoal during a cycle that took approximately 12 hours.

The tentative results from the more recent work at Laxton by Crew (1998) give a slightly higher yield: 500kg of ore and 600kg of charcoal could have produced 100kg of bloom in one 24 hour smelting cycle (these ratios have been used to calculate the amount of ore and charcoal required for the annual British output in chapter 1). Annual production of bar iron from this site is put at 30 tonnes per year (based on an assessment of the size of the slag heap and assuming 60% yield on the bloom consolidation). Comparing this with our annual figure for the industry of 5400 tonnes (chapter 1), this site would have produced about 1/180th of the total industry requirements.

Cleere and Crossley (1985: 81) project a peak total output of 750 tonnes per annum during the period AD 150–250 for the whole area of the Weald. Other sites would have contributed to the overall production, and whilst the total might struggle to achieve 5400 tonnes, this figure is certainly of the right order. If Aiano (1975: 40–41) and Millet's (1990: 185) estimation of (respectively) the consumption and population are each 20% too high, then the total annual production would have been 3456 tonnes, or 4.6 times the total annual production from the Weald.

4

THE BLACKSMITH

Social standing

Before we move on to consider what the blacksmith did, we should try to get some idea of the man himself. The examination of an iron artefact can reveal the skill of the craftsman who made it, and sometimes the techniques by which it was made, but it does not give any indication of how he acquired his craftsmanship or his position in society.

Aiano (1975: 48) makes the interesting point that most pagan religions had a smith god (Vulcan in the case of the Romans), which suggests a level of respect and status. However, the blacksmith was a tradesman, a worker who supported not only the ruling upper classes, but also the many other industries and trades. Thus he was firmly a member of the lower class. Aiano (1975: 48) reports:

> Under the Empire craftsmen's guilds increased in number. They were formed for a variety of purposes, not only for commemoration of the dead and mutual aid, but also for business purposes, and for religious and purely social objects. One guild of blacksmiths from Rome had among its members a high magistrate, M. Sutorius M. L. Pamphilus, according to *CIL* VI 1892.

Taken together, this evidence would tend to suggest that whilst a member of the lower class, the blacksmith was an important member of the community, who was held in respect by his peers.

Training

Until very recently craftsmen were usually trained by the system of apprenticeships. Where the apprentice was not part of the family, his own parents would pay for their son to learn under the guidance of a trained craftsman. Since the lower classes were correspondingly of lower-wealth, it was often the case that crafts were kept within the family, thus avoiding this expense (in whatever form it took). This arrangement has considerable advantages; if one considers the case of a blacksmith whose father and grandfather practised the same trade, then the amount of accumulated knowledge that he could learn from and pass on to the next generation would be considerable. Anyone growing up within a family of blacksmiths would be receiving training perhaps without realising it from the very beginning of his life. Additionally, if the apprentice was part of the family, there would be a greater loyalty to their 'employer', and the logical progression would be that they would take over the 'business' and support their parents when they became too frail to work.

The apprentice system consists of on-the-job training, starting from an early age. The apprentice would initially undertake menial tasks such as keeping the smithy tidy, fetching and carrying, lighting fires and so on. He worked alongside the master craftsman, who gave him instruction and gradually increased the amount of work that he was able to carry out on his own. At the end of the apprenticeship, which would last for several years, the next stage was to become a journeyman who moved from one smithy to another in order to gain varied experience. All apprentices, even those who were studying under members of their own family, undertook this part of the training. Eventually the student would progress to being a master himself, and the training cycle would begin again.

Dress

There are a number of representations of the smith from antiquity. Probably the most famous picture is that found at Pompeii in the House of Vettii (**colour plate 3**), which shows the cherub smiths heating a work piece in a furnace. Other representations include a carved relief sculpture that is now housed in Aquileia museum (**6**), and

6 *Roman relief sculpture of a blacksmith at his forge (now in Aquileia Museum)*

7 *Pottery fragment found at Corbridge showing a blacksmith at work (fragment size 137mm top to bottom)*

a fragment of pottery that was found at Corbridge (**7**). There are also numerous statues of Hephaistos catalogued by Brommer (1978). In all these images, the blacksmith is seen wearing his short, loose fitting tunic-like apron over one shoulder, and he is invariably depicted as bare armed and bare chested, a cool style of dress in what must have been a hot environment. It also allowed both some protection from the sparks, and a freedom of movement, which would have been important to the blacksmith. (As a blacksmith himself, the author has often been asked how he avoided being burnt. The answer is quite simple, he didn't, being burnt is just part of the job!)

The role of the striker

Throughout antiquity and right up to the middle of the twentieth century, blacksmiths worked with at least one assistant or *striker*. The striker(s) provided the hammering power needed to forge the iron into the required shape. Additionally, there would be many forging operations where it was necessary for the blacksmith to hold the iron in one hand and a tool such as a chisel or fuller in the other, thus requiring the striker to hit the tool head with a hammer in order to complete the operation. Under normal working conditions the maximum number of strikers that can work with one blacksmith on a big job is three; it is not practical to fit more than four men around one

8 *Hephaestos in his forge assisted by three strikers*

anvil (**8**). It is interesting to note that in both the scene of Hephaestos in his forge (**8**) and the relief from Aquileia (**6**), the smith is shown seated. It is in fact quite easy for the smith to work in this position if assisted by a striker or two.

The blacksmith and his strikers work together as a team; if the blacksmith wants the sequence of blows to be three heavy blows followed by one light blow he will lay a hot iron on the anvil and with his own hammer will strike the anvil with three (relatively) heavy blows followed by one light blow. He will then hit the iron with his own hammer on the spot where he wants the blows to land.

The number of personnel a blacksmith can employ

If we consider a military establishment, a blacksmith could have what would be an ideal situation as far as a workforce is concerned. A single blacksmith would be supported by three strikers, and a man (or apprentice) to manage the fire. This would allow the smith to work to his maximum advantage; he directs the strikers where to land their blows, and the fire manager sees that the fire is run correctly. By having a person in charge of the fire, it would be possible to work on several pieces at once: the smith could work on one piece, whilst a second was being brought to forging temperature, and possibly a third at the edge of the fire was being slowly heated. Once the first piece was too cold to continue working, it could be returned to the hearth and heated whilst the second piece was worked on. In addition to this personal team of assistants, there is no reason why other less skilled forging work, e.g. *barsmithing* could not be undertaken concurrently by other teams of semi-skilled workers. It will be shown by consideration of the Inchtuthil nail hoard (chapter 6) that the production was likely to have involved a sizeable team of personnel.

Fuel

Chapter 3 has discussed charcoal production, which was the principle fuel used in antiquity; but it was not the only one. Although it is true that coal is unsuitable for smelting iron, this does not apply to the forging process. It is in fact a far superior fuel for forging than charcoal, because it burns hotter and smaller quantities are required. It is possible that blacksmiths made use of sea coal in area such as the North East coast of England and where it was outcropped on the surface.

It is also possible to do a limited amount of forging using wood, although it is impossible to conduct certain operations such as *fire welding* (*forge welding*), which require a high temperature.

It is possible to produce charcoal during forging operations. A log may be placed at the back of the fire, and as the fire burns the outer layer of the wood becomes charcoaled. This is then scraped into the fire until the unburned wood beneath is exposed. The log is then returned to the fire, and the process continued until the log is burnt away and replaced. In this way, the Roman blacksmith would be able to make a portion of his own charcoal, and so reduce his running costs. Military blacksmiths working in the field on campaign could well have used this system.

The hearth

It has been assumed that forging was carried out in open hearths, which would be raised to a convenient height from the ground. The temperature would be controlled by bellows forcing air through a tuyère into the centre of the fire. Pictorial evidence (**colour plate 3 & 9**) suggests that that a box type 'enclosed' hearth would also have been used.

Work by the author described in chapter 8 has shown that this type of enclosed hearth would produce considerable savings both in terms of fuel consumed and the amount of material loss during forging caused by oxidisation. Such structures were probably permanent in civilian smithies and could readily be made from clay with or without a temper. A military blacksmith could easily construct such an enclosed hearth in a very short time (for example, two working days).

Blacksmith's tools

By the foundation of the Roman Empire iron had been in use for about 500 years, and most of the iron working tools had developed to a stage where no further improvement was necessary – this is still the case even today. By way of example, the tongs used by Roman blacksmiths (**6, 7**) are identical to those used by their modern counterparts. Indeed, apart from the electric rotary fans, which have replaced hand pumped bellows in delivering air to the fire, a Roman blacksmith would be quite familiar with everything in a modern forge. The tools most commonly associated with the blacksmith are the *anvil*, hammer and tongs (**colour plate 4**). In addition to these the smith would have had a series of *punches* (drifts), *fullers*, *flatters*, *swages* and *sets* (**9**).

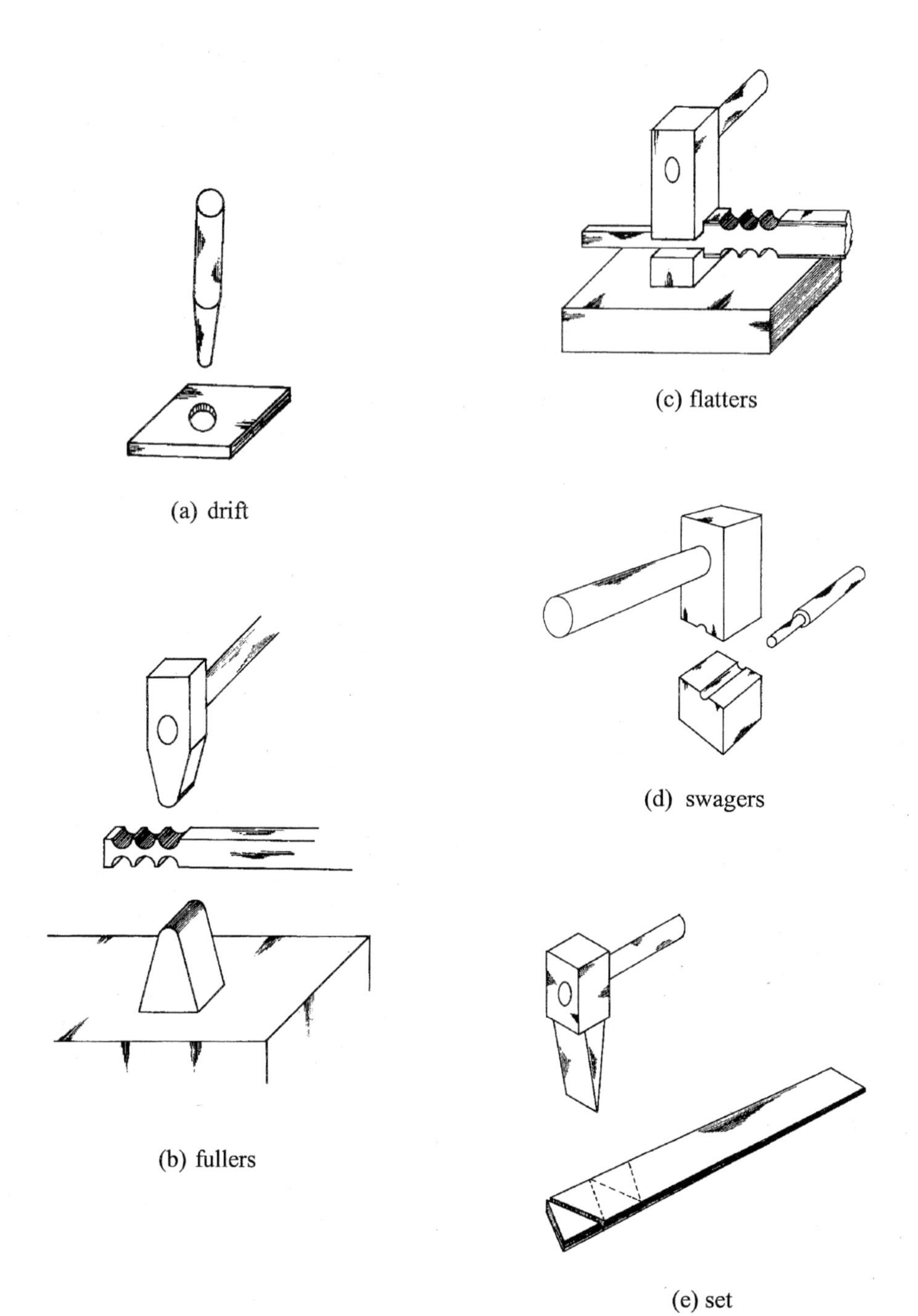

9 *A blacksmith's tools*

Anvils

Roman anvils were square or rectangular blocks of iron tapering towards the base, which was dished to provide four feet (**10a**). Examples of this type have been found in Pompeii. The most common form found in Britain is tapered and designed to fit into an *anvil stump*, and some of these anvils weigh more than 50kg – a valuable piece of iron (**10b**). Another type, which is not a very common find, are those with pointed *bicks* (**10c**), which would be mounted in a hole in (for example) a tree stump. This version was usually for specialist use; why they were not in wider use is unclear, as this type of anvil enables the blacksmith to perform a larger range of work at a single work station.

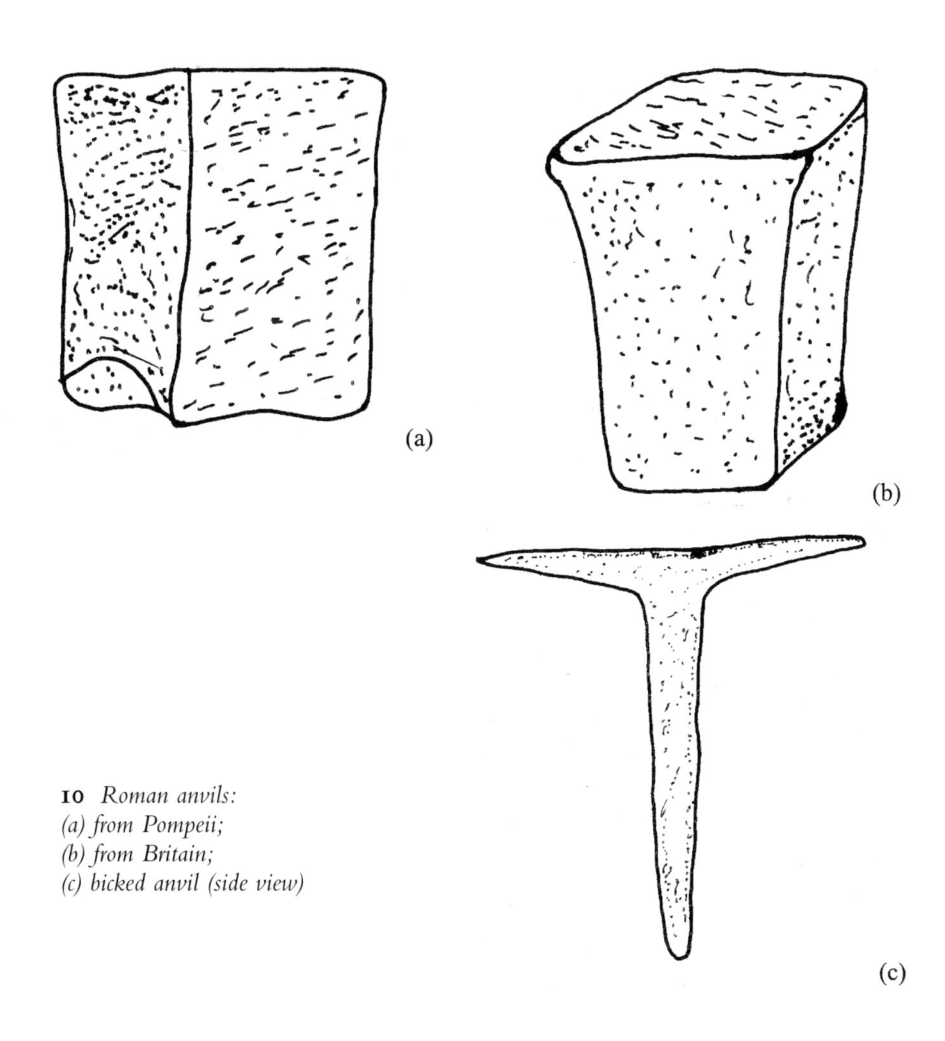

10 *Roman anvils:*
(a) from Pompeii;
(b) from Britain;
(c) bicked anvil (side view)

Hammers

The blacksmith would have had a range of special hammers, the number of which depended upon the type of work he did. A minimum number would be two, one which could be used in one hand, and a heavier sledge hammer for striking work (**8**). Another type was the *cross pein hammer*, which had a rounded face on one end of the head, as shown in **11b**.

Tongs

Tongs (**6**, **7**) would only be used where necessary, the blacksmith preferring to hold the cooler end of the work piece which had not been in the fire – this allows a much better feel for how the iron is behaving under the hammer. Furthermore, it would be much safer to be able to hold the iron directly, eliminating the possibility of it slipping out of the tongs (Sim 1992). We shall see in the next chapter how the blacksmith's tongs could be used in the essential work of consolidating the smelted bloom.

Punches and drifts

Punches were used for making (usually) round holes. Where a more precise diameter was needed, the hole was then finished using a drift to bring it up to size (**9a**).

Fullers

Fullering is a technique used to decrease the cross-section of the work piece locally and increase the length. A pair of fullers was used, the bottom of which was mounted on the anvil by means of a peg hole, the top fuller being a cross pein hammer. With the work piece sandwiched between the two fullers, the top one was then struck (**9b**).

Flatters

Flatters were used in a similar way to fullers, in order to make an uneven surface more level (**9c**).

Swages

Swages, or a pair of swages, were used to form a round on a square section bar. The diameter of the round would be determined by the swage (**9d**).

Sets

A set is a chisel-shaped tool with a wooden handle, which would be struck with a hammer in order to cut hot sheet or bar (**9e**). In addition to the arrangement shown in (**9e**), an alternative mode of use was to fix the set to (for example) the anvil and, holding the work piece over it, hit down onto the set (c.f. **78e**). This method had two benefits: it required one person rather than two to hold the tools and work piece steady, and it was easier to use accurately for operations such as splitting a bar.

Manipulating the iron

Fire welding or forge welding

Until the discovery of oxyacetylene welding in the nineteenth century, the only way to weld iron to iron was by the method known as either fire welding or forge welding. In this process the two pieces to be joined must be heated to a very high temperature (yellow heat 1100°C); it is important to have this just right, as at this temperature the metal is very soft but not molten, and is in its most *plastic* state (almost like modelling clay). The two pieces are then placed on top of each other and hammered with heavy blows. The hammering forces any slag out from between the two pieces and then fuses or welds them into each other (**colour plate 5**). Fire welding is, and always has been, a highly-skilled operation requiring considerable practice to reach a level of proficiency. If the temperature is too low, the parts will not weld: if it is too high then the metal will burn and the resulting weld will be brittle. Gordon (1968: 135) observed that 'The successful makers and shapers of iron learned to sense many factors that we now need laboratory methods to detect'. This is especially true in fire welding, because it relies on the skill of the operator to be able to judge the exact moment when the metal is at the correct temperature for welding. The usual means of determination is by eye, and observing the colour of the iron (**Table 2**); and in the case of fire welding, the correct temperature is also shown by small bursting sparks. If the process is carried out correctly, then the welded section will be as strong as the parent bar. Many blacksmiths were judged by the quality of their fire welds.

Table 2 Colour of iron heated to different temperatures in a forge

Colour	Temperature (°C)
dark brown	550
brown red	630
dark red	680
cherry red	780
light red	850
bright red	900
yellow red	950
yellow	1100
snowball white	1300

When fire welding, it is important that the material is clean and as free as possible from surface contamination such as iron oxide. In modern operations, the surfaces to be joined are often coated with a flux to help dissolve the oxide film and prevent further oxide from forming. Even with the assistance of fluxes, each time a fire weld is made between two pieces, large quantities of iron – up to 50% of the material – may be lost.

It is not known if fluxing was used in ancient fire welding. A series of three experiments conducted (by the author) investigated whether fire welds carried out using different fluxes left any identifiable residues in the material. Scanning Electron Microscope (SEM) analysis of welds made using fluxes showed no traces (Sim 1994: appendix 1). In the Roman period, fluxes are known to have been used for both hard and soft soldering of bronze, brass and iron (Aitchison 1960: 214); therefore as the necessity for fluxing was recognised it is possible it was used in the fire welding of iron but no trace would remain.

Upsetting

Upsetting is a technique used to increase locally the section of the work piece being smithed. The bar (in our example) is heated at the point where it is desired to increase the section, and then the end is struck with the hammer; the cool material either side remains unchanged, whilst the hot and softer material compresses and bulges (**11**). Upsetting could be applied equally well to the end of the work piece (as for example in the production of nails).

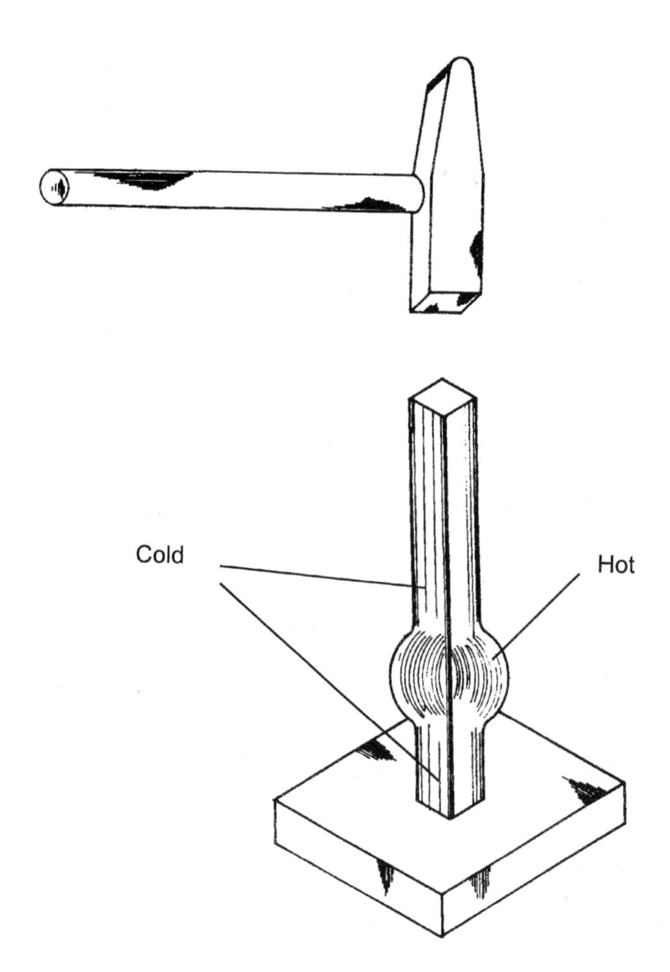

11 *Principles of upsetting*

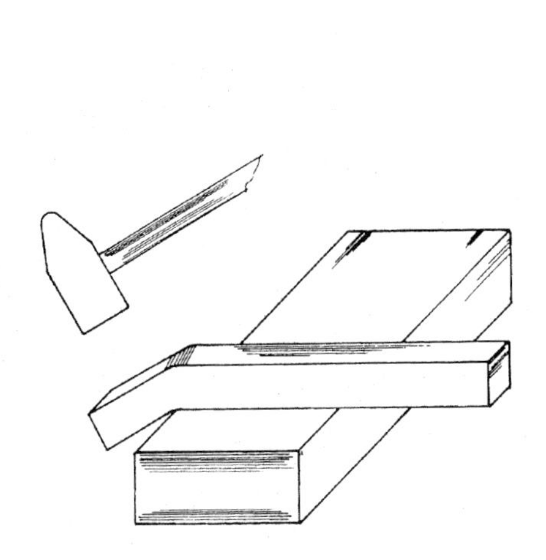
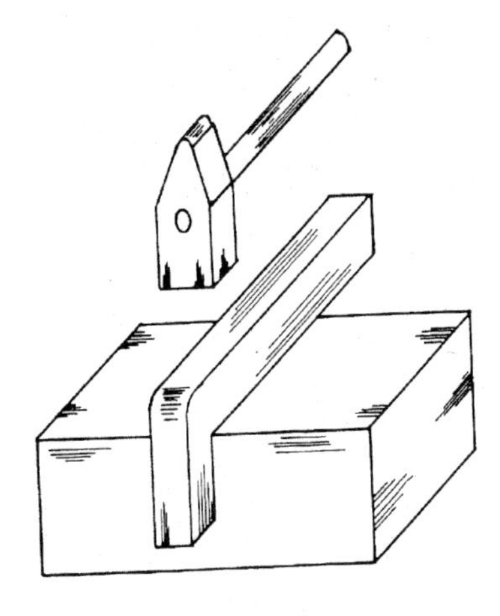

12 *Bending a bar*

Drawing down

Drawing down is the opposite process to upsetting: the cross-section of the bar is reduced leading to an increase in length. A simple example is forging a long point on the end of a bar.

Bending

The operation of bending is usually carried out at bright red heat (900°C), but can be performed at room temperature on smaller sections of bar (**12**).

Hot cutting

In the time before power machinery this was the quickest method of cutting iron – a 25mm^2 bar for example can be cut through in seconds. A chisel is put on top of the red-hot iron and hammered through (**13**). Alternatively, the hot metal is placed on top of a fixed chisel set and hammered onto it (as described in the use of sets).

The military blacksmith

The Roman army obtained its iron goods from a number of sources. There were factories (*fabrica*), some of which were run by private enterprise, that specialised in particular items such as shields or swords or arrows, as well as others that may have supplied a range of arms and armour. Once a military post was established, these *fabrica* were set up within the military system, although not always within the fortress walls. Iron in the form of billets would have been obtained from regional sources, and other worked items could also be acquired from local craftsmen.

There were times however when the legions had to be self-sufficient, such as when they were on campaign. Within the Roman army there were soldiers who trained in

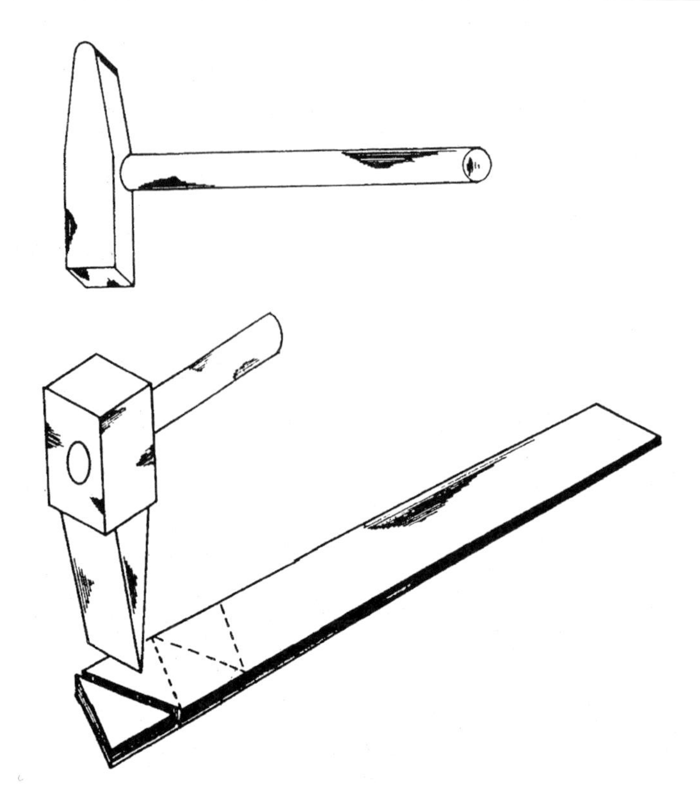

13 *Cutting iron using a set*

crafts – *Immunes* – in return for which they were given release (i.e. they were immune) from various duties and parades. Provided they had the raw material, the legionary blacksmiths would be able to supply new items as well as carry out repairs or modifications to existing equipment. As already mentioned, there would be a ready supply of men to support these operations and act as strikers and fire managers. Experiments conducted by the author have shown that simple levels of blacksmithing can be taught quite easily.

5

Bloomsmithing and Barsmithing

It has been shown in chapter 4 that the product of the smelting process is a bloom of iron containing a quantity of slag. In order to transform the raw product of the bloom into a workable material from which items may be manufactured, it must be smithed to remove the slag and produce a consolidated billet of iron, a process called *bloomsmithing*. Once the billet of iron has been produced, it can be further worked to obtain bars of a size ready for artefact manufacture; this is *barsmithing*. This chapter will discuss the methods of bloomsmithing and barsmithing, and provide some indication of the level of labour required to produce the consolidated iron.

Bloomsmithing

The product of the bloomery process is a mass of iron interspersed with slag; **colour plate 6** shows a typical piece of bloom which has been cut in two, while **14** is a micrograph of the same example. The iron appears as the light grey, whilst the darker material is the unwanted slag. In order to consolidate the bloom, it is necessary to drive out the slag, whilst maintaining the integrity of the bloom. The pieces of iron in the bloom are driven together by *fire welding* (see chapter 5). This is carried out in a hearth; the metal to be joined is heated to approximately 1100°C, at which point it is very soft but not molten. The slag needs to be at a temperature at which it will be fluid enough to be forced out upon hammering the bloom, but not so liquefied that it flows out on its own – if this happens, the resulting voids considerably weaken the bloom, which will fall apart as it is handled.

Work by the author (Sim 1998a) has shown that the most efficient means of refining the bloom to produce a consolidated billet of iron is to exploit the fact that the bloom will tend to break along the weaknesses caused by the slag inclusions. Once the bloom has been broken into small manageable pieces (which is easily achieved while the bloom is still hot on removal from the smelting furnace), the individual parts may be processed before welding the whole together into a billet. Work by the author has shown that if the bloom pieces are worked by simply striking with a hammer to consolidate them, however much care is taken it is difficult to obtain a yield of more

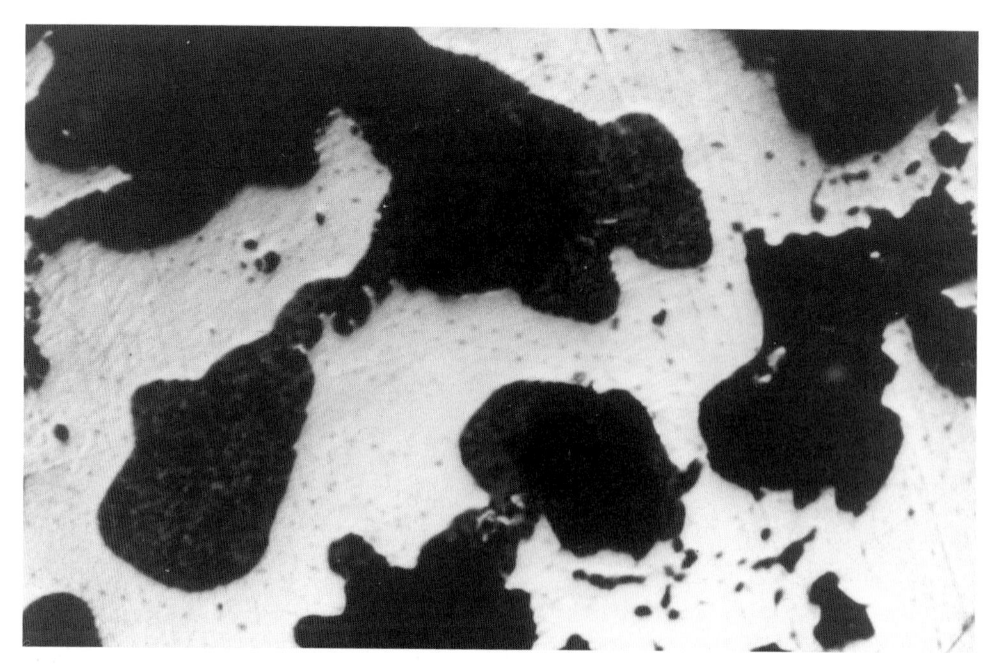

14 *Micrograph of a piece of bloom x 35, polished and etched in 2% nital solution. The light colour is the iron, the dark the slag inclusions*

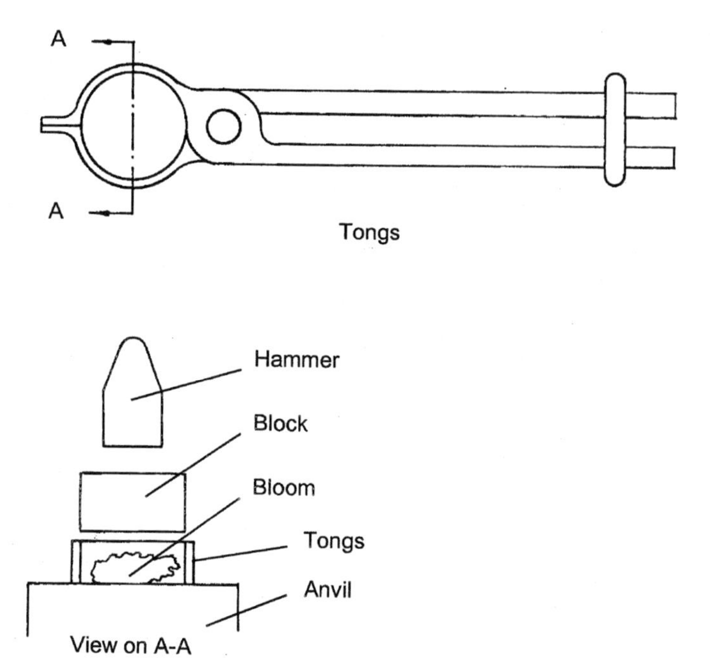

15 *Method of constraining bloom during fire welding to avoid disintegration*

16 *Billet found at Newstead fort.* Copyright Trustees of the National Museums of Scotland

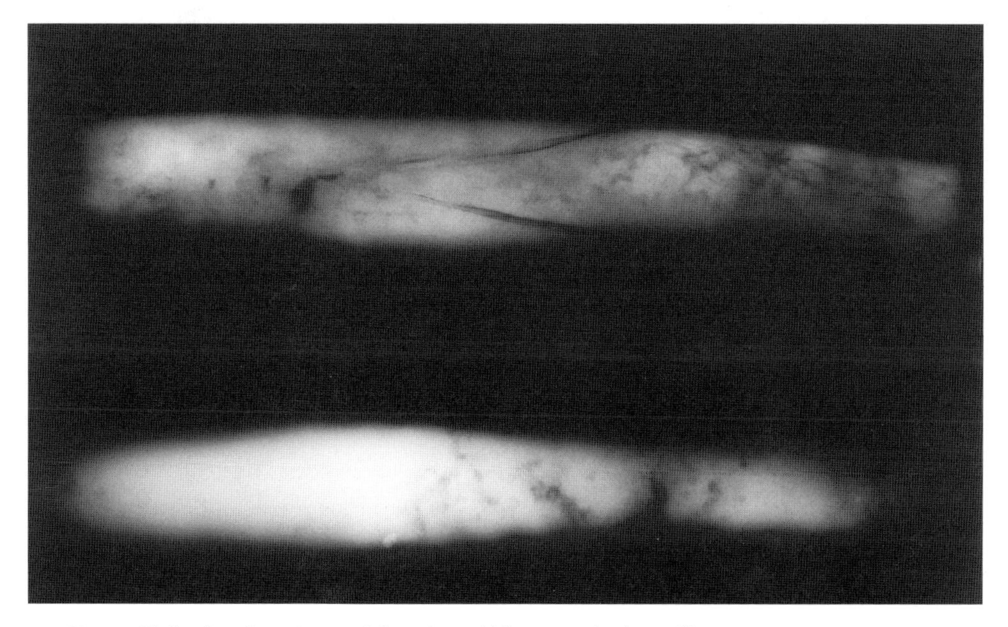

17 *X-ray of billet found at Newstead fort: the weld lines are clearly visible*

than 25% of the original bloom weight. If they are constrained so that they cannot just disintegrate, the yield is nearer 90% by weight (Sim 1998a) (**15**). The tongs with which the blacksmith is traditionally depicted are ideal for this process of constraining the bloom during striking (**6**, **7**). In addition to a much higher yield, the production time is dramatically reduced as the process requires far less delicate hammer work. The study showed that bloomsmithing by the traditionally-received method of working with a large bloom indicated a production time of 17 hours per kg of consolidated iron, whereas the constrained method led to 0.5 hours per kg – an improvement of factor 34. It should be noted that one man operating on his own conducted the experiments quoted here; however, they do serve to demonstrate a feasible technique. As we have seen in chapter 5, it was usual for a blacksmith to employ a staff including at least one striker. It is therefore highly likely that this production time would be reduced still further by a supported, systematic approach.

Further credence for the method described above may also be found in the archaeological record. An iron billet from the Roman legionary fort at Newstead is evidently made up of a number of smaller pieces (**16** & **17**). Other billet evidence, although of a later date (ninth to eleventh century), in the form of finds from Haithabu (northern Germany) show that they too were made up of many small pieces (Thomsen *et al.* 1971). Agricola, writing in 1556, also makes mention of blooms being cut into small pieces, and Tylecote (1976: 41) has suggested this was done prior to forging.

Fire welding a billet

Chapter 5 has discussed the process of fire welding, and the procedure for welding a billet would be exactly the same. Practical experience of fire welding a billet found that as the blocks heated up, their surface became sticky, because the slag melted and became a treacle-like substance. This stickiness helped to hold the block on the bar when it was in the fire. Welding time was very short, and three hammer blows were usually enough to cause welding. Large amounts of liquid slag came out at high speed causing burns to the smith's hands (**colour plate 5**). The surface of the bar was scraped clean after each weld to assist in subsequent welding. As the billet got larger, so welding became easier and the oxidation losses smaller. The heat from the billet raised the temperature of the blocks, in addition to the heat from the fire, and this reduced the welding time. With the help of an assistant, it would be possible to work two bars at a time.

A section through an experimental piece of iron produced is shown in **colour plate 7**. It can be seen that the quality (purity of the iron) was very high at the bottom of the bloom, and decreased towards the top, this was because the material at the base had been worked more and so more slag had been expelled than from the iron at the top (which had only been through one welding cycle). Figure **18** shows a micrograph of the consolidated bloom shown in **colour plate 7**. Comparison may be made with a piece of Roman iron (**19**), and shows that the quality in terms of slag inclusions are of a similar level.

Size of billets

Several billets have been found at the Legionary fortresses of Stageath (Frere and Wilkes 1989) and Newstead (Curle 1911) (**16**, **colour plate 8**). The principle dimensions are listed in **Table 3**.

Table 3 Size and weights of iron billets found at the legionary fortresses of Strageath and Newstead

Location	Dimensions (mm)	Weight (kg)
Strageath	300 x 65 x 65	7.3
	360 x 60 x 60 (each end tapers to 40 x 40)	5.7
	450 x 60 x 70 (each end tapers to 30 x 30)	6.9
	340 x 60 x 60 (each end tapers to 50 x 50)	7.4
Newstead	390 x 60 x 60	7.0
	340 x 60 x 50	6.0
	340 x 60 x 50	6.5

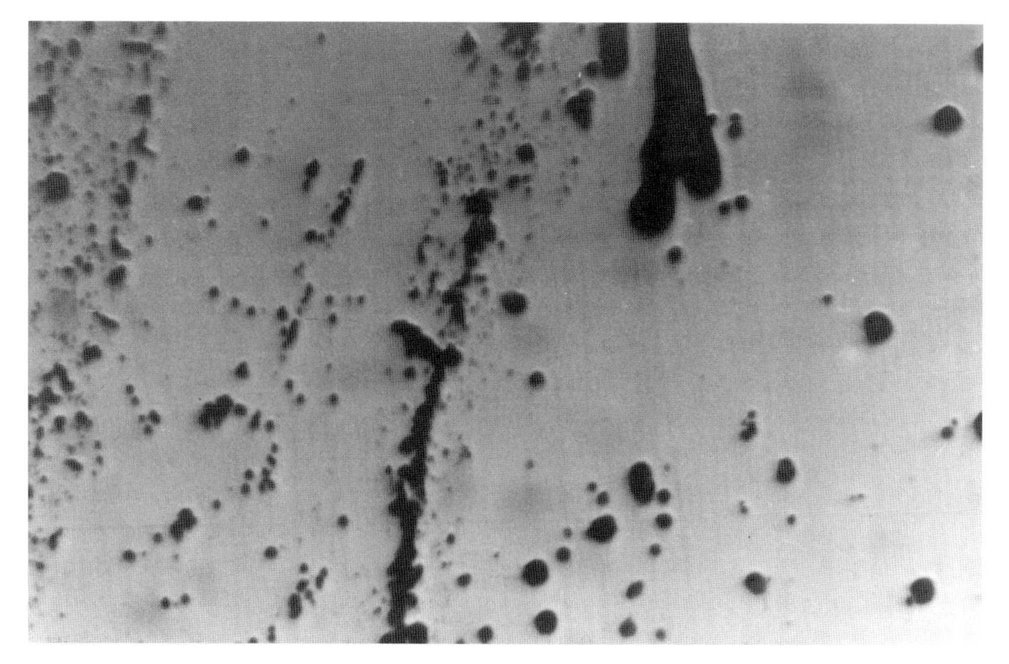

18 *Micrograph of consolidated bloom x 35, polished and etched in 2% nital solution. Note the slag inclusions are smaller — c.f.* **14**. *The vertical bands show where the layers have been added*

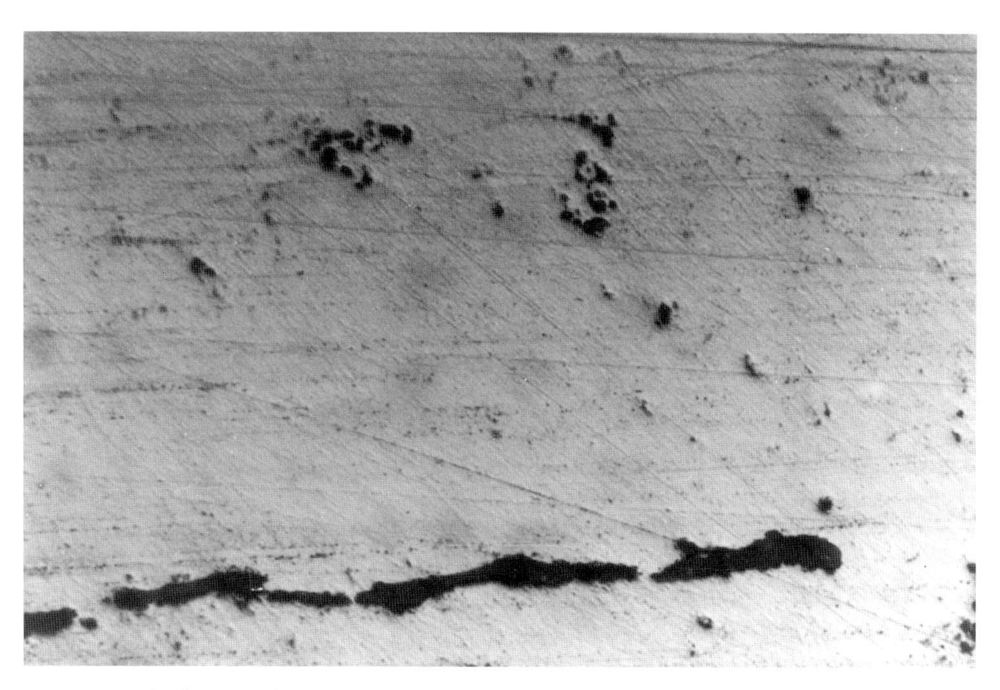

19 *Micrograoh of a piece of Roman iron x 35, polished and etched in 2% nital solution. Note the horizontal black stripe of slag inclusion near the bottom*

Table 4 Duration of forging operations during production of stock sized bar from a billet

Heat No.	Time to reheat (mins:secs)	Time under hammer (mins:secs)	Cumulative time (mins:secs)	Dimensions (mm)
0	-	-	-	55 x 28 x 136*
1	19:17	2:23	21:40	45 x 30 x 136
2	6:28	2:01	30:09	42 x 28 x 146
3	14:50	1:45	46:04	38 x 23 x 150
4	5:54	1:58	53:16	37 x 34 x 160
5	8:10	2:11	63:37	35 x 40 x 160
6	11:41	2:17	77:35	33 x 23 x 170
7	5:20	2:41	85:36	32 x 26 x 185
8	7:31	2:25	95:32	30 x 28 x 195
9	7:53	1:52	104:37	30 x 28 x 200
10	3:40	0:34	108:11	30 x 28 x 203
11	6:40	3:46	118:37	29 x 26 x 210
12	9:37	3:50	131:24	28 x 25 x 216
13	9:36	5:00	145:06	25 x 25 x 220
14	13:10	5:00	163:07	22 x 22 x 230
15	10:52	4:42	179:04	20 x 20 x 250
16	15:06	3:20	197:30	15 x 26 x 290
17	10:44	4:00	212:14	15 x 15 x 320
18	10:14	2:40	225:18	15 x 13 x 330
19	10:02	2:34	237:02	13 x 13 x 360
20	9:53	2:26	249:21	11 x 11 x 390
21	9:27	2:41	261:29	9 x 9 x 500
22	8:46	2:10	272:25	7 x 7 x 650
23	9:46	2:56	284:27	6 x 6 x 800

* NB the billet forged in this experiment was initially tapered (55 x 28mm at one end and 45 x 28mm at the other) before being forged to the more uniform sections listed in this table.

It can be seen that the billets were of a fairly uniform size and shape that would be readily handled, and sufficient for the production of most artefacts. There would have been little point in making them any larger, as there would have been losses associated with production only for them to be cut and material lost again. It is interesting to note that the Haithbu billets mentioned earlier also show a high degree of conformity in both size and shape (**colour plate 9**). In the few cases where larger iron artefacts were required, such as bathhouse beams, several billets were welded together. The uniformity of both dimensions and weights suggest that these billets were of standard form for supply to the Roman army.

Barsmithing

The consolidated bloom in the form of the billet was too large for the manufacture of most artefacts, and was forged down to a series of bars, the dimensions of which would depend upon the artefact to be produced. Practical experience (Sim 1994) showed that in order to heat the raw billet in a reasonable time, it would probably be cut for working in half or into thirds (using a hammer and set). **Table 4** (opposite) gives an indication of the cumulative time required to manufacture bars of various sizes, and **Table 5** (below) the time for the manufacture of a range of sheets from bars. This information is useful, as it gives us an idea of the time taken to perform the first step in the artefact production which will be discussed in the next chapter; it is also interesting to note the scale of the change in the dimensions. During the forging process, the billet lost 20% of its weight and about 85% of its volume. This discrepancy was caused by the fact that there was additional slag and air exclusion from the billet, as well as material loss due to oxidation.

Table 5 Forging times for sheets or iron from bar stock

Heat no.	Time (mins : secs)	Dimensions (mm) width x thickness x length
0	0:0	30 x 28 x 195*
1	10:05	32 x 26 x 207
2	16:13	35 x 20 x 222
3	20:41	37 x 16 x 237
4	23:45	40 x 13 x 257
5	27:20	44 x 11 x 276
6	28:31	47 x 8 x 280
7	32:44	50 x 6 x 307
8	34:45	58 x 5 x 317
9	41:00	60 x 4 x 323
10	45:12	60 x 3 x 352

* ref. Table 4 heat 8 column 4, shows that the time taken to forge this billet is 95 minutes 32 seconds

Quality control

It is not known exactly what form this took in the Roman iron industry, or if there were quality standards for Roman iron. Structural items (such as chain for example) would have had to be made from iron of a high quality or it would fail, whilst the material of the tip on an arrow may be of a much lower standard and still function effectively. There is an obvious trade-off between the amount of time spent forging a billet to refine the iron, with the attendant material losses and the material properties.

Given that there seems to have been a standard size billet which the Roman army used, it would also be reasonable to speculate that they did indeed have some kind of quality control. Crew (1991) has suggested that the Iron Age currency bars are a form of quality control. If so, then it is possible that a similar standard could have existed in the Roman world, however, its form is uncertain.

6

ARTEFACT PRODUCTION

This chapter discusses the last stage in the production of iron artefacts: shaping the bars into their final form. I have tried to give as broad an overview of the Roman iron industry as possible, and discussed in chapter 1 the huge variety of artefacts, which would have been made.

Although it is probable that the Roman army only accounted for a fraction of the consumption of the output of the British iron industry, in many ways it may be thought of as a microcosm of the industry. Vegetius (*Epitoma Rei Militaris)* observed:

> [II, 11] In addition the legion has craftsmen, carpenters, builders, carriage-makers, blacksmiths, painters and other tradesmen for constructing buildings, for preparing the machines, wooden towers and other equipment used to storm enemy cities or defend our own, for constructing new or repairing broken weapons, vehicles and other kinds of catapults. They used to have workshops for making shields, armour and bows, in which arrows, missiles, helmets and all kinds of armour were produced. For the chief concern was that there should be no deficiency in the camp of anything that seemed essential for the army . . .
> [II, 25] To be brief, the legion must carry with it everything believed to be essential for any type of warfare, with the result that wherever it sets up camp it makes an armed city.

When not on campaign, the Roman army spent most of its time stationed at barracks in settlements which were either permanent or semi-permanent, and where a soldier's requirements for shelter, clothing and food and drink would be the same as any other citizen. Richmond (Angus *et al.* 1962: 956) describes the Roman legionary fortress at Inchtuthil:

> [The fortress] covers 50 ac. of ground. It was defended by a ditch and wall of dressed masonry, the wall being backed by a rampart. The four gateways each had twin portals, flanked by timber towers 20ft square. The internal buildings were also in timber, the building technique used being timber framing reinforcing walls of wattle and daub, while the roofs were mostly of oak shingles, but in some

buildings they were tiled. The internal buildings comprise 64 barrack-blocks, capable of holding some 5500 men (the complement of the Roman legion), a headquarters building, a drill-hall, six granaries or food-stores, a hospital, and a workshop, the main streets being bordered by colonnades behind which lay a row of storerooms.

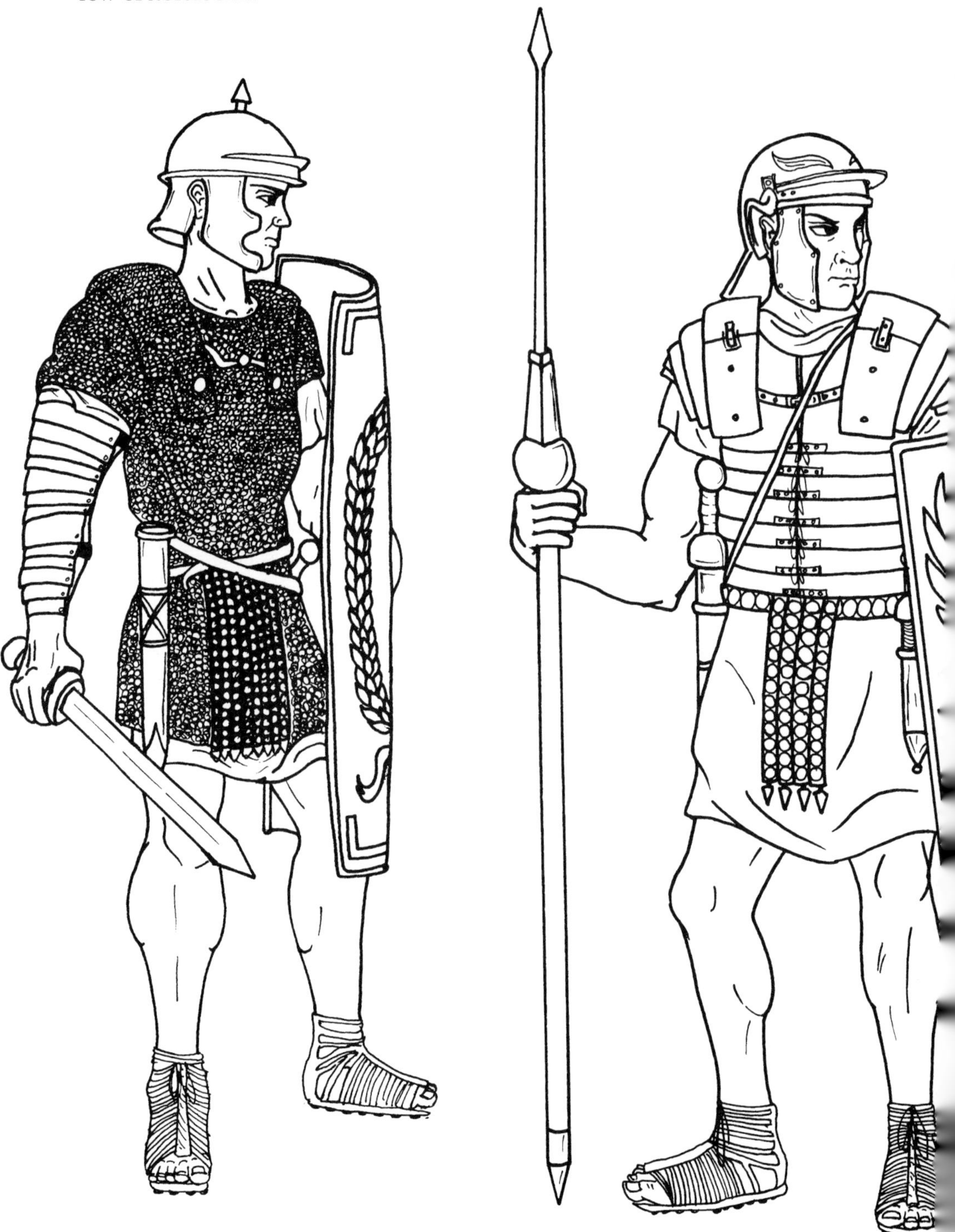

20 *(opposite left) Legionary of the first half of the first century* AD *armed with* scutum *(shield), helmet,* lorica hamata *(mail shirt), sword, dagger and* pilum. After Connolly 1981: 305

21 *(opposite right) Legionary of the second half of the first century* AD *armed with shield, helmet,* lorica segmentata, *sword, dagger and* pilum. After Connolly 1981: 308

22 *(left)* Aquilifer *of the mid-first century* AD *armed with helmet,* lorica squamata *(scale armour) and sword; he carries the Eagle of the Legion.* After Connolly 1981: 306

Drawings by H. Hazelby.

In addition to the military settlements a civilian area (*vecus*) would form, which provided the soldiers with drinking establishments, shops and other services the soldiers needed. It is likely that most weapons and armour were supplied to the army from *fabrice*, or were produced by the legionary smiths. It is possible that the manufacture of weapons by local smiths was not encouraged, in order to guard against uprisings; but local industry would have been able to supply a number of other more domestic items if required. In addition to the legionary's arms and armour, on campaign he would carry other iron items: an entrenching tool, a *dolabra* (a type of pick), shovel, axe, sickle, saucepan and a knife to eat with. Finally the boots a legionary wore (*caligi*) were made of leather with hob nails, millions of which must have been required across the empire as a whole, and presumably which needed regular replacement.

In the first part of this chapter I will consider the manufacture of items of arms and armour which the blacksmith would have produced (**20**, **21**, **22**; **colour plates 10** & **11**). These may be grouped broadly into two categories: disposable and non-disposable. Disposable weapons were typically projectiles: arrows, spears, javelin, *plumbatae*, catapult-bolts heads and *pila*, which whilst they could be reused if recovered, could easily get lost or damaged beyond repair. These weapons had to be cheap and by implication quick to manufacture, using a minimum quantity of material. At the other end of the spectrum, non-disposable weapons took a great deal of time to produce, and were consequently items of great value, such as a *gladius* (sword – especially the pattern-welded sword), shield and armour (including chain mail).

The second part of the chapter considers the production of a range of items which not only the Roman army but the civilian population would be likely to use, such as axes, iron tyres for cart wheels, knives, hammers and nails. The appendix lists some (the list is not to be considered exhaustive) of the museums in the United Kingdom with significant collections of Roman iron artefacts. There are three fundamental methods of manufacturing items from metal: casting, machining and forging. Tylecote (1987) attests that the Romans did not manufacture cast iron. There is some evidence of cast iron in the archaeological record however, although it is the subject of debate as to whether it was made deliberately or by accident. Work by the author has shown that the Romans could easily attain temperatures in excess of 1600°C in their furnaces, thus not ruling out the possibility of its use. However, the majority of artefacts are made of wrought iron or steel (an alloy of iron with carbon).

Machining for the removal of large quantities of material was not available, since milling machines and shapers were unknown. The Romans did however have the use of a pole lathe (**23**), which was capable of turning wood and although this tool would not have had the power to remove large amounts of metal at a single cut, it could have been used for finishing metallic objects such as *styli* (Sim 1997a), shield bosses and helmets.

The most practical method of shaping, which remains so today, is forging. This was the process used to manufacture the artefacts described here. In order to generate a consistent set of experimental data for the purposes of comparison of manufacturing times, the following assumptions were made:

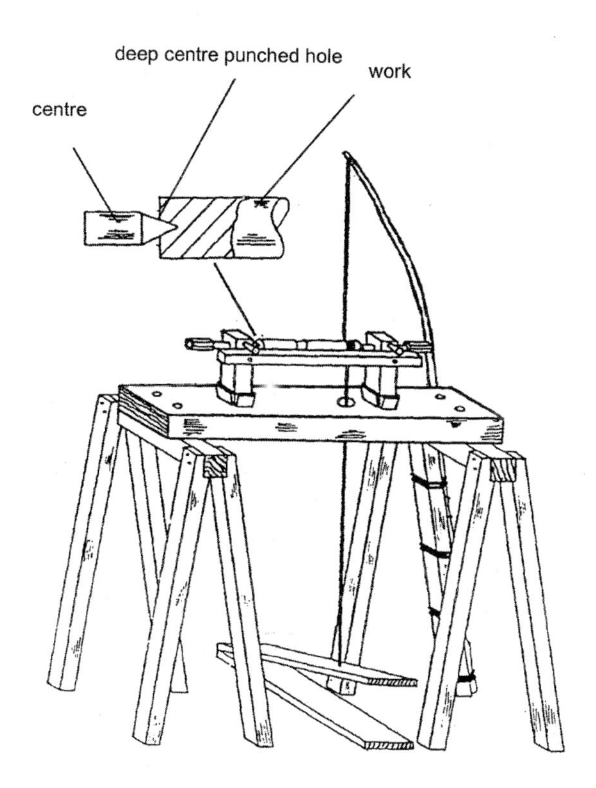

23 *Pole lathe*

- All the items were made as if they were mass-produced.
- The blacksmith worked with only one striker, although in practice, as discussed in chapter 5, a blacksmith can work with up to three. The blacksmith used a 2kg hammer, and the striker a 10kg sledge hammer.
- Wrought iron was used, as there is no evidence for the use of steel for disposable weapons.
- The iron was received in billet form to be forged into appropriate bars or sheet, in order to make blanks from which the weapons could be forged. It is also assumed that there was minimum of material wastage.
- The items had to be produced in the minimum amount of time and with minimum fuel consumption.
- Production was likely to be such that individual operations could be performed by semi-skilled labour.
- No items were hardened.
- Charcoal was used as a fuel throughout (although there is strong evidence of coal being used as an alternative in forging).

Additionally, as no evidence has so far come to light for the use of mechanical processing in the Roman period, none was utilised in the experimental work (the possibilities of mechanical processing will be discussed in more detail in chapter 9).

Manufacture of disposable weapons

Flat-bladed projectile heads

The flat-bladed type of head covers arrowheads, catapult-bolts (although there are other designs of these) javelin and spear heads (**colour plates 12, 13** & **14**).

Arrowheads

The Roman army made use of archers, but not in the same numbers as became common in later warfare such as at Agincourt. The archers were from a part of the army known as the *auxiliaries*, who were specialists in certain types of weapons unsuitable for the style of fighting in which the legionaries of the heavy infantry were trained. The archer shown in **colour plate 15** is equipped according to information found on Trajan's column. The bow is made from laminated layers of wood, horn and sinew (termed today a 'composite' bow), a very powerful weapon which can have a killing range of well over 200m. Equipped with such a bow, an archer could discharge 12 arrows in a minute with ease.

The number of archers or auxiliaries attached to each legion varied, and so it is not possible to give a precise number: we may assume a figure of 100. In an engagement where 100 archers fired 12 arrows a minute for five minutes, 6000 arrows would be shot. The logistics of supplying this quantity of disposable weapon are formidable, and it can be seen that any type of arrowhead that is both quick and cheap to make will be highly desirable. This type of consideration would also be true of the other projectile type weapons, particularly the *ballista*-bolts, and to a lesser extent the javelin and spear.

Catapults

Roman catapults of all sizes and types, whether bolt-shooters (*catapultae*) or stone-throwers (*ballistae*), derived their power from two separate bow arms inserted into two rope torsion springs usually made from animal sinew. These highly tensioned and torsioned springs were mounted in strong hardwood frames reinforced with iron or bronze plating. The smallest sizes of *catapultae* were often termed scorpions, the larger scorpion (*scorpio maior*) having a spring diameter of about 75mm, the smaller scorpion (*scorpio minor*) one of about 45mm. The Xanten-Wardt frame is an example of the latter, the Spanish frame from Ampurias of the former size.

The range of these catapults far exceeded those of contemporary hand bows and crossbows. Agesistratos, an expert artillery engineer, is credited with reaching a range of three and a half stadium lengths (647m) with a *scorpio maior*; the average legionary artillerymen may perhaps have regularly achieved ranges slightly less than this. They would be able to shoot with a high degree of accuracy because of the stable construction of *catapultae*, and the fact that the stock could be tilted up and down and traversed through 360°, allowing rapid changes of aim and a wide arc of fire. Legionaries could be taught to operate catapults in a few hours, whereas the skill and accuracy required by an archer using a hand held bow takes much longer, years, to perfect. As the range of ammunition described above would suggest, these machines were used in varied situations: against personnel as well as in sieges and naval engagements.

The scenes on Trajan's Column show that by AD 101-2 the legions were fielding a dramatically improved design of bolt-shooter with a spring-frame entirely of metal, and characterised by an upper strut with a semi-circular arch. The smallest size of arch strut bolt-shooter, the *manuballista*, is described in a Greek manuscript (Wilkins 1995 and 2003), and probably used the same size of rope spring as the *scorpio minor*. Scene XL on the Column shows *carroballistae,* larger arch strut catapults mounted on mule-drawn carts, shooting over the heads of advancing legionaries. Each legion had 55 of these (Vegetius *Epitoma Rei Militaris* II.25). Experiments with modern reconstructions of arch strut catapults have achieved a rate of fire of four bolts per minute. An advancing enemy under fire from 55 *carroballistae* would thus be showered with 1100 bolts in 5 minutes! Experiments by the author (with Alan Wilkins) have shown that the whole catapult-bolt (head, shaft and fletching) can take an hour to make. As with the arrows, with so many rounds being fired in such a short time the problems of supply are formidable. The broad head type of catapult-bolt described here is very simple to manufacture, and needs no sharpening because the amount of energy it contains on impact will allow it penetrate anything it hits. For further work on Roman catapults see Wilkins A. (1995) Wilkins A. and Morgan L. (2000) Wilkins A. (2003) Wilkins A. and Morgan L. (2012).

Manufacture of flat-bladed projectile heads

The types of projectile heads described below are all of the same basic design; they are produced from a single piece of metal with no joints, varying only in size. They are made by producing a strip of iron with a width equal to the length of the finished weapon from point to socket. The blank is cut into triangular pieces, and formed into weapons as described below.

The starting point is a billet of iron (**24a**) which is forged into a rough blank of rectangular cross-section (**24b**); using a flatter this is forged into a smooth-sided strip (**24c**). The width of this is equal to the length of the weapon head from point to socket, and will of course vary from weapon to weapon.

Using a hot set, a triangular blank is cut from the strip (**24d**). The cut edges are chamfered from the cutting, but this can be removed with a coarse rasp. Using a bottom swage and a cross pein hammer, the flange is partly formed (**24e, f**). The socket is closed up around a tapering mandrel (**24g**) to produce the finished item (**24h**).

This type of weapon could be produced in a very economical way, both in terms of material consumption and time. The way in which the blank was cut (**24d**) would lead to very little wastage. The fact that the weapons were made from a single piece of material means that there were no material- and time-consuming fire welds during production. The time needed for manufacture may be considered commensurate with a mass-produced item; for example, while the production of the spear type head took 46 minutes to forge (**Table 6**), the time taken to finish was somewhat longer at 79 minutes – but it is unlikely that the blacksmith would have undertaken this work. It is quite easy to imagine a production line of semi-skilled labour producing such items.

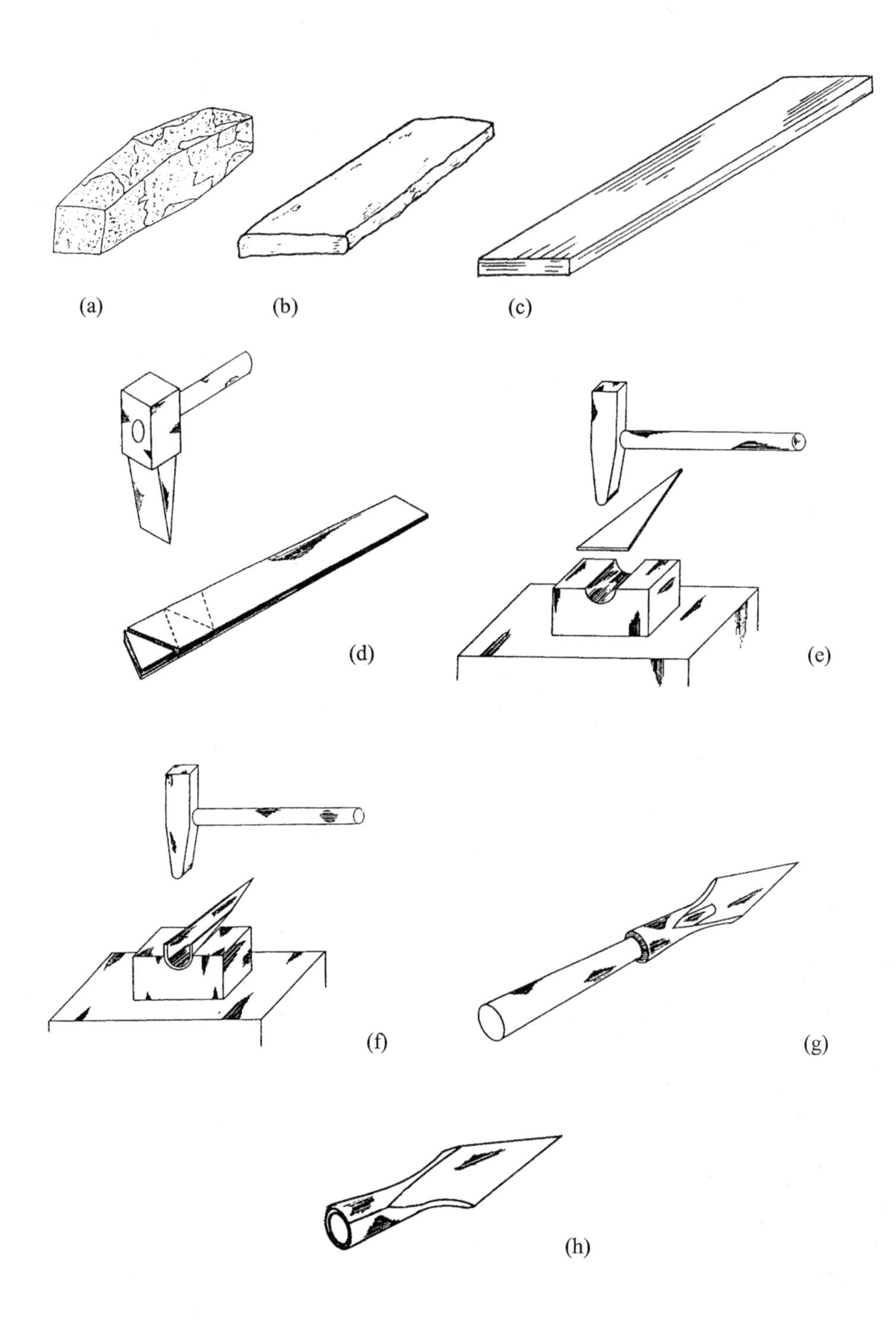

24 *Stages in the manufacture of an arrowhead: (a) billet; (b) forged bar; (c) flattened bar; (d) cutting blanks using a hot set; (e, f) forming the socket; (g) finishing the socket on a tapered mandril; (h) the finished head*

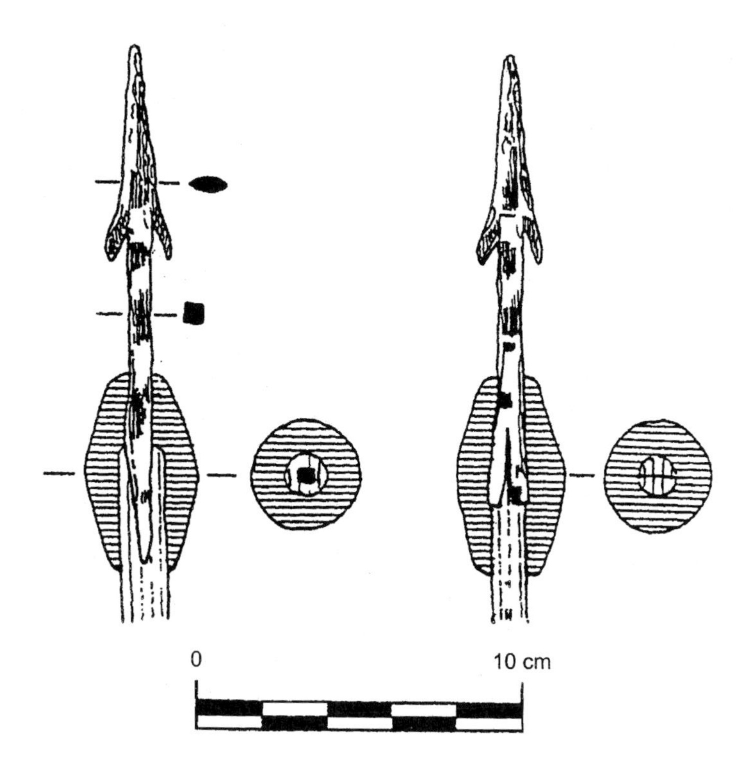

25 *Different types of* plumbatae

The plumbata

The *plumbata* was a projectile carried by heavy infantry and light-armed troops alike. Vegetius (*Epitoma Rei Militaris.*) II.15-16) states that they carried five, held behind their shields. It was believed that they were delivered by throwing underarm but experiments by the author has shown that thrown over arm, *plumbatae* are more accurate and can achieve a greater distance.

The barbs prevented the head from being pulled out of the wound, whilst the lead weight stopped it being pushed through. It was a very effective weapon and had the added advantage of being reasonably quick and cheap to make.

There are two types of *plumbata* head: those with a socketed head into which the wooden shaft is fitted and then some times pinned, and those with a plain tang that is fitted into the shaft (**25:** c.f. also Sherlock 1979 and Griffiths 1995). These two versions vary only in the method of fixing the head to the shaft.

The different options for manufacture are discussed by Sim (1995). The methods presented here are the quickest and cheapest, and therefore considered the most likely to have been used. The construction can be divided into four operations: forging the iron head; making a mould to cast the lead weight (this needs only to be done once as it may be reused many times); preparing the ash shafts; and casting the lead weights on the shafts.

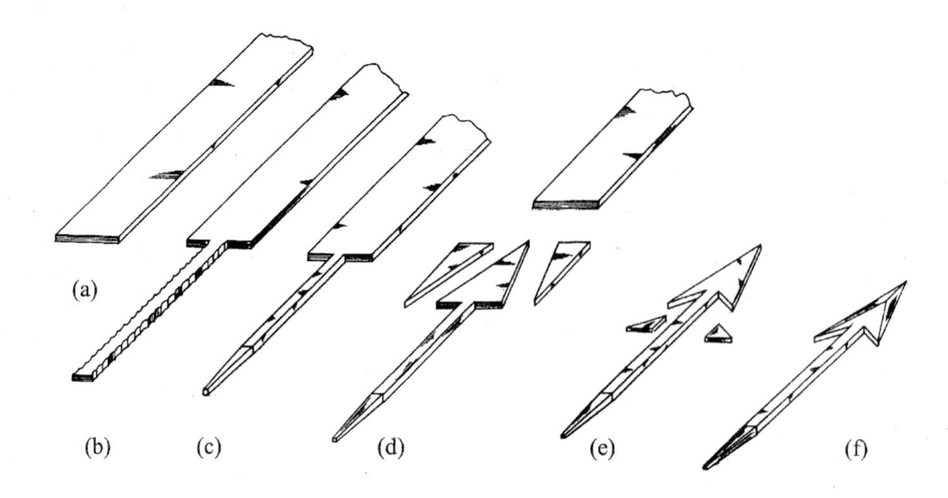

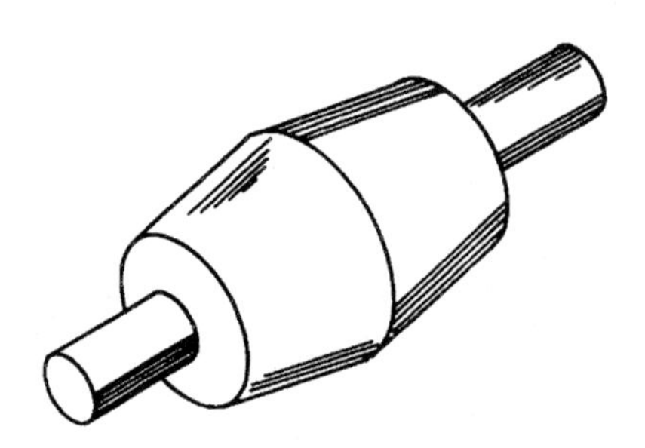

26 *Stages in the manufacture of a* plumbata *head: (a) bar; (b) the tang is rough forged; (c) the tang is forged smooth with a square tapering point; (d) the point is cut from the parent bar; (e) the barbs are formed; (f) the head is filed to shape*

27 *Wooden pattern for a* plumbata *mould*

Manufacture of a plumbata *head*

A piece of flat-wrought iron bar measuring 6 x 25mm was used (**26a**). First the tang was rough forged using the edge of the anvil and a cross pein hammer (**26b**); it was then forged smooth into a square tapering point (**26c**). The blank was cut from the parent bar and two wedge shaped pieces of metal were cut off to form the point. This was achieved by cutting the metal halfway through and then turning it over and cutting from the other side. From this procedure, it can be seen that the cutting edge had started to form (**26d**). A hot set was used to cut the head to form the barbs, and when they were cut out, the set was used as a lever to prise the barbs out a little (**26e**). The cutting edges were forged down (but not to a razor edge, which would burn during forging). When cold, the iron was filed to give the head sharp edges and point (**26f**).

The procedure would be the same for the socketed heads, with the exception that the end of the bar would be flared first, then the shanks and head forged, finally, the flared end would be rolled to shape to form the socket (as for the spear or arrow; **24**).

Casting the lead weight and assembly

For a long period the method of casting the lead onto the wooden shaft was the topic of much discussion. The difficulty was that it was assumed that when liquid lead was poured onto the wooden shaft it would burn the shaft through, thus making the

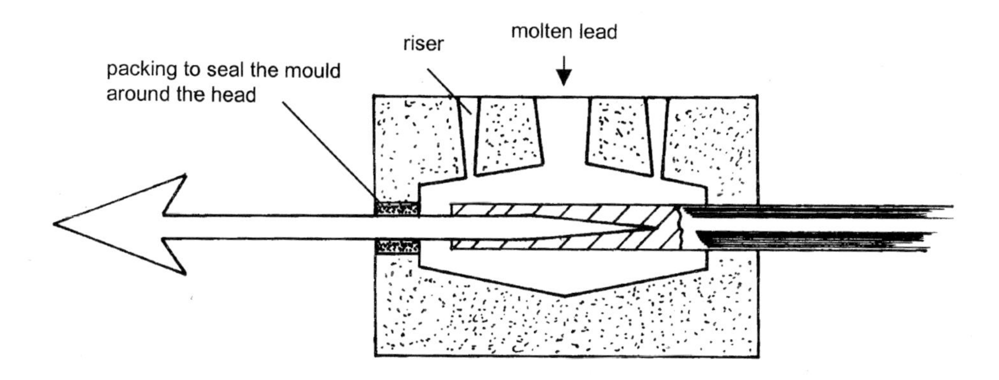

28 Plumbata *in mould ready for lead casting*

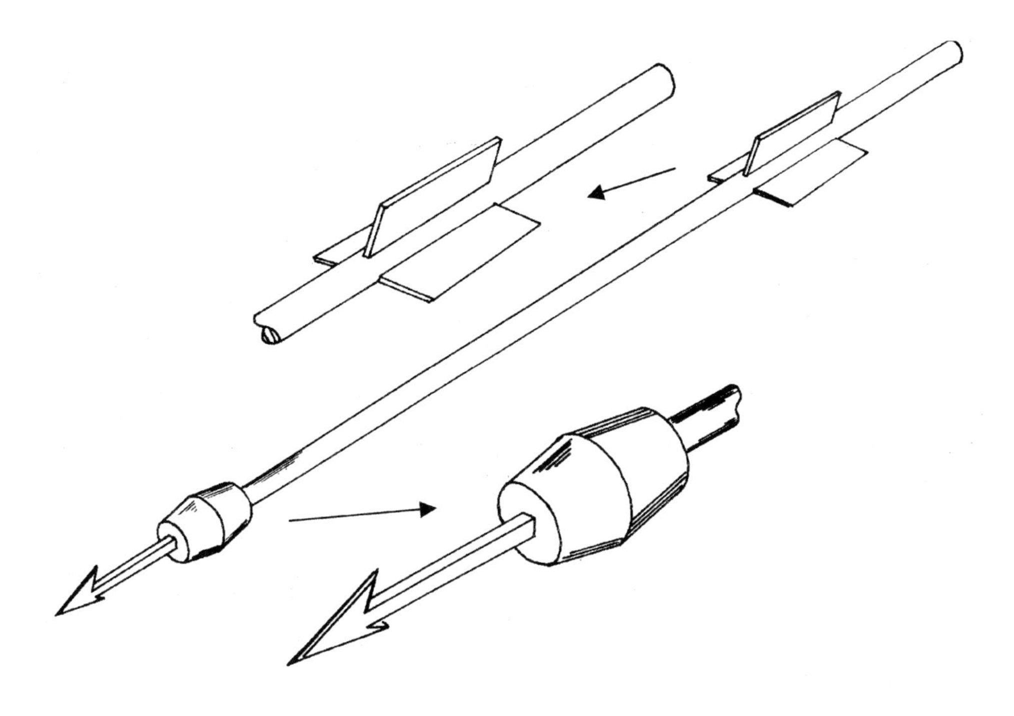

29 *Finished* plumbatae *taken from mould with flights added*

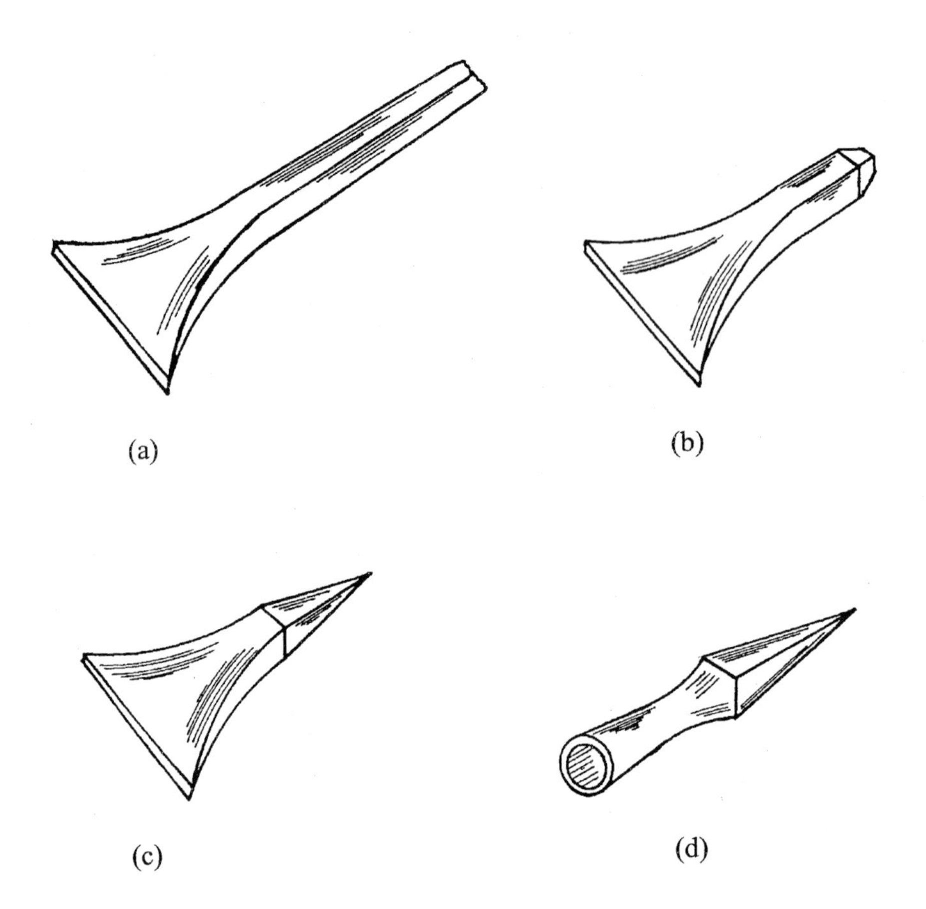

30 *Stages in the manufacture of a square pyramid-type bolt head: (a) flaring the bar for the socket; (b, c) drawing down the point; (d) forming the socket (as* **24e–g***)*

weapon useless. The author has shown that the casting of lead onto a wooden shaft is a simple and straightforward operation, well within the skill set of any metalworker or armourer. (Sim 1995)

In the first set of experiments to replicate *plumbatae* the moulds for casting the weights were made from plaster (**27, 28**).

Over the course of the next few years more experiments were conducted with making and testing *plumbatae* (Sim 2012). One of the facts to emerge was that in all the many field trials with replica *plumbatae* the wooden shafts broke on four out of every five *plumbatae* thrown. On one level this breaking has the advantage that the enemy cannot retrieve them and then throw them back. The disadvantage is that those recovered from the field of battle will have to be repaired in large numbers.

After the initial trials showed that only a small number of castings could be made with plaster moulds, it was decided to try different materials to see if the number of castings could be improved.

Table 6 shows the results from experiments with different media used to cast *plumbata* weights.

Table 6 Experiments with various media used to make moulds

Experiment number	Material	Treatment	Number of castings produced	Comments
1	Plaster	Dried at room temperature for 48 hours	11	Started to deteriorate after 3 castings
2	Plaster	Dried in warm room for 48 hours	6	Started to deteriorate after 2 castings
3	Plaster	Dried at room temperature for 48 hours	6	Repeat of experiment 1
4	Plaster	Dried at room temperature for 72 hours	5	Started to deteriorate after 2 castings
5	Plaster	Dried in warm room for 72 hours	5	Started to deteriorate after 2 castings
6	Plaster mixed with grog	Dried at room temperature	6	Started to deteriorate after 3 castings
7	Puddle clay	Dried at room temp till leather hard. Put in charcoal embers for six hours	2	Started to deteriorate after 2 castings
8	Puddle clay mixed with fine sand	Fired in a pottery kiln	5	Started to deteriorate after 1 casting
9	Cement mixed with sand	Dried at room temperature for 48 hours	2	Started to deteriorate after 1 casting

As can be seen from **Table 6** the best results were obtained using plaster but even this was unpredictable. In one experiment 11 castings were made; in another using the same plaster only 3 castings were produced. All the materials varied from one mould to the next.

There are several disadvantages in using these types of mould.

They are time-consuming to produce. Each mould requires approximately one hour to produce but all of them require considerable amounts of time for setting and drying. Moulds to cast liquid metal in have to be free from all moisture. The liquid metal coming into contact with any moisture will cause the liquid to form super heated steam and thus will cause an explosion. Wet clay and wet plaster have to be dried slowly to avoid cracking and so there would have to be a constant supply of moulds in various stages of manufacture if *plumbatae* were made in any quantity. This is uneconomical and wasteful. The use of this type of material to make moulds will cause problems when *plumbatae* have to be repaired in the field. Transporting heavy material such as clay is a logistical problem and no one can rely on there being clay in the place where armies may find themselves. Ever if local material was available the processing of it during times of conflict would have been a difficult task.

These experiments have demonstrated that casting *plumbata* weights using what is considered to be common media available at the time has considerable disadvantages and has led the author to consider a different approach.

The use of metal moulds

Justification for a different approach

Clay and plaster are not the only material that moulds could be made from; one alternative is that moulds were made from metal.

The use of two part metal moulds to cast metal in is well known from early times. Bronze moulds for casting bronze axe heads are known in Britain from the Middle Bronze Age (1400-100 BC) (Tylecote 1976) and several other examples of the use of metal moulds demonstrate that their use was common and well understood. There is an multi part mould for casting socketed arrow heads from Mosul (Marion1961) There is also a copper mould from Coppa Nevigata in Italy (Tylcote 1976, 33). This shows that the use of metal moulds has a long history and was a well-established method of casting that must have been common knowledge to Roman metalworkers.

It has been assumed that *plumbata* weights were cast onto the head and shaft using moulds made of clay or plaster. To date no findings from the archaeological record have supported this assumption. On the other hand clay and plaster do not survive well in the archaeological record so there is little possibility that any evidence to support the use of clay or plaster will emerge.

It is of course possible that clay moulds were never used at all and metal moulds were used from the start of the manufacturing of *plumbatae*.

The limitations of clay moulds became very quickly obvious to the author during experiments and there is no reason to suppose it would not become apparent to Roman metalworkers just as quickly. Any manufacturer will always try to find ways of improving his methods of production and with the knowledge that metal moulds have been in use to cast metal it seems likely that this would have been considered as an alternative by Roman metalworkers.

Copper and brass were common metals in the Roman period and there was a plentiful supply of both metals. Copper is an ideal metal for making this type of mould from. It is a very good conductor of heat and casting lead onto wood requires that the heat be conducted away from the wood as quickly as possible.

The laws of thermo dynamics states that heat energy moves from hot to cold. The heat will be conducted away from the lead through the copper mould to the material that surrounds the copper, probably damp earth or damp sand. This will be very rapid and the heat from the lead casting will be conducted away from the wooden shaft quickly before it has time to heat up and burn. This has already been demonstrated (Sim 1995). In fact a copper mould is likely to transfer heat faster than a clay or plaster mould. Damage to the copper mould from liquid lead will be negligible. Lead melts at 326°C and copper melts at 1000°C, because of the rapid cooling of the mould the lead is not in contact for long enough to raise the temperature of the mould for long enough for it to cause any damage.

It makes sense to invest in the time to make a mould that will have a long production life. It was decided to make moulds from copper to determine if the amount of time to make such a mould would be cost effective.

The experiments

Given that lead was used in huge quantities in the Roman period the techniques associated with the methods of working it would be familiar to any Roman maker of weapons.

Adhering to the principle of only making reproduction from the materials available at the time and using only the tools from the period it was decided to make the mould from copper.

Two Cones

The shape of the *plumbata* weight made in the first set of experiments is that of a double frustum of a cone joined at their largest diameter. Such a shape could be made by joining two frustums together. It is first necessary to draw the frusturum to actual size as shown below.

The development of the frustum of a cone is shown overleaf.

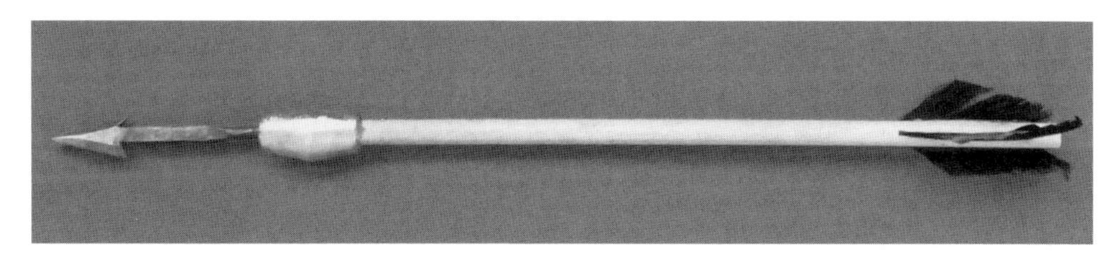

31 *Modern copy of a* plumbata

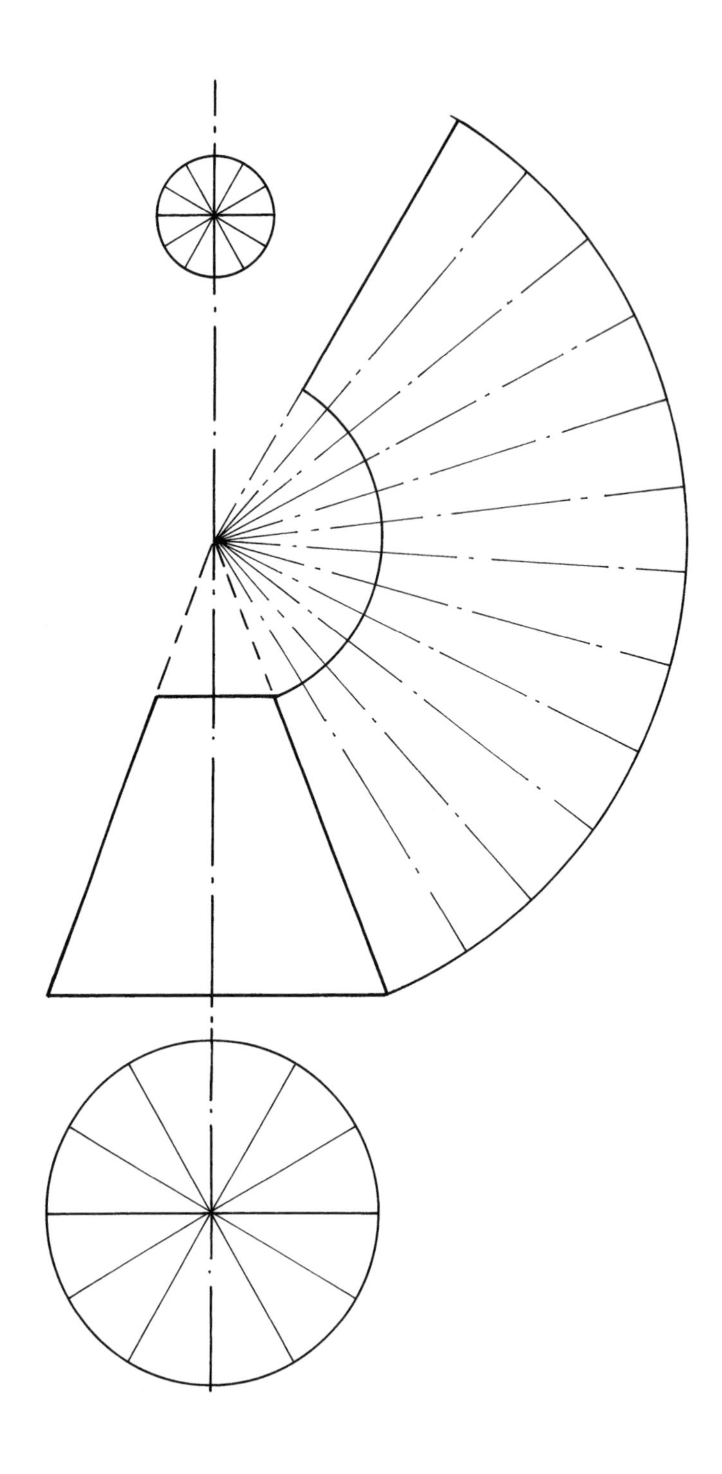

32 *Development of the frustum of a cone*

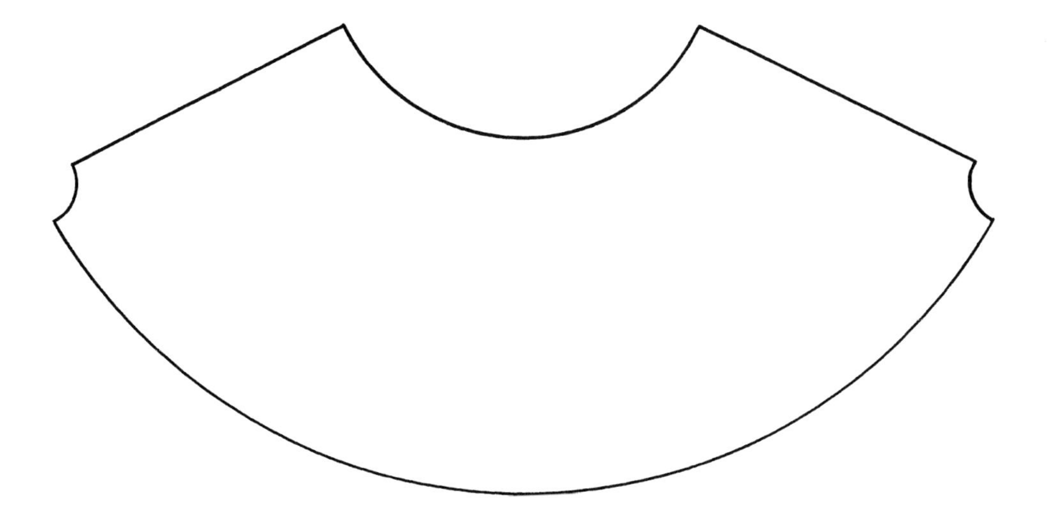

33 *Development cut to shape from a copper sheet*

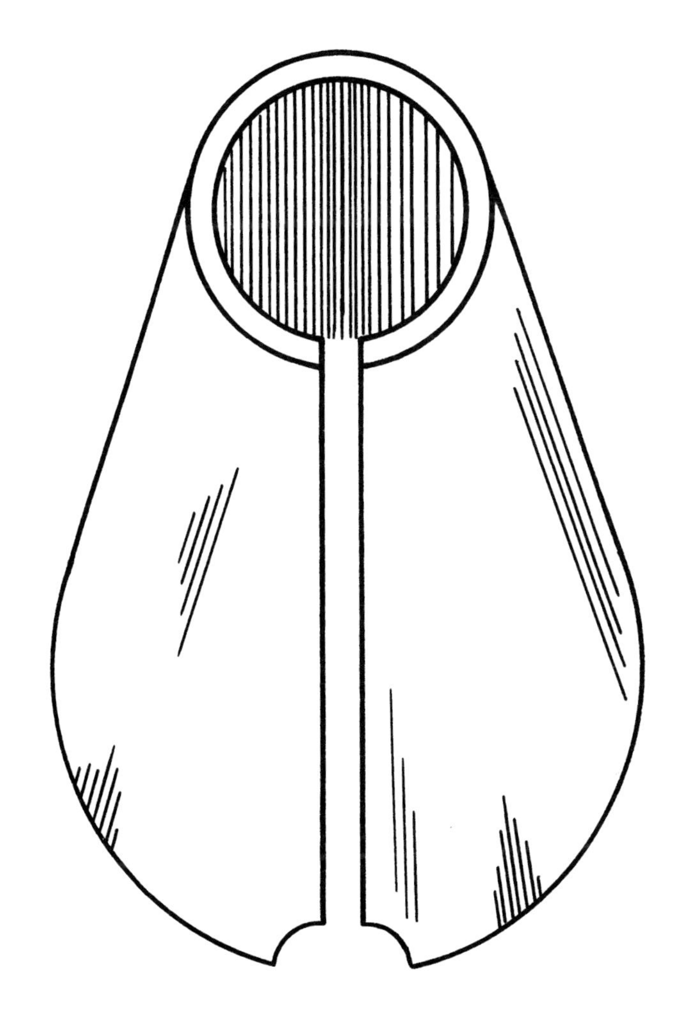

34 *Copper sheet folded into a frustum of a cone*

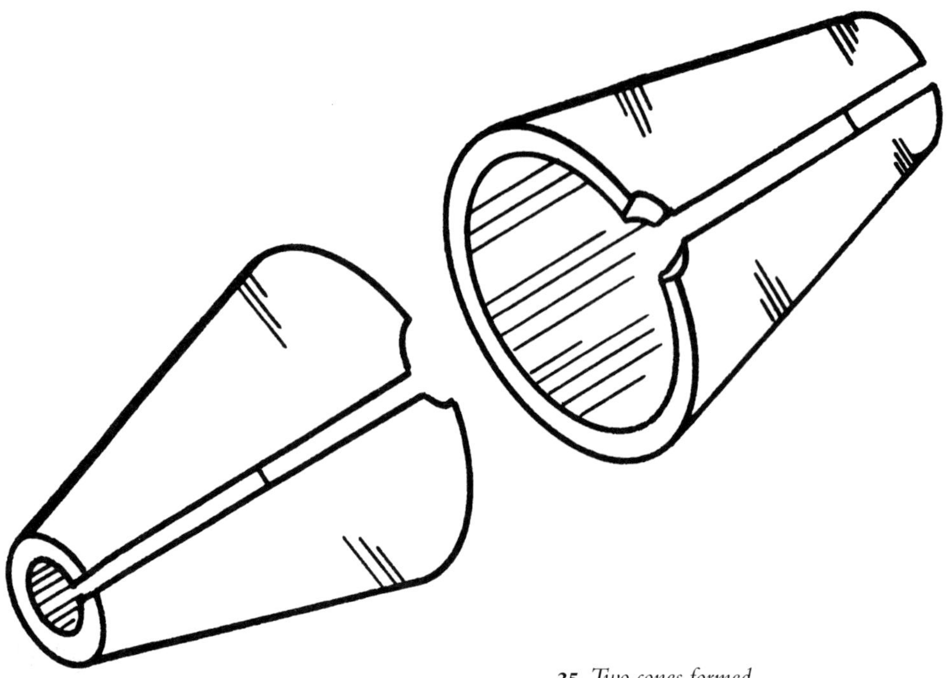

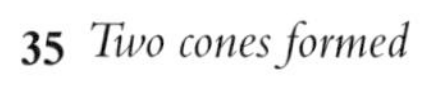

35 *Two cones formed*

36 *Two cones soldered together*

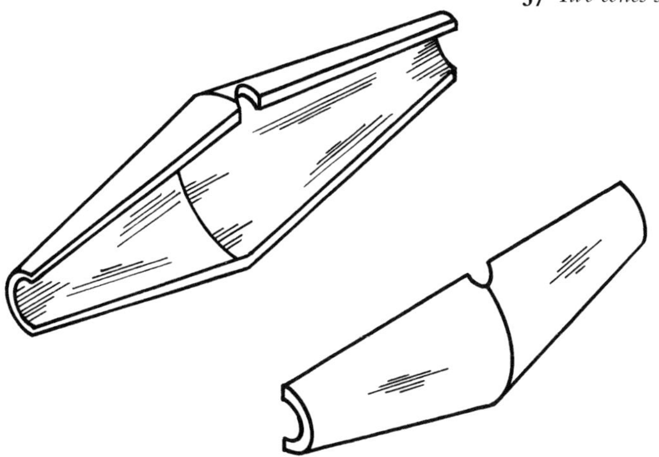

37 *Two cones separated down the long axis*

38 *The finished mould*

39 *Casting produced from metal mould*

This sequence of operations shows that the making of such a mould is a piece of simple metalwork that any competent metalworker could easily carry out. The production sequence shows a careful drawing of the development of the cone. The author has worked in a tinsmiths shop and has seen tinsmiths cut developments of cones by eye with no marking out. The cones fitted perfectly. Roman sheet metalworkers and tinsmiths would be no less skilled.

The total time to produce this mould was 53 minutes.

At the time of writing this mould has produced 63 castings with no visible change to the appearance of the mould's inner surface.

Most two piece moulds are fitted with registers to make sure both parts of the mould are correctly aligned when brought together. In this mould it is unnecessary because the wooden shaft and the shank of the metal head align the two halves of the mould on its long axis and the alignment on the short axis is done by eye.

As well as a long life this type of mould is easy to transport and a legionary could easily carry one in his equipment. It is unlikely that these moulds would survive as a pair in the archaeological record but if one side was found on its own it seems unlikely that its function would be obvious.

It is possible to carry the pattern for a clay mould but it is uncertain that suitable clay or other material would be available at the destination (the pattern is light but carrying clay would be heavy and there is no guarantee that where you arrive there will be any clay or anything else to make a mould out of). There is also the time to make a mould and cure it before it can have liquid metal poured into it to be considered. (See Making *plumbatae* in the field.)

The second two hemispheres

The mould made from two truncated cones requires a soldered joint, though this is a simple matter for any competent metalworker. It is possible that there are times (when in the field) when the necessary equipment for soldering might not be available. Therefore it was decided to investigate the possibility of producing a mould from a single piece of sheet copper.

It was decided to make *plumbatae* with a spherical weight. The reasoning behind this approach is that Vegetius describes legionaries carrying five *plumbatae* inside their shields. Although no description of size is given, common sense dictates they would not be so heavy as to make manoeuvering the shield difficult or so bulky they would interfere with manoeuvering the shield during combat.

The sequence of operations was as follows:

The mould was made from sheet copper 1.0mm thick.

Using a pair of dividers a circle 50.0 mm in diameter was drawn. The circle was cut to shape with shears to produce a disc.

The disc was annealed. A dome headed wooden mallet was used to hammer the disc into a concave hemisphere in a wooden block. This produced a hemisphere with rough edges. The hemisphere was placed on a flat piece of sand stone and rubbed with a circular motion until the edges were smooth. This was then repeated to produce a second hemisphere and the edges were smoothed until the edges of both hemispheres

40 *The finished mould*

41 *Casting produced from metal mould*

fitted with no gap. The two pieces placed together did not form a true sphere but a flattened sphere. Such a weight would be much easer to carry inside a shield and so it was decided to keep this mould and use it for tests.

There are three holes in the rim of the spheres two opposite each other to accommodate the shaft and the head. The third at 90° to the other two is for pouring the liquid metal into the mould. There were made using a circular file.

Total production time: 54 minutes.

This procedure was repeated for four different sizes of hemisphere. The production time was eventually reduced to 43 minutes.

Making the cylinder type

It is possible that the weights made from a double frustum could have been cast as a cylinder then hammered to shape. The mould shown in Fig. 42 was made from a single piece of sheet copper.

Both halves were produced in 41 minutes. The weight was cast producing the cylinder shown in figure 43. It was found that the head and shaft were loose. To tighten them up they were hammered on an anvil while being rotated, which produced the tapering cone shown in figure44 This is an identical shape to that produced in the first set of experiments. This raises the question, were the original *plumbatae* found at Burgh Castle (Sherlock 1979, 101) produced by this method?

42 *Two halves of a cylindrical copper mould*

43 *Cylindrical casting*

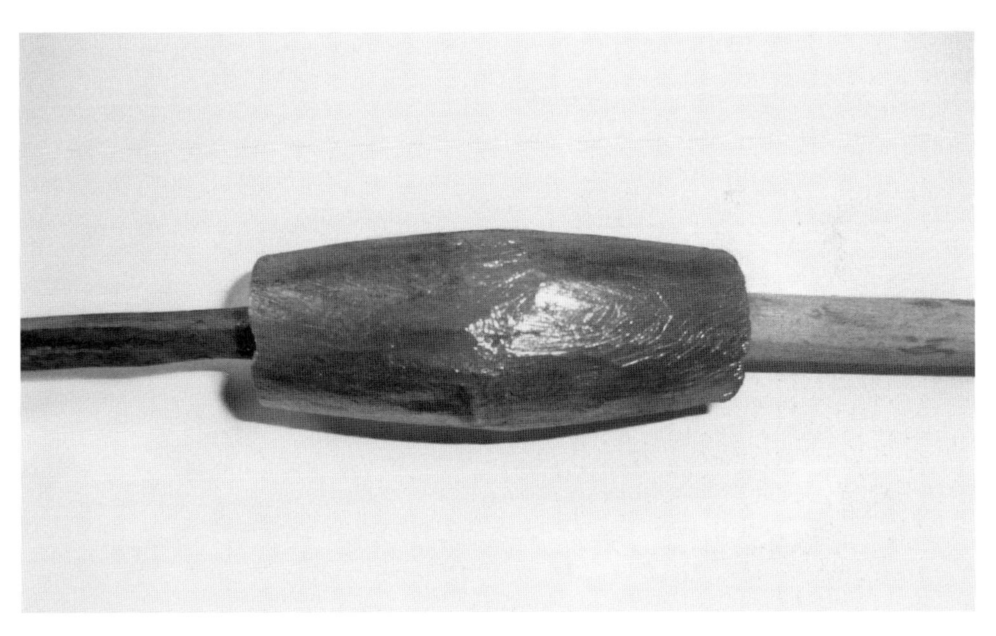

44 *Casting after hammering*

45 *The method of casting by burring in sand*

46 *Cast weight and mould*

Casting the plumbata

There is no necessity to clamp the two halves of the mould together for casting. The metal is poured in slowly and provided the mould is packed tightly into the sand or earth surrounding it there is enough to hold the two halves together.

At the time of writing, over 70 castings have been made using this method and there have been no separating of the moulds and no spillage of liquid metal during any of the castings. The mould shows no sign of deterioration.

As clay moulds take 20 minutes to make and require time to dry or if fired, fuel to fire them. The experiments with making clay and plaster moulds have shown that each mould takes a minimum of one hour to make and has a very short life. It seems the outlay of 54 minutes plus the cost of copper (it can be made from any scrap) is a worthwhile return on the investment. The hemisphere design is made from a single piece of metal and is very simple. If a different shape was required then a punch of that shape could be made in either metal or even hard wood. It would be hammered into a lead block thus producing a die. The sheet metal would be placed in the die then the punch would be hammered onto the metal driving it into the die and forming the shape.

Conclusions

Experiments have shown that making moulds for casting *plumbatae* from materials such as clay or plaster is a time consuming and very inefficient method of production. The existence of metal moulds for casting metal objects has been known since the bronze age and it is suggested that it would have been known to the Roman workmen.

Metal moulds are very robust and would be capable of producing many hundreds of castings. They are also easy to produce, cheap to make, have a long life span and are easy to transport.

It has been shown that a simple and very efficient mould can be made from copper sheet and such moulds can be produced using only basic metalworking techniques. It is not work needing a highly skilled craftsman.

These experiments have been conducted to show the minimum time and materials that would be needed to make these moulds. It is possible that some form of attachment such as a chain could have been added to keep the two halves of the mould together or they could have been attached to tong ends for faster production.

From their appearance it is unlikely that such items found in the archaeological record would be identified as moulds for casting *plumbatae.*

This *plumbata* was made using only the tools and equipment available during the Roman period. The supply of large numbers of these weapons would not be a difficulty for either an individual manufacturer supplying the army or for a legionary workshop. Both would have easy access to all the materials necessary to produce *plumbatae.*

The weights were cast onto the shafts and heads using a mould, which may have been made by turning up a wooden pattern on a pole lathe (**23**, **30**) and then using this to form it. The material which would have been used to produce the mould is uncertain, but they would probably be made from clay mixed with sand (Tylecote 1987) or plaster (Sim 1995).

The tanged type of head was fitted by heating the tang to a dull red colour and burning it into the shaft. A small hole was first drilled in the end of the shaft to act as a guide. The shaft and head were positioned in the mould (**28**), which would be preheated before the lead was poured in (this would stop the lead chilling and blocking the mould as soon as pouring commenced). After cooling, the excess lead from the mould could easily be removed (and recycled). The *plumbatae* would be finished off by fletching. Note that the flights are not at the end of the shafts (such as on an arrow), as it is likely that this is where the *plumbata* was gripped for throwing (**29**).

The socketed type heads were fitted to the shafts using a knife to shave them to fit the sockets. A bow drill could be used to drill a hole in the socket and through the shaft, following which a pin would be put in the hole and then riveted in place. The casting of the weight would be applied in exactly the same way as for the tanged type.

The total loss of iron due to forging and filing was 19%, about average for this type of process. A typical manufacturing time of 35 minutes was found for the tanged type of head, whilst the socketed head took slightly longer at 41 minutes.

The bolt head (square pyramid)

The catapult-bolt head manufactured in this experiment was based on an example illustrated by Manning (1985 V144, pl. 80). This is a common type, with a pyramid-shaped point and a tapering socket (**colour plate 18**). A length of bar was heated to a yellow-red heat (950°C), and one end flared into a fantail shape (**30a**). A further heat was taken to the same temperature as before, and the head was cut off the bar with a hot set (**30b**). In one heat, the pyramid point was forged to shape (**30c**). Using a bottom swage and the cross pein end of the hammer, the socket was partly formed and then closed over a mandril on the anvil using the hammer (**30d**). When the metal had cooled down to black-red heat, the point was hammered to impart a smooth surface finish. As with the flat blade type weapons, this method of manufacture was simple and involved little loss of material. Three bolt heads were made in an average time of 53 minutes (**Table 6**).

The pilum

The *pilum* underwent many changes in design during its history, including alterations to the tang and the length of the shaft, and the addition of a lead weight (c.f. **20**, **21**). Its basic design was a pointed head on a slender shaft fitted to a wooden shaft. The head was of the square pyramid type, which would make a hole in a shield thus allowing the smaller shank to pass through. *Pila* were meant as throwing weapons, but if necessity demanded they could be used as spears.

Manufacture of a pilum

A billet of iron was rough forged into a bar of square cross-section, and further forged between swages to produce a bar 700mm long by 13mm² (**47a–c**). This was enough material to make one *pilum*, and conveniently is long enough to handle when forging without resorting to the use of tongs. The end of the bar was heated to a light yellow heat (1000°C) over a length of 90mm. On removal, a length of up to 40mm at the end was quenched in cold water, and the adjacent hot part upset (**47d**). A total of eight heats was needed to complete the upsetting. The section that was upset was drawn down to a square point (**47e**). Using a *fuller* and *cross-pein hammer* the length behind the head was reduced in section before being evened out with a flatter (**47f,g**). A large radius was left under the head so as not to weaken it during the *fullering*. The tang was produced by *fullering* and the use of a flatter. Using a pointed punch, and then a tapering drift, the two holes were made in the tang. The radius under the head was removed by filing to provide a square shoulder. The rest of the forging was brought to size by filing, and the finished surface was produced with various grades of file (**47h**). Production was halted when the item had a clean finish – although additional finishing could have been undertaken, it would not have enhanced the performance of this weapon in any way.

Production took rather longer than the other 'disposable' type weapons, approximately 10.5 hours from billet to finished product. Of this 4 hours 41 minutes was spent filing (an activity which would probably not have been undertaken by the blacksmith); the actual forging of the artefact took just over two hours once the bar had been produced.

The production of the *pilum* presents no technological problems; it is straightforward forge-work, of a fairly simple kind. The weapon was forged to as near the finished size as possible in order to minimise the amount of time-consuming work involved in finishing by filing. Even so, 18% of the metal was removed to bring about the finished item. It is assumed that, as this weapon probably had only a short life span, polishing was not an appropriate process, since it would fulfil no practical purpose, and only add to the cost (although legionaries might have polished their own *pila*, in order to enhance their appearance when on parade). From an operational point of view, the design of the *pilum* is simple, yet very effective. The tip is strong and sharp and would penetrate most materials with ease, even without a hardened point (the hardening of iron will be discussed later). The design is such that when the *pilum* strikes an object it will penetrate, and allow the thinner shaft to pass through the hole, however, the design is such that the relatively long tapering shaft tends to bend. Caesar (*De Bello Gallico* I.25) describes *pilum* heads bending and rendering the shields of the enemy useless:

> Caesar had all the horses – starting with his own – sent away out of sight, so that everyone might stand in equal danger and no one have any chance of flight. Then he addressed the men and joined battle. By throwing down spears [*pilum*] from their commanding position the troops easily broke the enemy's phalanx, and then drew their swords and charged. The Gauls were much hampered in action because a single spear [*pilum*] often pierced more than one of their over-lapping shields and pinned them together; and, as the iron bent, they could not pull them out. With their left arms thus encumbered it was impossible for them to

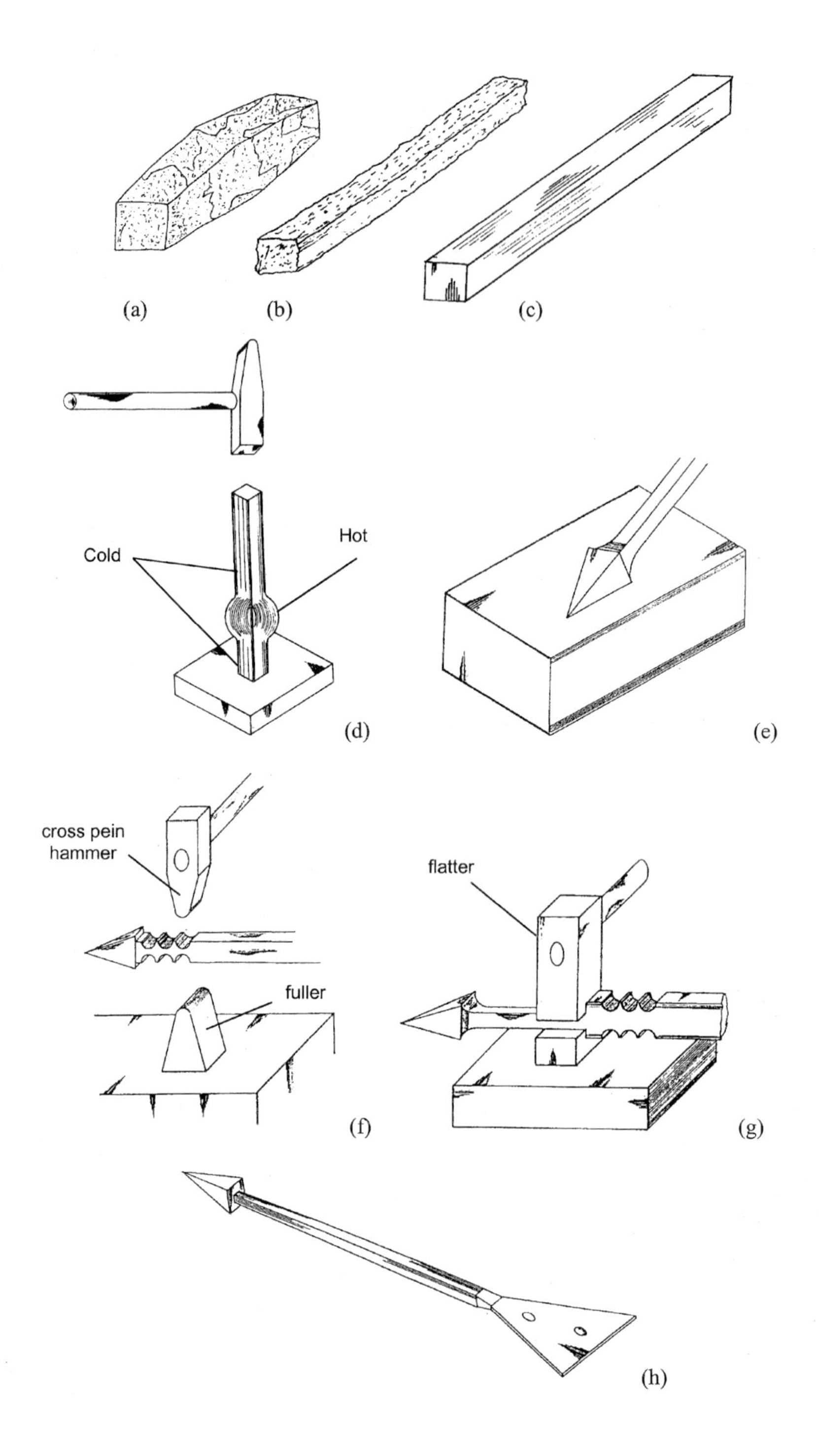

47 *Stages in the manufacture of a* pilum*: (a) billet; (b) forged bar); (c) flattened bar; (d) upsetting the end to form the point; (e) shaping the point; (f) reducing the shaft; (g) flattening out; (h) flare opposite end and punch two holes*

> fight properly, and many, after repeated attempts to jerk their arms free, preferred to drop the shields and fight unprotected. At length, exhausted by wounds, they began to fall back towards a hill about a mile away.

It has been suggested that this attribute, which may almost be described as a self-destruct mechanism, was a design feature to prevent the immediate reuse by the enemy (as a returning projectile). Whilst possible, this seems unlikely: it is unusual to design a weapon to fail, especially in such an unregulated way. Testing by the author of the type of *pilum* described here found some bending during some of the experiments. It seems safest merely to say that under some conditions a *pilum* will bend. Of those used in battle that were recovered, some would be damaged beyond repair, but others could be straightened by the blacksmith for reuse, and the unhardened points would be easy to resharpen. Irreparably damaged weapons would be recycled, as the material would be of good quality and far too valuable to abandon. A production time of 10 hours 26 minutes for each *pilum*, together with a fuel consumption of 13.5kg, shows that this was not a cheap weapon to produce; but as it was manufactured over a considerable period of time and passed through several modifications in design, one is led to the conclusion that the effectiveness of the *pilum* justified its expense.

The fire arrow

The destructive power of fire is known to most humans and the Romans exploited it to the full. Fire was used in sieges, pitched battles and naval engagements and is equally destructive when used against people or buildings. Most of the artillery pieces used in antiquity were capable of discharging incendiary devices, sometimes in the form of pots filled with flammable materials such as bitumen, sulphur, liquid tar and oil (Vegetius *Epitoma Rei Militaris.* IV.8), or possibly with other materials of which we have no knowledge.

The fire arrow discussed here is in the form of a cage, which it is thought was filled with bitumen that was then set alight and shot. When the arrow struck its target the burning pitch would be thrown over the immediate area, thus optimising the spread of the fire (an arrow that has only a rag soaked in burning material will tend only to ignite the small area it strikes.)

The fire-arrowhead described is based on examples illustrated by Robertson *et al.* (1975: 32) and Manning (1985: 177). The cage is made from three lengths of iron, welded at each end. One end forms the point, while the other is fixed into the shaft (**50d**). Almost certainly these arrowheads were used only once, and again, economy would no doubt play an important role in their design. The heads would need to be of a sufficiently large size to hold adequate incendiary material to keep burning long enough to set the fire once the target was struck – some of the charge would burn up during flight, especially due to the rush of oxygen induced by the passage of the arrow through the air.

Manufacture of a fire arrow

Three pieces of iron, typically 6mm in section and 140mm long, were fire-welded at each end (**50a**), and the welds were then drawn down into points (**50b**). The assembly was given a clockwise twist of 270°, which was then turned in the opposite direction to open it out and form a cage (**50c**).

The forging time was 23 minutes, and a further 7 minutes were taken to file the point and the shoulder end to fit in the arrow shaft, giving a total of 30 minutes for each arrow. This production time seems quite high. Given also the length of material required for each head was 420mm (of 6mm section), reference to **Table 4** shows it will require 149 minutes to forge enough material for each arrowhead from a billet. Hence, the total production time is 179 minutes (almost 3 hours).

Discussion of disposable weapon manufacturing techniques

The weapons considered here are all expendable, therefore it seems there are two important criteria to take into account in their design: efficient performance and production costs. All the weapons discussed (apart from the fire arrow) were forged from a single piece of material, entirely without joints and using the minimum amount of metal. As joints tend to be a source of weakness, their elimination may have been a deliberate factor in the design, or more likely, demonstrate an avoidance of fire welding, a technique which leads to considerable loss of material (chapter 6). Production can be considered in two stages. In the first, the raw material, be it billet or scrap, is forged into a suitable blank (chapter 6); in the second, the weapons are produced. The items discussed thus far are all simple to make, and if the manufacturing was divided into individual tasks they could be made by semi-skilled labour: certainly the bars for all the items can be prepared by such workers. It is not unreasonable to assume that these objects were made in large quantities, and then stored ready for use: the Inchtuthil hoard of nails (nearly one million nails weighing 7 tonnes – Angus *et al.* 1962) would certainly indicate mass production in advance of specific demand. The storage of iron items in such a way as to prevent rusting was known in antiquity. Pliny (*Natural History*) suggests the use of such substances as liquid tar, bitumen, red lead, white lead and gypsum. It should also be noted that if iron is left as forged, the oxide coat will give a limited amount of protection.

Hardening is a process that is carried out to provide a long-lasting cutting edge, and so is not necessary on a disposable weapon. Gilmour and Tylecote (1986: 242) state the examples of Romano-British spearheads that they examined showed no evidence of hardening (hardening and heat treatments will be discussed further in chapter 8.) It is likely for several reasons that this was a deliberate policy by the Romans. In many of the wars of conquest (though not in the civil wars), the Roman army was fighting opponents who used little or no body armour. Weapons made of wrought iron could be given a cutting edge that was just as sharp as that of hardened steel, and were equally capable of causing fatal injury in battle. The difference here between the two materials is that the wrought iron will not *hold* the edge, whereas hardened steel will. Since however the weapons were disposable, they only had to hold their edge for a short time. Furthermore, field experiments by the author showed that where a weapon did get damaged – for example, a javelin head was bent and blunted when it hit a rock (**colour plate 19**) – it could be brought back to serviceable condition in less than a minute. If this weapon had been made from hardened steel it would need much more time, and the services of a skilled blacksmith to repair it.

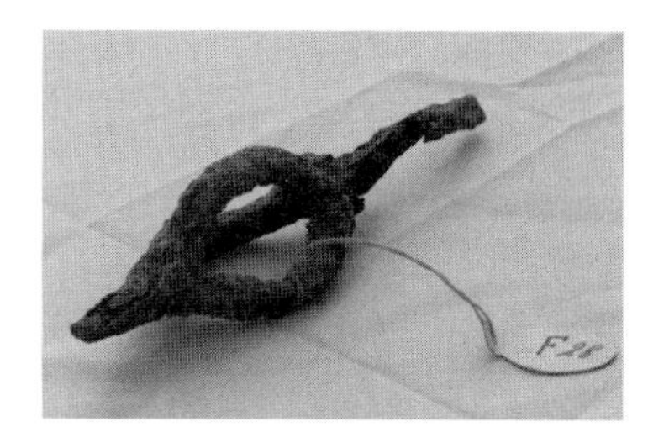

48 *Original Roman fire arrow*

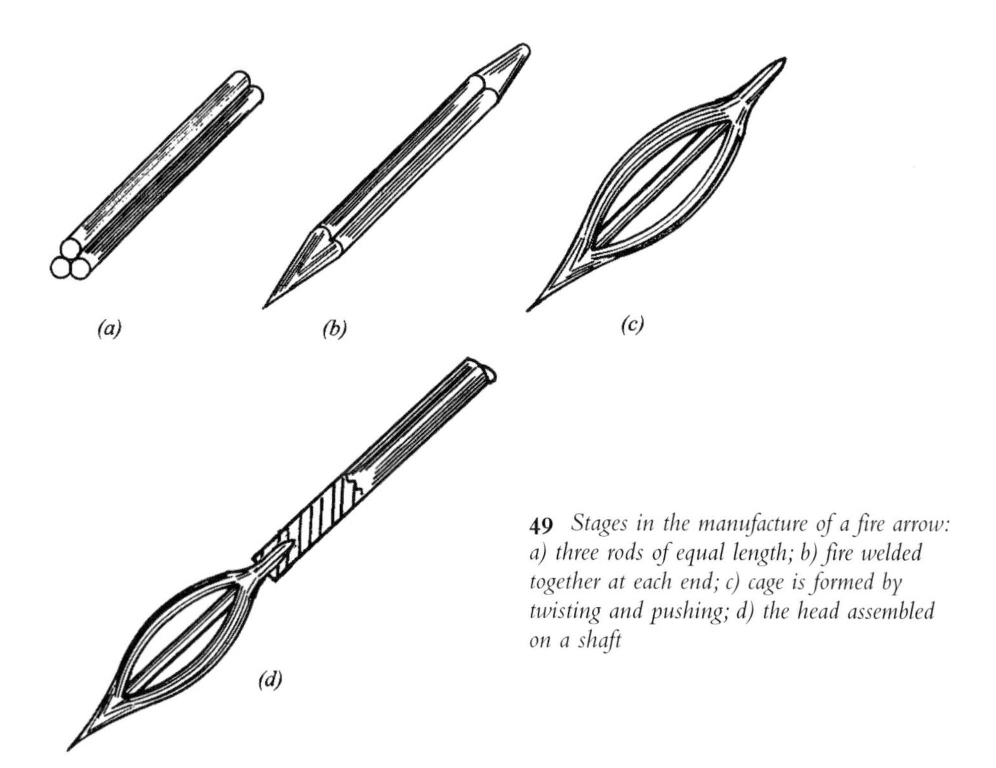

49 *Stages in the manufacture of a fire arrow: a) three rods of equal length; b) fire welded together at each end; c) cage is formed by twisting and pushing; d) the head assembled on a shaft*

50 *Modern reproduction*

So far as the pyramid-shaped heads are concerned, it has already been noted that the configuration of both the *pilum* and the pyramid bolt head are such that they will penetrate almost any material. Thus a hardened point would not increase their effectiveness, unless they were to be used against very thick plate armour.

Table 7 Forging and finishing times (h : m) for disposable and non-disposable weapons

Item	Forging time billet to blank	Forging time	Finishing time	Total time
Spear	0 : 54	0 : 46	1 : 19	2 : 59
Flat bladed arrow	0 : 30	0 : 05	0 : 02	0 : 37
Flat bolt head	0 : 31	0 : 05	None	0 : 36
Javelin	0 : 54	0 : 45	1 : 19	2 : 58
Plumbatae	0 : 40	0 : 14	0 : 11	1 : 05
Pyramid bolt head	0 : 35	0 : 18	None	0 : 53
Pilum	4 : 38	2 : 07	3 : 41	10 : 26
Fire Arrow	2 : 29	0 : 23	0 : 07	2 : 59
Gladius	4 : 46	2 : 00	30 : 00	36 : 46

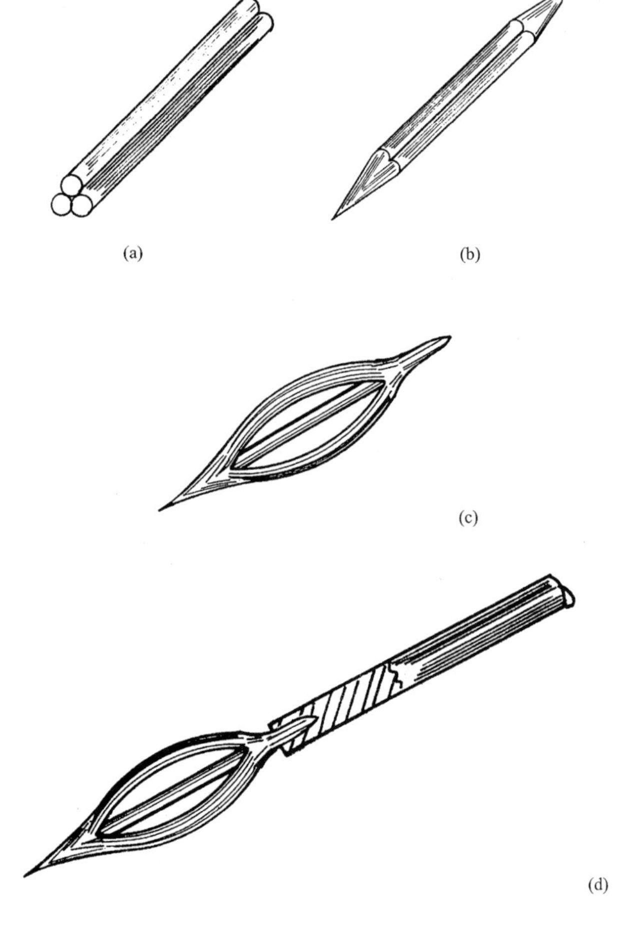

49 *Stages in the manufacture of a fire arrow: (a) three rods of equal length; (b) fire welded together at each end; (c) cage is formed by twisting and pushing; (d) the head assembled on a shaft*

To summarise, the recovery of any weapon operating as a projectile is always in doubt, and so it is reasonable to suggest that those discussed in this section were made to be used only once or a few times. Study has shown how they could be produced using the minimum amount of iron, and the methods of manufacture available at the time are reflected in the design of the weapons. The iron was first formed into blanks, from which the weapons were subsequently forged. As the blank forging operation is very time consuming, it is possible that some of this work was done by unskilled labour. The time needed to produce large numbers of each weapons leads to the conclusion that blacksmiths assisted by a number of semi-skilled strikers and finishers conducted the forging.

Making a copy of a Roman caltrop

Caltrops have been described as weapons to be used against cavalry for laming horses but they are equally effective against the soles of human feet. A caltrop is made of four sharp tines positioned so that when it falls there is always one tine at 90° to the surface it lands on.

A deep wound to the sole of the foot is not only extremely painful but will also make walking almost impossible. In combat the wounded man or animal is effectively removed from the fight. Although the wound would not prove immediately fatal the risk of infection in a deep wound was high and pre-Lister 1865 (antiseptic medicine) there was an 80% death rate from war wounds.

The origins of the caltrop are uncertain but examples from the Roman period have been found at the Prysg Field site at Caerleon, Nash Williams (1932), Newstead, Curle (1911) and Wroxeter, Burhe Fox (1913 & 1914).

The caltrop is still in use today (usually by police forces) to puncture the tyres of cars. In 1993 the author saw caltrops for sale to the general public in a hardware shop in Rome. That this weapon is still in use today is a testament to its effectiveness.

A disposable weapon

A caltrop fits into the category of disposable weapon because it is manufactured with the intention of being used once and probably not recovered (Sim 1992). The concept of disposable weapons has been advanced to such a stage that much of modern warfare is built around it. Bullets from rifles, land mines, bombs from aeroplanes, hand grenades and cruise missiles are examples of weapons designed to be used only once.

As caltrops were often used by forces in retreat who scattered them indiscriminately in their wake to injure pursuing cavalry and infantry, they are likely to have been used in areas away from settlements or forts. Once dropped, it is unlikely that they would have been intentionally sought and recovered. If not trodden on, they would become buried in soft soil and corrode away. This helps to explain their low visibility in the archaeological record. Although they were probably made in large numbers, they are not common finds.

51 *Original Roman caltrops found at Wroxeter*

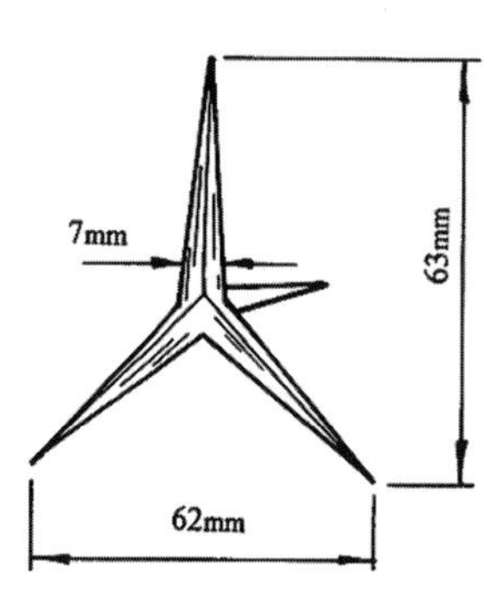

52 *Schematic dimensional drawing of the Roman caltrop found at Wroxeter*

53 *Replica caltrop made by the author*

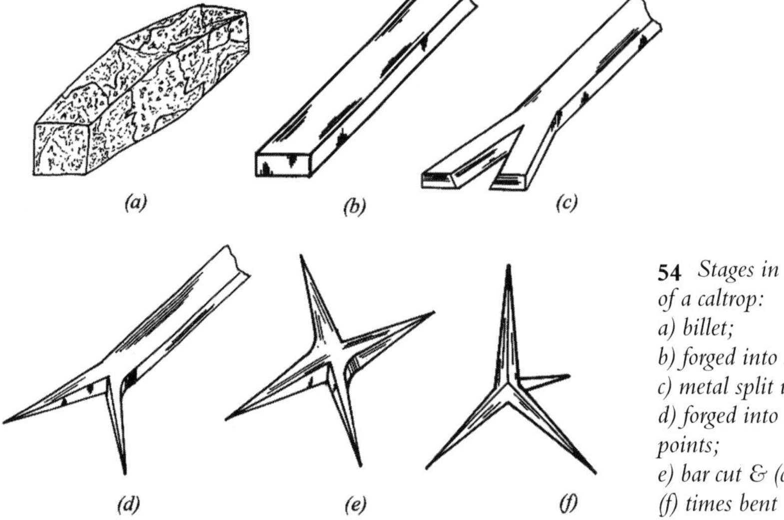

54 *Stages in the manufacture of a caltrop:*
a) billet;
b) forged into strip;
c) metal split using hot set;
d) forged into long square points;
e) bar cut & (c) & (d) repeated;
(f) times bent

Figure 54 *shows the sequence of operations to make a copy of the caltrop found at Wroxeter Burhe Fox (1913 & 1914).*

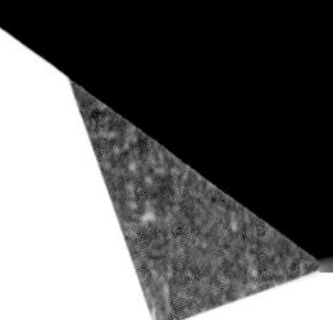

1 *Iron ore (haematite)*

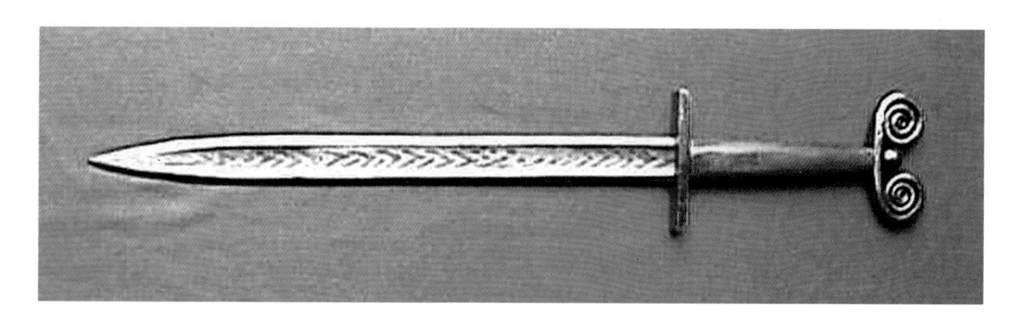

2 *Reproduction Roman sword made using traditional methods.* D. Sim

3 *Cherub smiths tending a furnace, from a wall painting in the House of the Vettii, Pompeii*

4 *Cherub smiths forging, from a wall painting in the House of the Vettii, Pompeii*

5 *Fire welding in Ironstone forge.* D. Sim

6 *Section through a piece of bloom iron. Magnification approximately x 1.2*

7 *Section through a piece of consolidated bloom iron*

8 *Iron billets found at the legionary fort of Newstead*

9 *Iron billets found at Haithabu (Northern Germany), c.ninth-eleventh century*

10 *Roman military parade*. Copyright Leg. II Aug.

11 *Roman commander, bodyguards and standard-bearers*. Copyright Leg. II Aug.

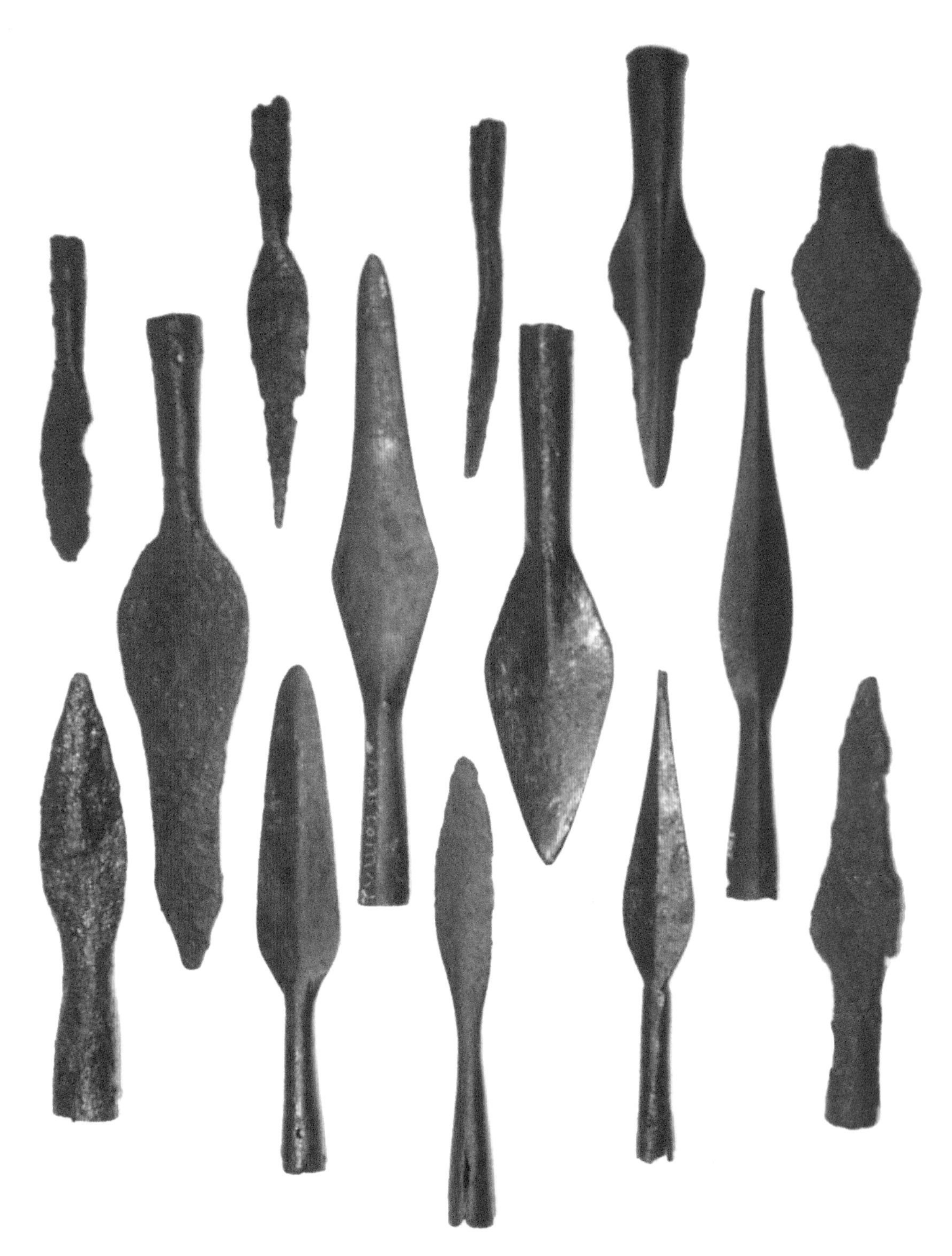

12 *An assortment of arrowheads found at Vindolanda.* Copyright The Vindolanda Trust

13 *An assortment of spearheads found at Vindolanda.* Copyright The Vindolanda Trust

14 *Roman spearhead (insert detail of socket showing mode of production)*

15 *Auxiliary archer, style of dress based on Trajan's column.* Copyright Leg. II Aug.

16 Manubalista. Copyright The Roman Military Research Society

17 *Three-span* catapulta. Copyright The Roman Military Research Society

18 *Pyramid* balista *bolts from Vindolanda.* Copyright The Vindolanda Trust

19 *Reproduction javelin head (unhardened), bent during field trials*

20 *Reproduction Roman* gladius

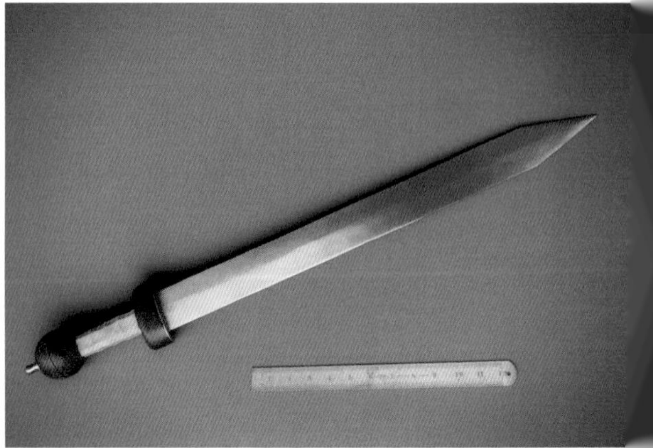

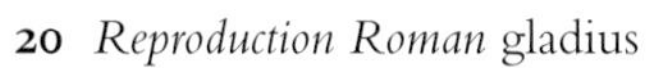

21 *Auxiliary cavalryman mid-first century AD*. Copyright Leg. II Aug.

22 *Roman legionaries. The legionary on the left carries his mess kit, a shield with goat skin protective cover and* pilum. *His companion is armed with* lorica segmentata, gladius, *dagger,* pilum *and shield.* Copyright Leg. II Aug.

23 *Piece of a Roman bronze chain mail coat, showing both solid and riveted rings*

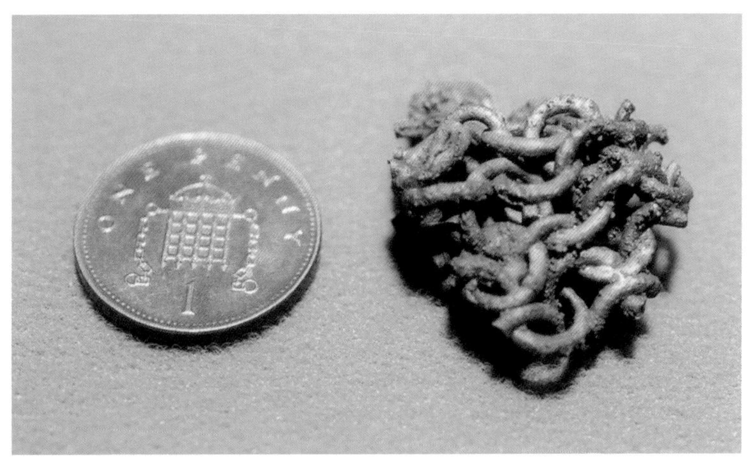

24 *Piece of a Roman iron chain mail coat*

25 *Roman iron tyre on cartwheel (reproduction) found at Pompeii*

26 *Detail of Roman iron tyre on cartwheel (reproduction) found at Pompeii*

27 *Roman hammer head made from iron billet*

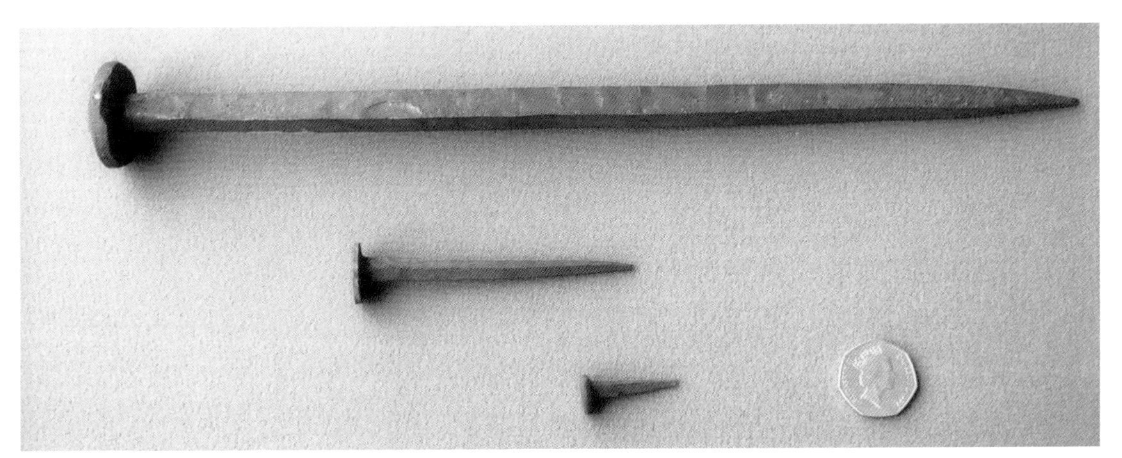

28 *Reproduction Roman nails based on those in the Inchtuthil hoard*

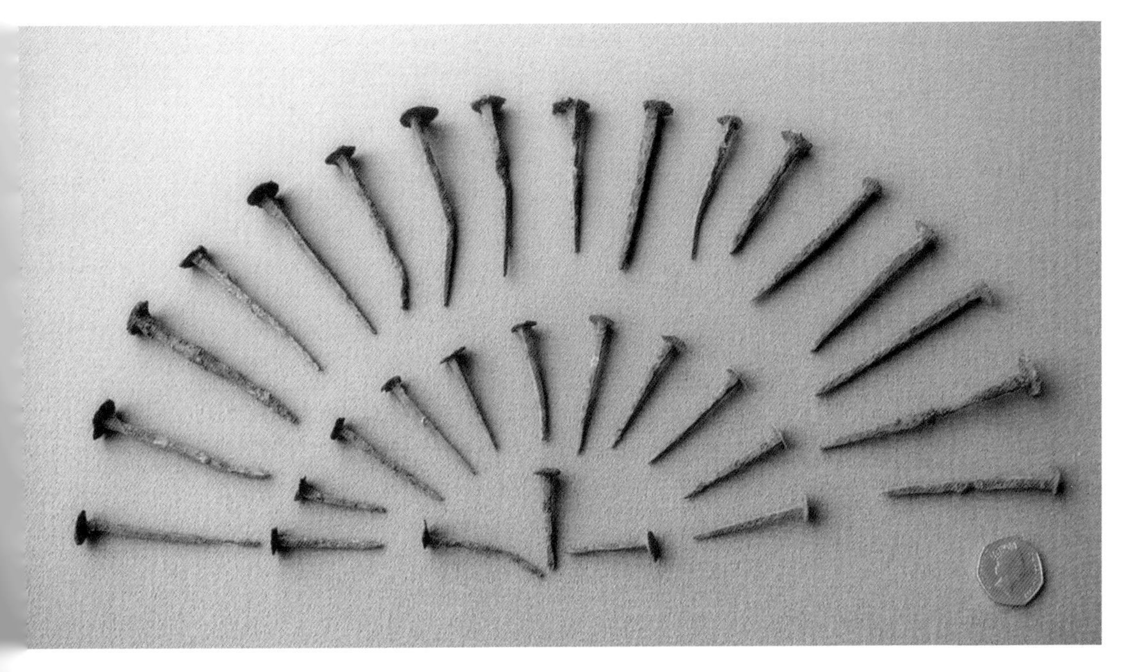

29 *Nails from the Inchtuthail hoard. Angus* et al. *classification types D (outer) and E (inner)*

30 *Nail from the Inchtuthil hoard showing poorly centred head.* Angus *et al.* (1962) classification type D

31 *Steel masonry tie from Pompeii*

The specific objectives of the experiments were to determine:
1. How long it takes to make a caltrop?
2. What is the simplest method of manufacture?
3. How much material is lost in manufacture?
4. How easy are they to make with the equipment available in the Roman period?

Macro examination and X-rays were used to determine the method of construction and although they are not definitive, there is a strong case to be made for the caltrop having been made from a single piece of metal.

Material

The caltrops examined were made of a ferrous metal; this was confirmed by the application of a magnet.

Due to their fragile nature it was not possible to carry out any hardness tests or to sample the caltrop for metallography in order to determine the exact nature of the material. However, from work undertaken by the writer (see Fulford, Sim and Doig, 2003 and Fulford, Doig, and Sim 2003) it is now possible to determine with more certainty the type of material used for many Roman iron artefacts.

As the makers knew that this was a weapon that would only be used once, cost would be a consideration. It seems likely that the chosen material would be the cheapest for the purpose. The material that fits this specification is likely to be the same as that used for making nails. Angus et al. (1962). This would be a low carbon steel with few slag inclusions which is similar to modern mild steel.

Possible methods of manufacture

There are three basic ways to make a caltrop. It can be made from:
1. one piece of metal.
2. two pieces fire-welded together.
3. two pieces joined by riveting.

The most cost-effective of these three options is making the caltrop from a single piece of metal.

Parameters of the experiment

The writer adopted the same criteria as in all his previous work on replicating ancient iron artefacts. The item has to be made with the minimum material loss, using the minimum amount of fuel and in the shortest time possible to achieve the results. Only the types of tools known to have existed in the Roman world were used. The forge was fuelled by charcoal, heated with hand-pumped bellows.

Sequence of operations

There is always more than one way to make any object and several methods were tried before the sequence of operations described here was finalised. The starting point is the billet (**54a**), which is how the blacksmith would have received his metal. This was then forged down into strip (**55b**). (Times for forging billets into bar can be found in Sim, 1992.)

54c. Shows the metal split using a hot set.
54d. Shows the two tines forged into long square points.
54e. Bar cut and operations 3c & 3d were repeated.
54f. Tines bent as shown.

The forging was then water quenched and the tines cold hammered.

Storage

It is impossible to predict at what stage of an engagement caltrops would be used. It not realistic to imagine that they would have been made as and when the need arose. Therefore caltrops must have been made in large numbers and stock piled, perhaps for months. During storage, iron items have to be protected to stop the formation of rust. A number of unprotected caltrops would rust and fuse together in a matter of weeks if not days.

The formation of rust and the need to protect iron from rust was known to the Romans. Pliny Natural History states; iron can be protected from rust by white lead (meaning tin) gypsum and pitch. Tin was (and still is) an expensive material and although it was used as a rust preventative on prestige items, it was too expensive to be used for items such as caltrops.

Rust is iron oxide and iron can only oxidise if it is in the presence of oxygen. Iron coated with anything that separates it from the atmosphere will not rust. There are many suitable candidates other than those mentioned by Pliny, such as lanolin extracted from wool, or animal fat which would have been in plentiful supply at the time. In 1995 the author conducted an experiment to determine the efficiency of animal fat as a rust preventative. Beef dripping (from the Sunday roast) was poured over a number of newly made copies of Roman nails and left to solidify. They have been checked over the intervening years and at the time of writing (December 2011) the nails are still in prefect condition. It is not stretching belief to expect the Roman blacksmiths to have developed a similar system.

Work hardening

In the sequence of operations the last stage was to forge the tines when the metal is cold; this is done to sharpen up the edges and smooth out the surface (a smooth surface with sharp edges will ease penetration). Cold working is a standard forging practice. (The effect of cold working is the subject of current research by the author and other workers). It was decided to test the hardening effect of cold working on the copy caltrops that had been made. This was done by using a Vickers hardness testing machine with a 10kg load.

Hardness of parent bar	69 VPN
Hardness of tine after hot working and air cooling	153 VPN
Hardness of tine after cold working	268 VPN

Cold working has made a considerable increase to the hardness and makes the weapon more effective at penetrating the sole of a leather shoe. It makes no difference to its penetrative power on unprotected flesh.

Discussion

The caltrop is a small forging so it would only be possible to have a blacksmith working with one striker. The forging of the tangs is not a simple operation and would require a trained smith to do it although the splitting (Fig.3c) and cutting to length could be done by unskilled labour.

The starting weight of the blank was 19g and the finished weight 18g. The amount of metal lost to oxidization in the forging was 5.3%.

The manufacturing time was 14 minutes working alone and 10 minutes working with a striker. Given a working day of 10 hours this means a blacksmith and striker could produce 60 caltrops in one day and 350 in a 5 day week.

A caltrop needs tines that will not bend under impact. As it is too expensive to make caltrops out of steel or carburised iron, the cheapest and most effective method is to work harden them.

Lilies (foot-piercing spike)

As can be seen in Figures 55 and 56, these deadly devices were hammered into short sharpened wooden poles that were then hammered into the ground, leaving only the iron barbed spike protruding. They were put in dense numbers around fortifications and when placed in long grass become almost invisible.

Experiments by the author have shown that even with a thick leather soled shoe the weight of a body is enough to drive the spike straight through the sole of the foot and out through the top.

The spike is fixed firmly in the ground and cannot be pulled up by hand. There is little possibility of the impaled man having the strength to pull his foot off the spike because of the barb. They are completely stuck and at the mercy of their opponents. A sitting or more correctly a standing target for archers or any one with any sort of missile weapon.

These were made in large numbers and the method of manufacture seems straightforward:

The billet was forged into a bar A.
The bar had long square points forged on both ends B.
It was then bent into a Z shape C.
Finally a chisel was used to cut the barb D.
The finished spike can be seen in E.
If this spike was made in large quantities, as seems likely, then they would have been stored in a manner that would prevent rusting (see Sim and Kaminski 2011). When in uses no rust preventing treatment was necessary. Indeed the more rust and dirt on the surface the more effective the spike would be in inflicting blood poisoning, if the victim survived.

55 *Stake before being driven into the ground*

56 *Only the barbed spike is visible above ground level*

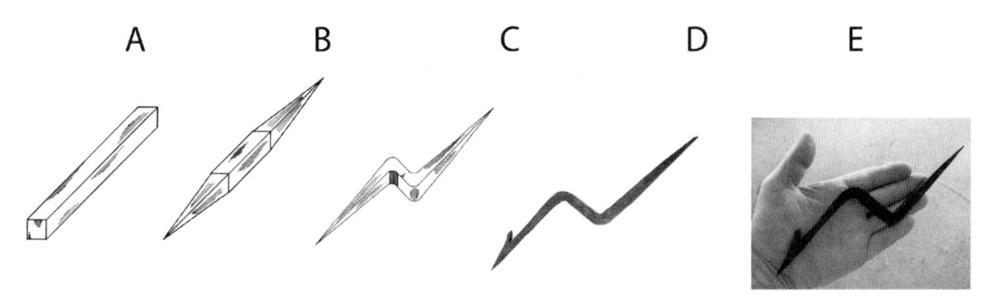

57 *Sequence of operations to forge the spike*

Manufacture of non-disposable weapons

Gladius

One of the fundamental differences between the Roman army and other fighting forces in antiquity is that the Romans were the first to use the sword as the major personal weapon: most other armies had favoured the spear.

There are two types of sword or *gladius* most associated with the Roman army; the *gladius hispaniensis,* with a long tapering point, which was gradually replaced by a *gladius* with a short point and a parallel blade known as the Pompeii type (**colour plate 20**). The style of fighting used by the Romans favoured the use of this as a stabbing weapon; the legionary was taught to aim at the centre of the body and strike up. A *gladius* has only to penetrate a human torso to a depth of 50mm to produce a fatal injury.

However, this does not mean that it was only used as a stabbing weapon; any sword made with double cutting edges can and will be used to slash when the circumstances demand it. Very little work has been carried out on the type and nature of the iron used to make a standard legionary's *gladius*, but that which has been done (Williams 1977) suggests that they were not hardened and tempered (the reasons for this will be discussed in chapter 8).

Manufacture of a gladius

Figure **58** shows the main steps in the making of a *gladius*. The starting point is a billet of iron; this is heated and cut into smaller pieces, which are then forged into a rectangular cross-section (**58a**, **b**). The *tang* (which inserts into the handle) is forged at one end, and the point at the other (**58c**, **d**). The point was formed either by forging down, or by cutting with a hot set: the former method wastes no material but takes a little longer to produce – but the difference is not significant, and it is the author's belief that it was the method used. Next, the edges are forged to a taper, giving the blade a diamond shaped cross-section (**58e**). At each stage the sword blank has undergone two types of forging: rough hammering to produce the form, and fine forging with swages and flatters to bring the sword to a shape and size as close to the finished size as possible. Forging operations are much quicker than finishing, and as much as possible is done to reduce to a minimum the amount of metal that has to be removed after

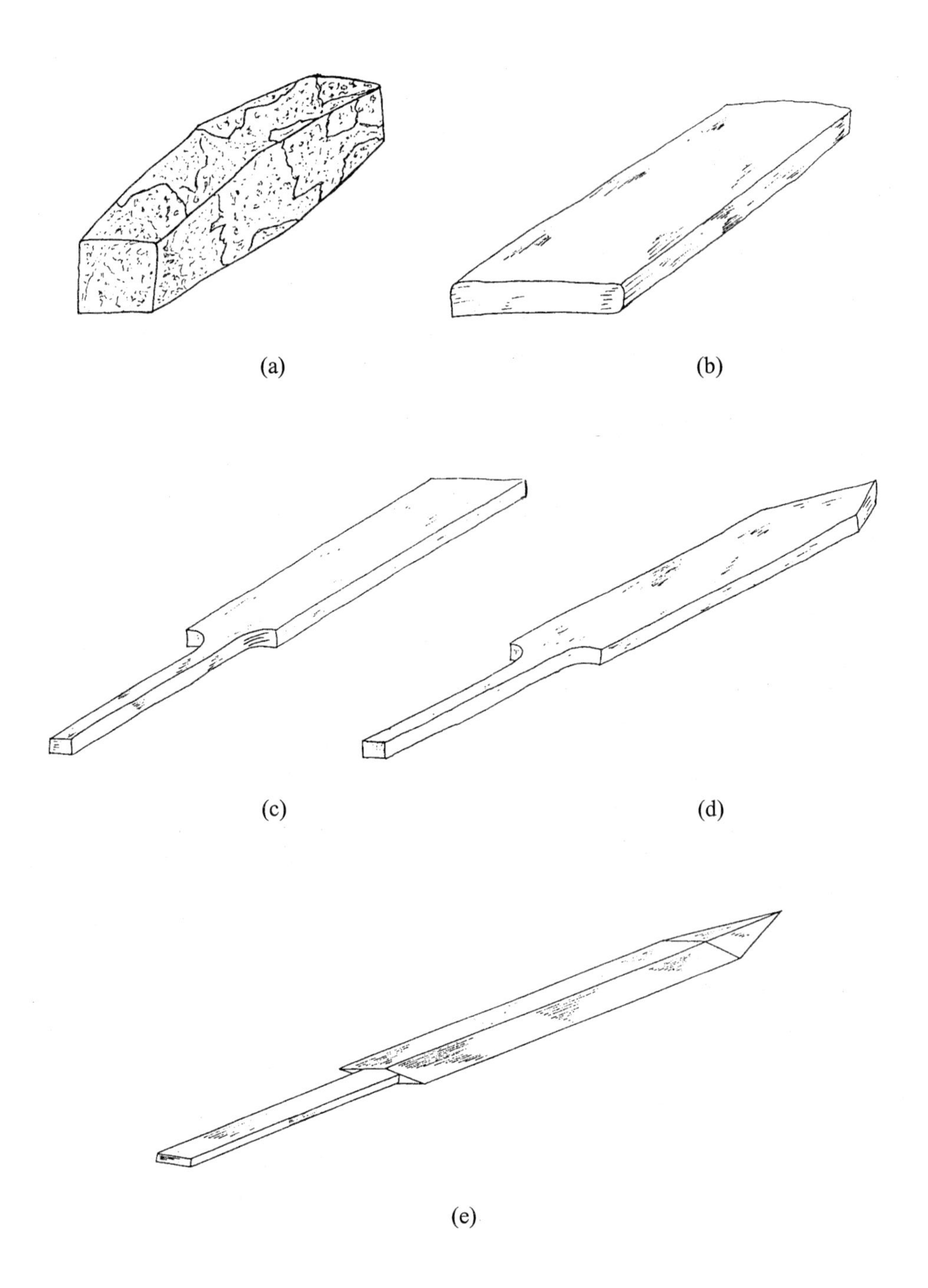

58 *Stages in the manufacture of a* gladius*: (a) billet; (b) forged bar; (c) forged tang; (d) forged point; (e) completed blade*

forging. The sword is completed by the use of files and abrasive stones to bring it to its finished form: **Table 6** shows that the finishing time for a *gladius* is huge – some 30 hours. Comparison with the production of the *pilum* shows their respective forging times to be surprisingly similar, whist the finishing time is a factor of ten greater. As with the disposable weapons, it is unlikely that the blacksmith would have been responsible for the finishing of the artefact, which in this case would probably be left to specialist cutlers.

Pattern-welded sword

The *gladius* described above would have been the standard legionary-issue sword. This section describes the production of a highly ornate weapon – the pattern-welded sword, which would probably only be carried by soldiers of high rank. It is discussed here because it shows the level of complexity that the Roman blacksmith could achieve. In the pattern-welded sword (**colour plate 2**) the initial blank is made up of a series of piles of iron with differing carbon content, which have been twisted and fire welded together. When such a construction is polished and etched the varying irons will etch differently, and a pattern will show in the blade. Gilmore and Tylecote (1986) show eight arrangements of piles and edging strips, but obviously the possibilities are endless (**59**).

At present there is insufficient evidence to determine if pattern welding was undertaken for decorative purposes or strength (Lang and Ager 1989), but there is a strong possibility that it was mechanically necessary, owing to the poor quality of the iron produced by the bloomery process. The author has examined swords from the Nydam collection (Engelhard 1866) and reached the conclusion that both points of view are valid. In some instances, the layer of pattern-welded material is so thin that it can only be a decorative feature, while in others, the whole thickness of the blade is pattern-welded and this might well increase the strength.

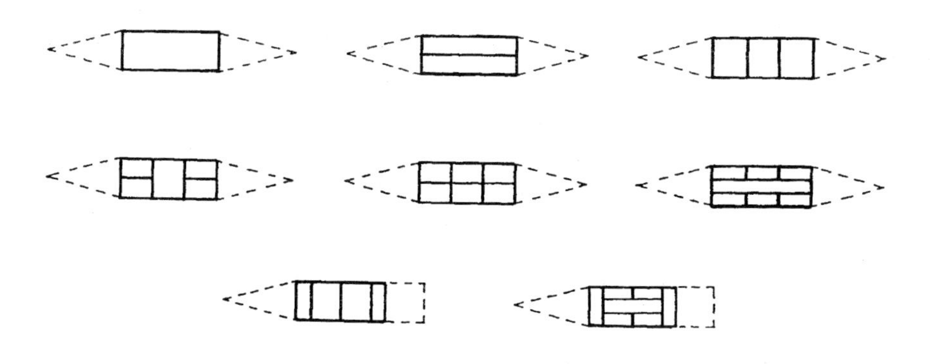

59 *Various arrangements of central core and edging strips of a pattern-welded sword.* After Gilmore & Tylecote 1986

Manufacture of a pattern-welded sword

Billets of different level carbon content (that is iron and steel) are forged into thin sheets, which are then fire welded into bundles of alternating iron and steel laminate (**60a**). In the design described here, three bundles are used to form the central core of the sword (**60b**). These are heated and twisted (two clockwise, one anti-clockwise) and then fire welded along their length to consolidate them. Following this, the bundles themselves are fire welded together (**60c**, **d**). A single strip of steel is bent to form the edge of the blade, which is then also fire welded into place (**60e**, **f**). Finally, the tang for the handle is forged (**60g**).

Although fairly quick to describe, the manufacturing time for the pattern-welded blank from which the sword is made involves a series of fire welds on the carefully twisted piles, and is about 110 hours! As with all fire welding, the process is a very skilled operation, requiring careful judgement of the correct temperature for the weld to take. Additionally, a considerable amount of material is lost through welding, which has to be allowed for at the beginning of production. Finishing was comparatively short, requiring only 10 hours (Sim 1998a: 73).

The shield

The shield was the first line of personal defence for the Roman soldier (the last was his body armour). Shields in the Roman army went through many changes in design, and those which the infantry used were different to those of the cavalry. However the concept was basically the same: a laminated wood body with central boss protecting the gripping hand. The cavalry man shown in **colour plate 21** carries an oval shield with a shield boss made from iron. The shield was held by a handle which was horizontal to the ground (**61**). The board was made of a laminated wood construction (Bishop and Coulston 1993: 58), often covered on both sides with leather, and was pierced to allow the hand to wrap around the handle. The boss was fixed outside the shield at this point to protect the fingers. The rim of the shield was banded with a thin metal strip (**20** & **21**). Roman infantry shields were large, typically over half the height of the man carrying it and although the main body was made of the relatively light wood, this meant that weight was a consideration (**21**). The central boss was made of either iron or brass and because of the weight problem, the thickness had to be kept to a minimum but be sufficient to protect the hand of the owner from heavy blows from swords or axes. It is worth mentioning that in antiquity most fighting was conducted hand-to-hand and although the Roman soldier was assaulted by arrows fired from bows, these could not deliver as much energy as a man at close range wielding an axe or sword.

As mentioned above, the shields were usually made of wood laminated to form plywood, with the handles strengthened by an iron bar. When not in use they were protected with leather covers made from goat skin, which at first seems quite an extravagant level of care (**colour plate 22**). The author and a colleague from the Department of Chemistry at Reading University conducted a series of experiments to determine the feasibility of a proposal that a glue 'casein' made from cheese could have been used to bind shields together (Bishop and Coulston 1993: 61). It was found to be very strong and would have been ideal for a shield but when exposed to the elements for two days (left outside in England in March), the glue broke down. This could well be the reason why Roman shields were given leather covers.

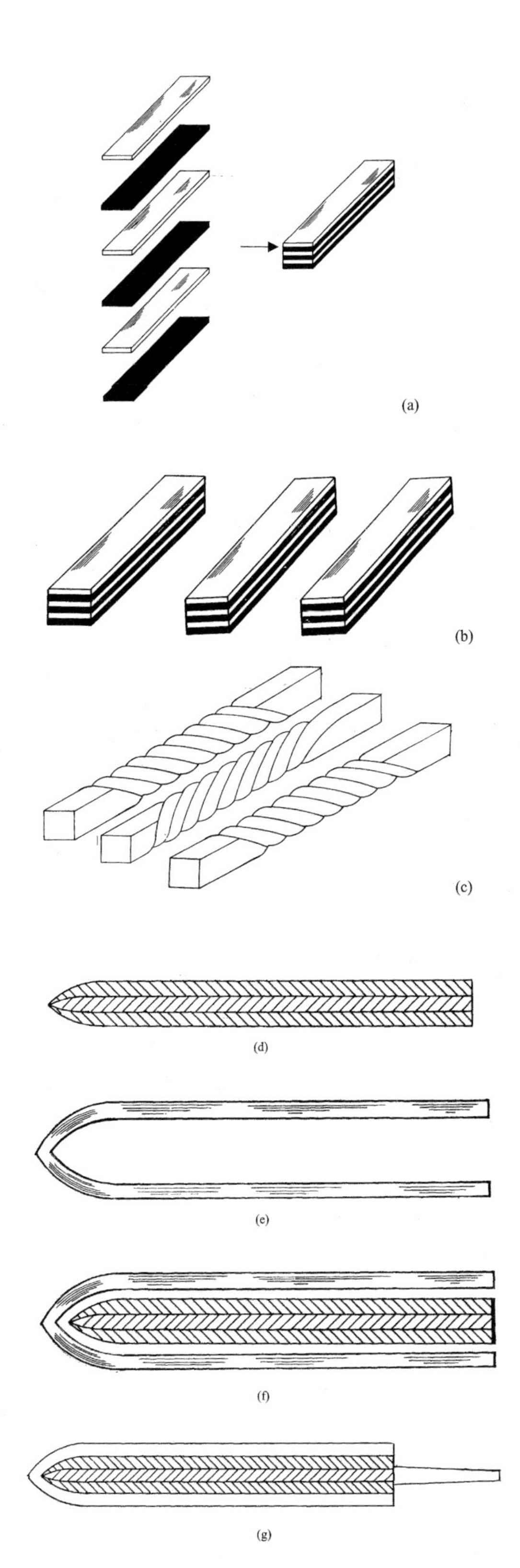

60 *Stages in the manufacture of a pattern-welded sword:*
(a) alternate strips of iron and steel are fire welded into piles;
(b) three piles are produced;
(c) the piles are twisted according to choice – in this example the outer two anti-clockwise, and the inner clockwise;
(d) the twisted piles are welded together;
(e) a steel edge is bent up from a single strip of steel;
(f) the strip is placed round the welded piles;
(g) the edge is welded on and a tang forged

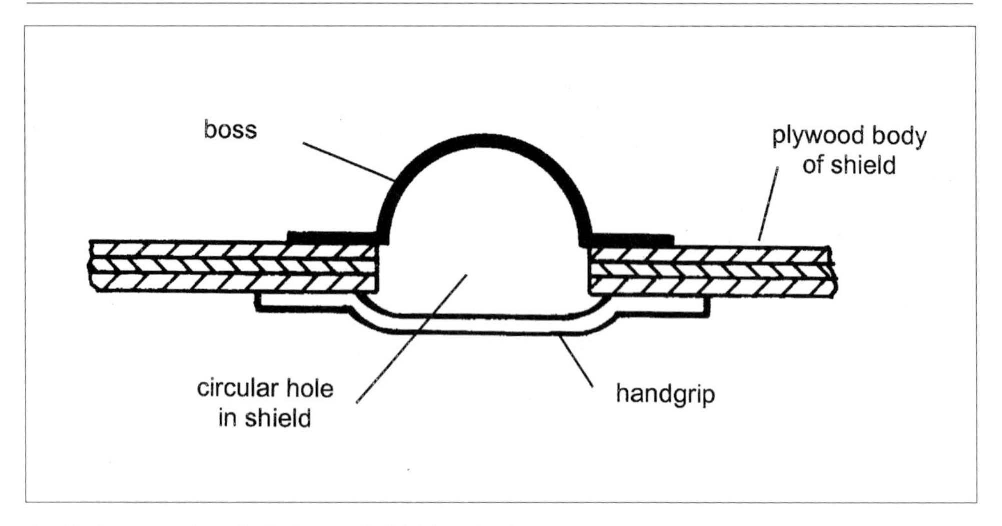

61 *Basic construction of a legionary shield (plan view)*

Manufacture of the shield boss

The shield boss was made from sheet metal. The production of this material is the subject of current research: some of the Roman sheet iron examined by the author shows a uniformity of thickness that suggests the use of sophisticated forms of production, such as rollers. A system of rolling used in the production of olive oil was well known in antiquity and it is therefore possible that a similar system may have been used to make sheet iron. However, it has to be noted that at present there is no specific evidence to support the use of rollers by the Romans. There is a further complication in the production and working of sheet iron, which is that the metal is very prone to cracking as it gets below four millimetres thick because of the slag inclusions. Examination of a piece of *lorica segmentata* and a strip of sheet metal of secure Roman date (both from Vindolanda) has shown the practice of welding two pieces of ferrous metal, one of soft, ductile wrought iron and the other of high carbon steel, was used in Roman times (**62**). In the case of the *lorica segmentata* the steel was on the outside, that is the side which would be facing the enemy. Such a composite material would combine the very desirable properties of strength and ductility for the production of sheet metal from which to form deep drawings such as shield bosses and helmets. The technique of joining a hard, stronger steel to a tougher iron body is often found in Roman tools such as knives and axes. Research is currently underway which it is hoped will reveal the extent of the use of the thin sheet kind of laminated metal structure described here.

The billet of iron is forged down into a sheet. When the bowl part of the boss is being formed the metal will be stretched, and in the finished boss the apex of the bowl will be thinner than the flange. Therefore it is important to profile the blank in such a way that it retains enough thickness at the crown of the bowl to be strong enough to protect the user (**63a**).

62 *Section of* lorica segmentata *showing an iron-steel laminate from Vindolanda (No. 5767). Magnification approximately x 100.* Copyright The Vindolanda Trust

The sheet is then cut into an approximate disc shape (**63b**) with a hot set and sledge hammer. It is not necessary to form a perfect disc at this stage: during the shaping of the bowl some deformation will take place, and it cannot be guaranteed that the bowl and the outer circumference of the flange will be concentric. Any error can be corrected later. The metal is heated to dull red and formed into a bowl shape by holding the blank over a ring and hammering (**63c**). This produces a bowl with an irregular surface, and these irregularities are hammered out over a ball stake (**63d**). From the centre a circle is inscribed on what will be the inside surface of the boss; this marks the finished diameter of the bowl. This circle is then traced with a small chisel, leaving a circular groove. This enables the smith to see the circle when the metal is hot, and acts as a slight weakening point where the metal will bend, making the formation of the flange easier. The metal is heated to red heat and the marked groove is placed on the edge of the anvil and hammered to form the flange (**63e**). It is then heated to bright red heat to punch the holes for the fixing nails (**63f**). The boss may then be nailed to a wooden board and set up on a pole lathe, where the outside edge of the flange can be turned to a smooth edge, concentric with the dome of the boss. It can be left on the pole lathe in order to remove the surface oxide with abrasive stones. Final polishing may have been made using a small cylindrical piece of wood that had been covered with tallow then rolled in fine sand.

Chain mail

The production of chain mail has been described fully elsewhere (Sim 1997b) but the rings – of which there are two basic types, involve very different and important manufacturing processes.

A typical chain mail construction will involve the linking of 'solid' rings (that is without joint) with welded or 'riveted' rings (**64a**, **b** also **colour plates 23** and **21**). The number of both types needed in the production will depend on the size of both the coat required and the individual rings. The size of the ring is assumed to be 7mm (Sim 1997b: 361 **Table 2**) and a 'unit cell' – that is the repeat pattern – (**65**) to be $15mm^2$, then a coat of size 0.6 x 0.8m (with front and back) would need approximately 35,000 rings (17,500 solid rings and 17,500 'riveted' rings). The length of wire to produce 17,500 rings would be of the order of 380m (which, if a $1mm^2$ cross-section is assumed would weigh 3.3kg, making the whole coat approximately 6.6kg).

Solid rings – punch and die set

The possibility of the use of shaped punches to produce the 'solid' rings used in a (bronze) chain mail coat was suggested by Biek (1963). Examination of some of the few rings (in suitable condition) available, and comparison of their dimensions has certainly given credence to this approach. Additionally, a consideration of the undoubted quality of workmanship shown in Roman coins and hence their dies implies that they had the necessary skill to produce a simple die set for punching rings. The work by Sim (1997b) showed how, by using simple techniques, a pair of punch and die sets could be made to punch both the inner and outer diameters of the rings (**66**, **67**).

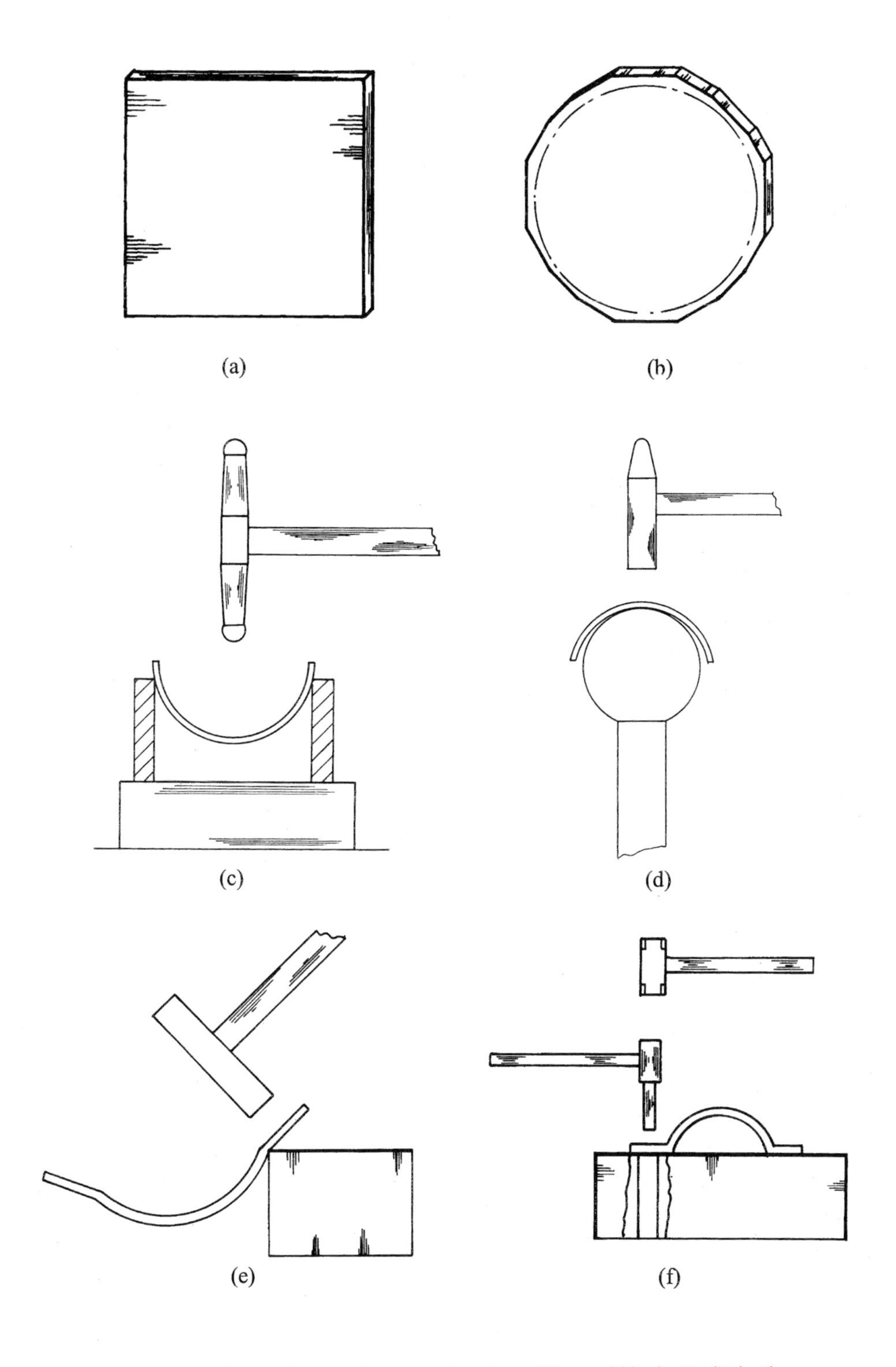

63 *Stages in the manufacture of a shield boss: (a) flat sheet; (b) round blank; (c, d) the dome is formed: (e) the rim is put on; (f) holes are punched for fitting to shield body*

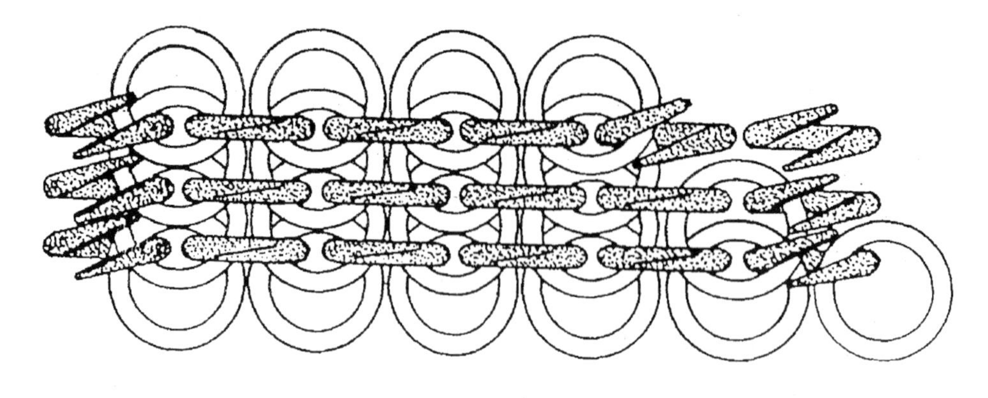

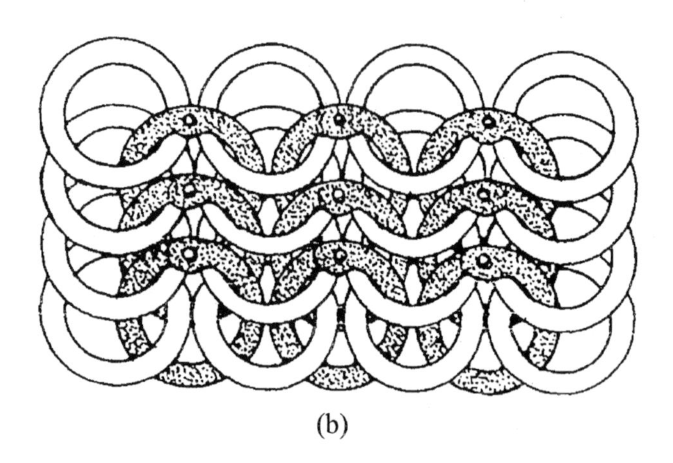

64 *Basic designs of chain mail: (a) solid and welded rings; (b) solid and riveted rings.* From Drescher 1981 fig. 3

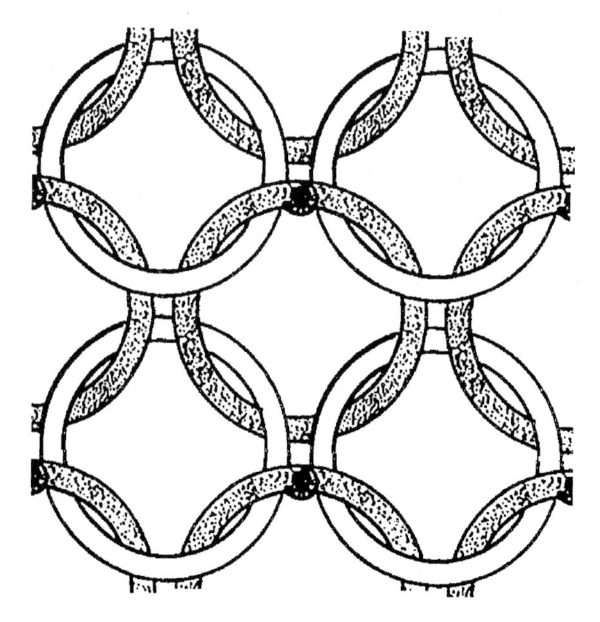

65 *Unit cell of chain mail showing both solid and riveted rings*

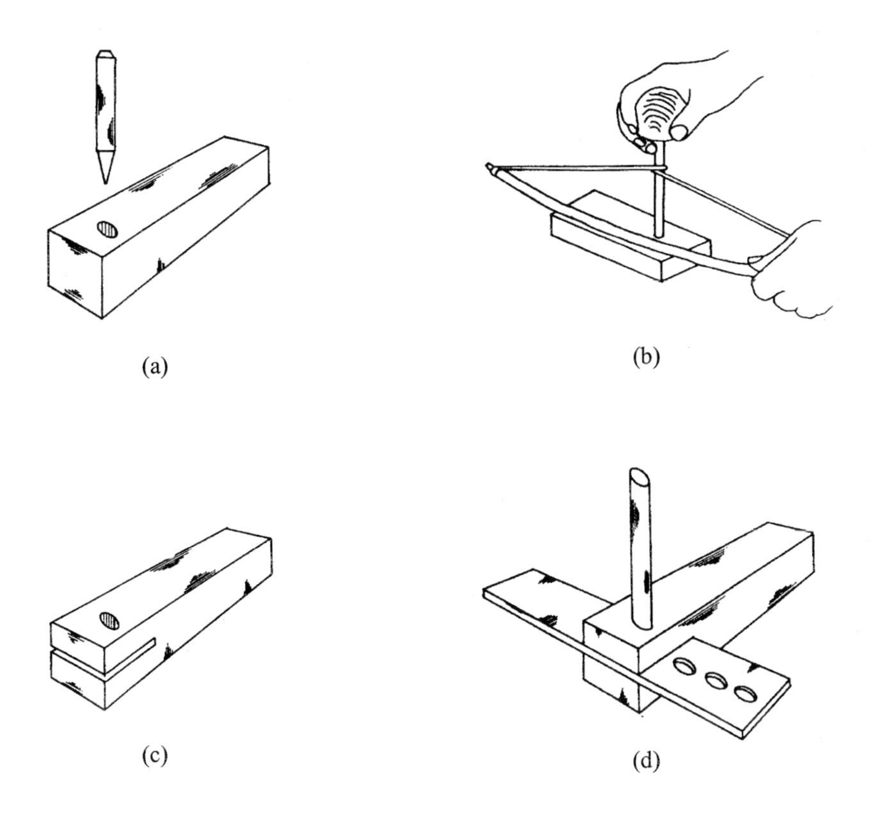

66 *Production of a punch and die set for making the internal diameter holes in a solid chain mail ring: (a) a tapered punch is used to make a hole through the die block; (b) the rough hole is* lapped *to bring it to size; (c) a slot is cut in the die to take the bar from which the rings will be punched; (d) the internal holes are punched out using a bar of the size used to lap the hole in (b)*

The first operation is to punch the inner diameter, a strip about 25mm wide and 1mm thick was used. The die for this would be made using a tapered punch to make a hole through a block of iron (heated to 950°C) (**66a**). For the die set to operate correctly, the punch must be a good fit in the die. If the punch is too big, obviously the set will not go together and so will not work. Equally if it is too small, as it punches, it will drag material into the gap between punch and die and jam. A good, well-finished hole may be obtained by a process known as *lapping*. Lapping involves the use of a bow drill to spin the punch back and forth in the hole. The Romans could have used substances such as ground glass or sand with water as an abrasive paste to produce a good fit and finish to the hole (**66b**). A slot would be needed to slide the iron bar through so that that the punch drives accurately through the hole below (**66c, d**).

The second set is similar in production, but involves stepped holes and punches (**67a**). The step on the punch may be produced using a swage (**67b**), this then being used to punch the hole in the die. These two may then be lapped as before to produce a

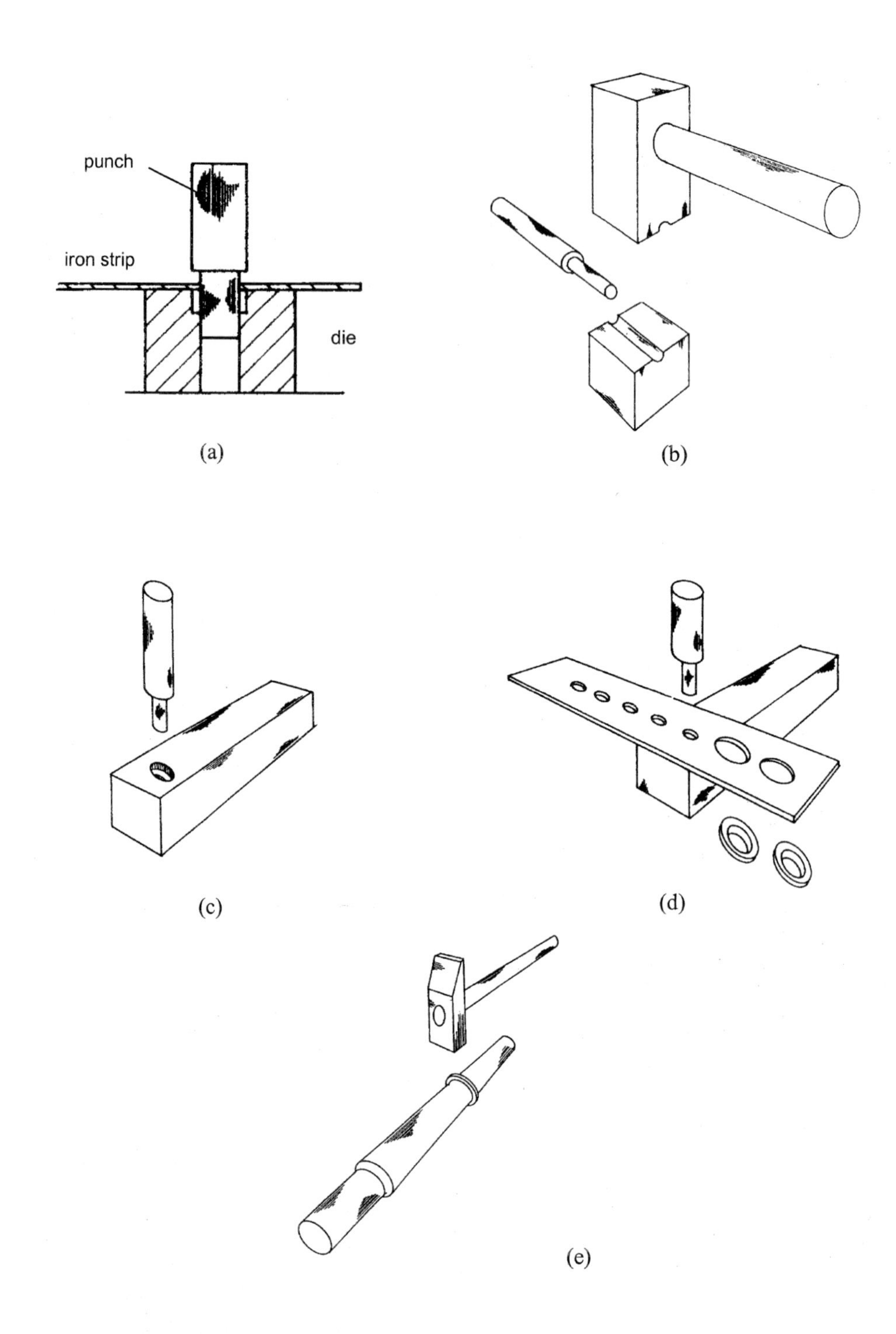

67 *Production of a punch and die set for punching out the solid chain mail ring: (a) basic principle – the inner diameter part of the punch locates the iron strip while the larger diameter will punch the ring; (b) the punch is swaged down; (c) punch and die set; (d) punching the final rings; (e) finishing by hammering on a tapered mandril*

well-fitting die set, from which the outer diameter of the rings may be punched (**67c, d**) and finished by hammering on a *mandril* (**67e**). Even with this level of tooling, it would have taken a considerable time for the production of the rings required – from the data Sim (1997b) supplies, 17,500 rings would take about 300 hours to punch and finish. Whilst the method proposed might not be exactly that used, it seems to be the only feasible technique to reproduce the dimensions (± 0.6mm) in the volume required.

Joined rings – wire drawing

The joints in the chain mail may be made in several ways: either simply by butting the ends together; by welding; or riveting (**64**). All rings must however be initially produced from long, thin strips of material, i.e. wire. The method of production again is uncertain, but given the volume required and the dimensional consistency, the only feasible method is wire drawing. Thomsen and Thomsen (1976) have noted that non-ferrous wires from Persia of sixth to fifth century BC could only have been produced by wire drawing. This, taken with the find of what appears to be an iron draw plate at the Roman fort of Vindolanda, and another from Altena, Germany (Thomsen and Thomsen 1974) would suggest very strongly that the Romans had the ability to draw wire (**68**). The draw plate from Altena (near Dusseldorf) sadly exists only as a cast, the original being lost, but shows a groove running on one side of the plate between the holes. This would have been used for lubricating the wire drawing process with, for example, bee's wax or animal fat. Draw plates such as these could easily have been made using a tapered punch, to produce wire of either square or round section (**69**). A series of holes of different sizes could be made with one punch driven in to different depths. The angle of the taper on the punch (and the thickness of the plate) will control the 'reduction ratio', that is the level of reduction in cross-sectional area as the wire is drawn through each hole. As the wire is drawn through it gets thinner and longer. The lower the taper angle the smaller the reduction in section each time the wire is drawn, however the loads required to draw it through each hole will be lower. Therefore to achieve a given reduction more holes must be used, but the work will be easier. Undoubtedly in practice the wire drawer would have experimented to find the best combination of reduction and required load.

68 *Draw-plate from the Roman fort of Vindolanda.* Copyright The Vindolanda Trust

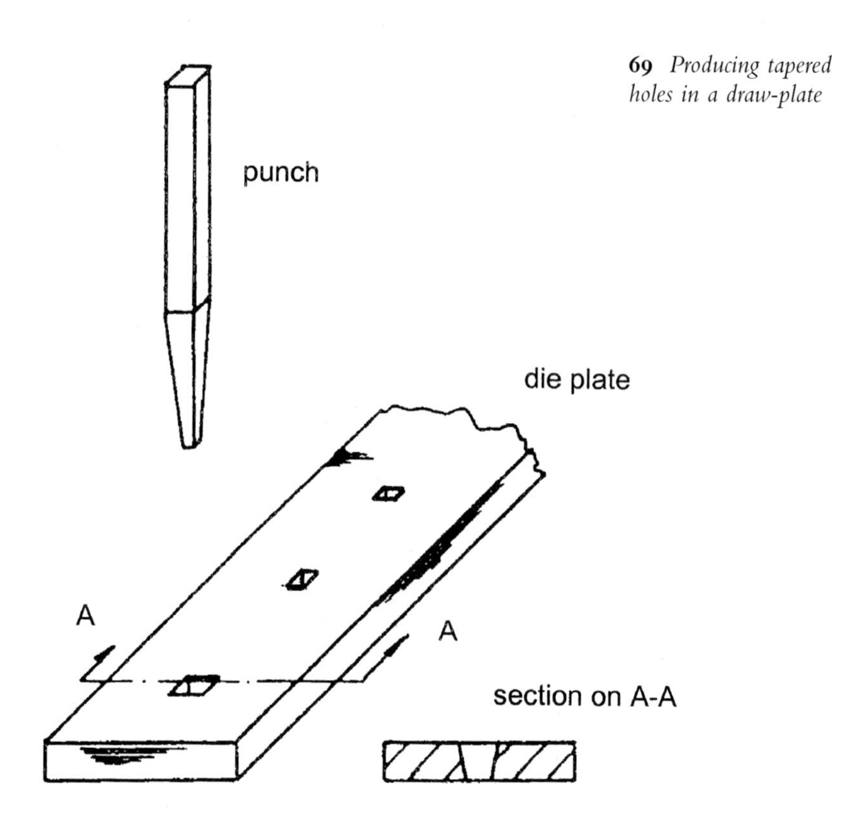

69 *Producing tapered holes in a draw-plate*

Once the wire had been drawn and the solid rings made, the coat had to be assembled. This would require a considerable amount of time, even if a simpler butted type style of joining ring were used. Bishop and Coulston (1993) note that the coats found near Hadrian's wall were of this type, and suggest that the assembly work might have been undertaken by off-duty legionaries rather than in a workshop.

Manufacture of domestic tools

Axe

It was mentioned earlier, and will be discussed in more detail in the next chapter, that the disposable type of weapons were left unhardened. However, for cutting tools which a craftsman might use for all his professional life, a more sophisticated approach was adopted: a hardened steel edge was combined with a tough iron body. Sim and Ridge (2000) report the use of a hardened steel edge on an iron plane blade used for woodworking. The manufacture of an axe (**70**, c.f. also Pleiner 1962), is described here. The *dolabrae*, a pickaxe type tool used by the legionaries (**71**) would have been made in a very similar manner. It had a sharp cutting edge at one end and a pointed tine at the other and was multipurpose, used for everything a modern pickaxe would be.

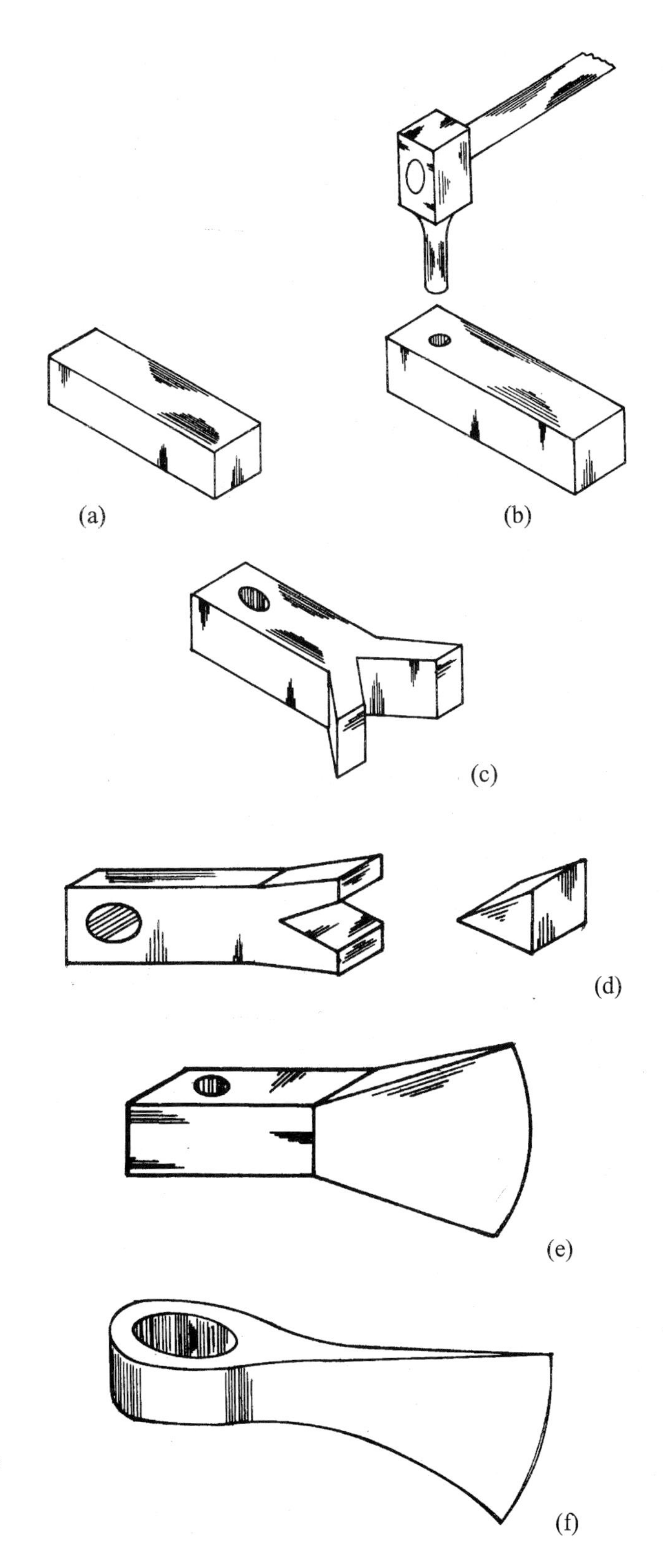

70 *Stages in the manufacture of an axe: (a) billet; (b) eye forged; (c, d) end split to receive wedge; (e) fire welded; (f) forged to finish*

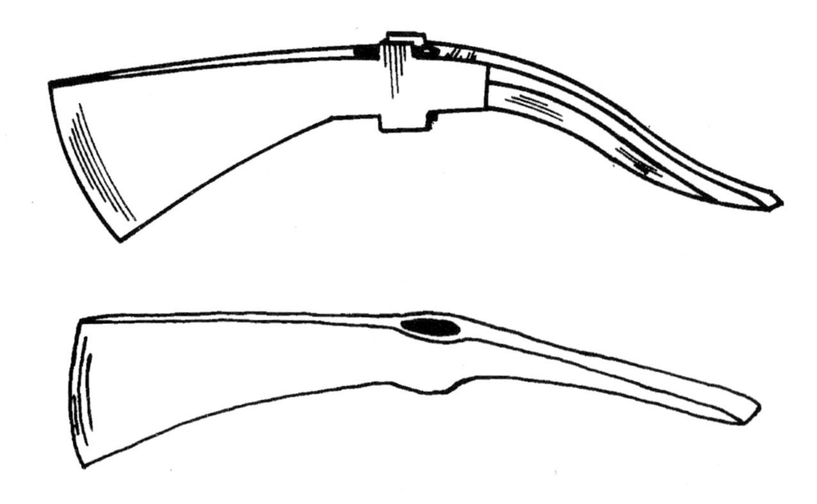

71 *Types of* dolabrae

Manufacture of an axe

The starting point is a billet which is forged down into a square bar of suitable dimensions (**70a**). A piece of steel (iron-carbon alloy) which will form the cutting edge is forged into a wedge shape. The iron bar is heated to yellow heat, and a tapered punch is used to forge the eye (**70b**). Using a hot set, the end of the bar is split open to accommodate the steel wedge (**70c**). This is driven into the opening, and the split sides hammered together to grip the wedge (**70d**). The edge holding the wedge is put into the fire and slowly brought up to welding heat, to ensure that the whole assembly is at the correct heat for a complete weld. This heat is indicated when small bursting sparks are seen coming out of the fire. The iron is removed and the weld made in three heavy blows. The first is directed at the centre of the join and welds the middle section, forcing any slag out of the joint. The second and third strikes are made either side of the first to complete the weld along the length of the joint, driving out any remaining slag. Since the iron is at such a high temperature, the steel edge of the axe deforms and starts to flare into shape as the weld is made (**70e**). If the blacksmith is assisted by strikers then the welding and flaring can be undertaken in one heat. A further heat is then taken to dark red heat, and the flared edge is smoothed out with a flatter (**70f**). The edge can now be hardened by heating and quenching in water.

Iron tyres for wheels

Transportation by wheeled vehicles was quite common in the Roman period, and regularly brought supplies and goods to many parts of the empire, including the number of garrisons maintained in Britain. The country was well served by a system of well-built and maintained roads, and it was this system that ensured troops could move quickly to any areas where trouble started. A Roman soldier was expected to be able to march 25 miles a day in full kit: it was important that the wagons could keep up.

These wagons were of a timber construction and had a number of iron fittings, including the rims or tyres on the wheels which acted both to hold the wheel together and to protect the rim. **Colour plates 25** and **26** show a typical construction. Although this example is from Pompeii, there are such tyres found in Britain, for example in the collection of material from the Silchester excavation. An iron tyre has to be made from a single piece that is welded together to form a continuous annulus. When finished, the inside diameter is made to be slightly smaller than the outside diameter of the wooden wheel. The tyre is fitted by heating to red heat, thus expanding it so that its increased diameter allows it to be placed over the wheel. It is then shrunk onto the rim by quenching with water. It is essential that the tyre is heated to a uniform temperature all over, otherwise it will be an ellipse rather than a true circle, and will not fit over the wheel. Nails are then driven through pre punched holes in the tyre to secure it to the wheel rim. Shrink fitting is still in use as a method of generating very high radial gripping forces between two components.

Knives

In Roman times, food was eaten with the aid of knives, spoons and fingers (the use of the fork for this purpose is not thought to have developed until the mid-fifteenth century, when it was introduced by the Italians – Mallalieu 1996: 111). The type of dagger carried by the legionary was large and wholly unsuitable for this. In addition to eating, the knife was essential for the preparation of food, and there are a bewildering number of versions and shapes that have been developed for specific purposes in cooking. A study of the types shown by Manning (1985) in his catalogue from the British Museum gives a good idea of the range of knife designs used in Roman times (**72**). It is probable that every individual carried his own eating knife, and it seems likely these were personal belongings. Such an item might also have been seen as a status symbol, and no doubt knives with patterned handles or with some work on the blade were favoured by those who could afford them. It is not clear what material such knives were made from but it seems possible that they were made from iron and were either carburised or had a steel edge welded to them to create a good cutting edge.

Hammers

Almost every craft that requires the use of hammers has developed special versions to fulfil particular needs. This was so in antiquity, as can be seen from the lists of hammers documented by various authors (Ohlaver 1939, Manning 1976, 1977, 1985 & Gaitzsch 1980). The ancient blacksmith would have made hammers for labourers and other craftsmen as well as for himself.

Examination of a Roman hammer head from the Silchester collection (ref. 07510 yc 169) showed it to be very similar to a modern day example, the main difference being the form of the 'eye' which takes the handle (**73**). In the Roman head this was in the form of a round linearly tapering hole (the frustrum of a cone), whilst a modern day head has an eye which is waisted in the middle and opens out at each end (**74a**). In order to secure the head of the Roman hammer, the handle must protrude through the head to allow the wedge to operate (**74b**). This style of wedging is depicted in the

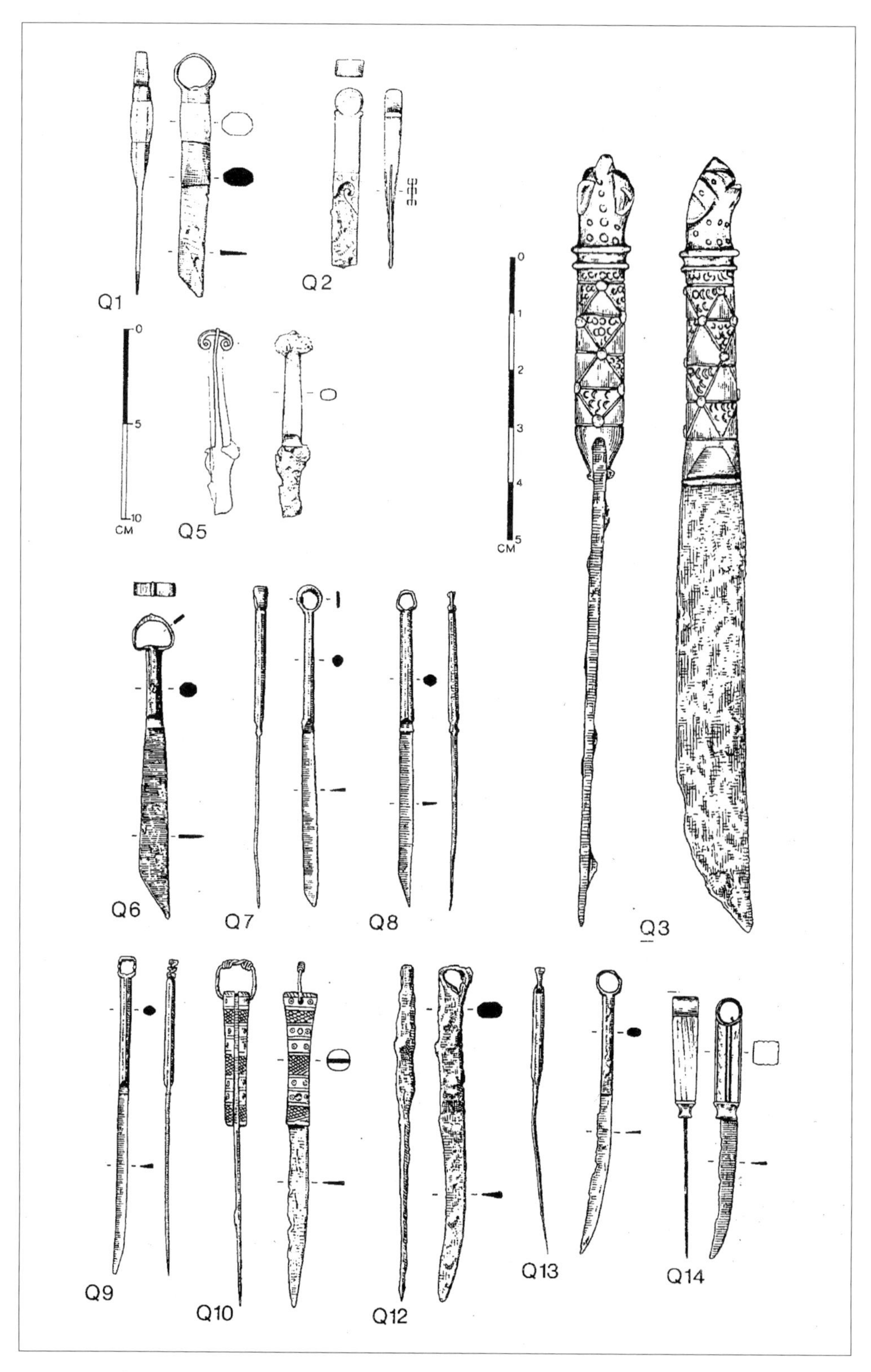

72 *Roman knives.* From Manning 1985

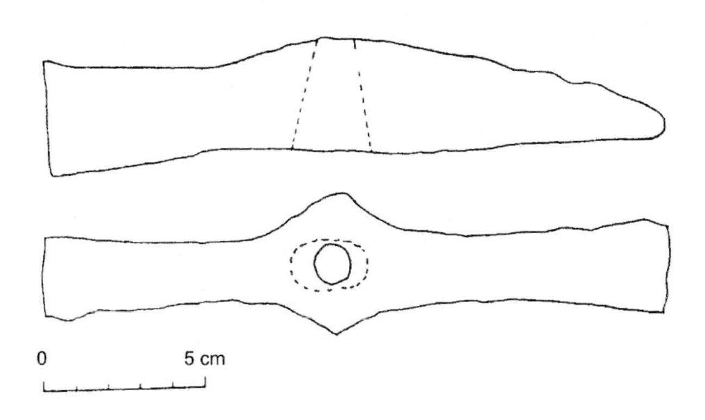

73 *A Roman hammer from Silchester.* Reading Museum No. 07510 yc 169

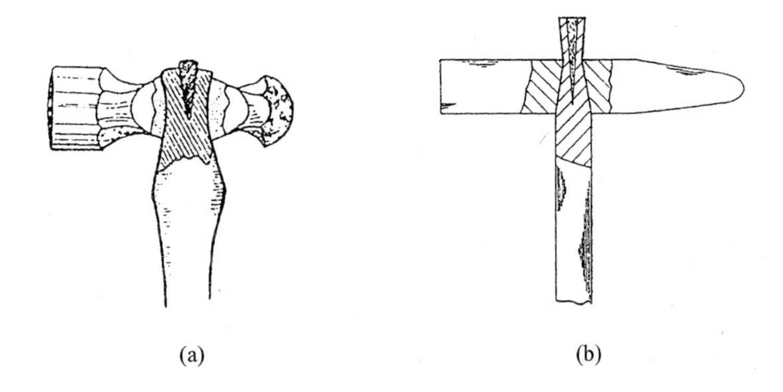

74 *Cross-sections showing hafting: (a) modern hammer; (b) Roman hammer*

mural *Vulcan's forge* at the Villa di Montalto, Rome, which shows two cutlers at work. The figure on the right can be seen holding a hammer with the shaft protruding through the head (**75**). A hammer in the cherub forge depicted in the mural in the House of the Vettii, Pompeii shows a similar design (**colour plate 4**).

Manufacture of a hammer

The starting point was a piece of well-consolidated wrought iron weighing 4kg. This was forged into a bar with a cross-section slightly larger than the final cross-section of the finished hammer (**76a**). The pein end of the hammer was forged, and a radius put on the end (**76b**, **c**). Following this, the position of the eye-hole was marked and a small hole punched through the thickness of the body of the hammer, followed by a taper punch to form the eye-hole (**76d**). The hammer head was then cut from the parent bar and the striking end was hammered flat (**76e**, **f**). To finish, the hammer was heated to dull red and the scale was scraped off using a chisel-ended scraper before quenching in cold water.

75 *Two cutlers at work, from* Vulcan's forge, *a mural in relief at the Villa di Montalto, Rome*

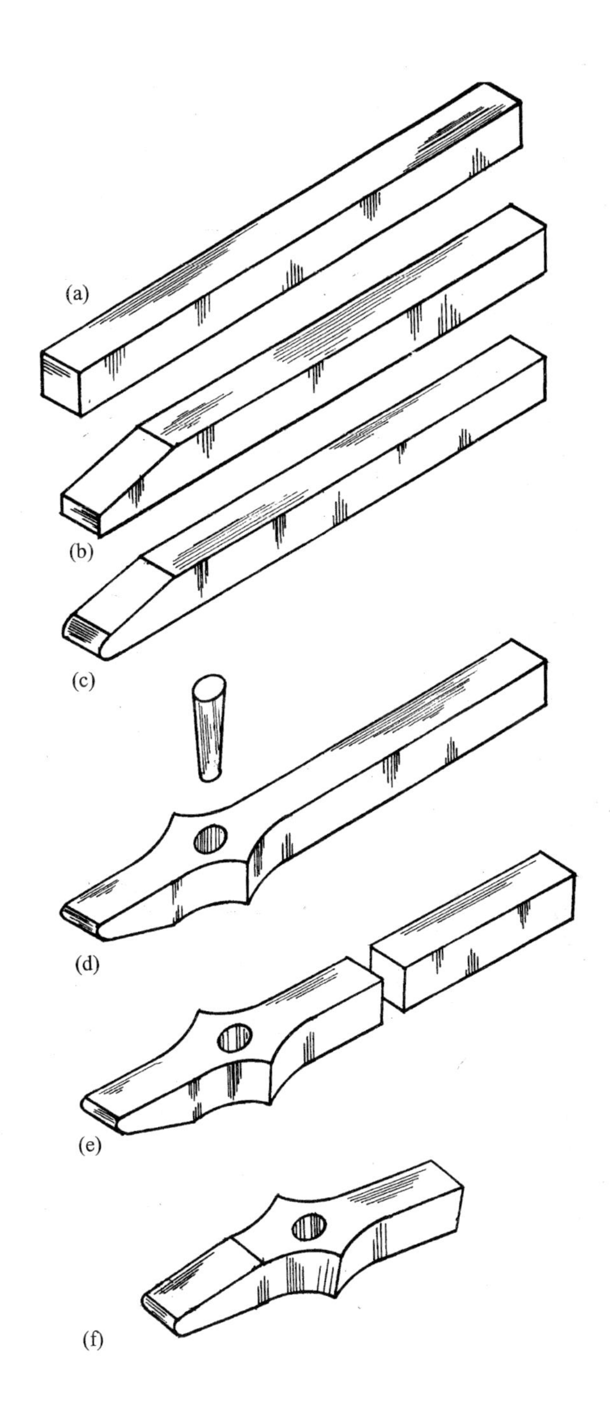

76 *Stages in the manufacture of a hammer: (a) bar; (b, c) pein end forged; (d) eye-hole punched; (e) cut from the parent bar; (f) finish forged*

The iron was forged into a hammer in a time of 1 hour 46 minutes. The only finishing work was the removal of superficial hammer marks on the two striking faces, which if necessary could be done with a file. The finished weight was 1.27kg. It is possible that the design of a Roman hammer may have been influenced to some extent by the size and shape of the billets from which it was formed; those from Newstead (Curle 1911) are of a very convenient shape and size from which to forge hammers of this size. Provided the iron was well consolidated, a very good hammer could have been made with a minimum of forging (**colour plate 27**).

A hammer made for forging hot iron does not need a hardened striking face, as the metal being struck is considerably softer than it is. If however the metal being struck is cold, and therefore as hard or harder than the hammer head, hardening is necessary. This is obviously also the case for other hard materials on which a hammer may be used (for example rock).

The hammer described above was subsequently used for the series of experiments to reproduce Roman iron artefacts. It was given no special consideration and was subjected to the same treatment as any other hammer used in the forge. In use, it had a very different feel from a contemporary hammer but was well balanced, and a steady hammering rhythm was easy to maintain.

No attempt was made to harden the head and, as the hammer was used in the forge on cold metal, mushrooming of the head occurred. This was remedied by cold forging the striking face back to its original shape, which was easy to do if carried out as soon as any spreading had taken place (Sim 1998b). It is interesting to note that the same mushrooming effect can be seen on hammer heads from Germany (Pietsch 1984 and Gaitzsch 1980), and in England, Hod Hill (Brailsford 1962). Presumably these heads were also unhardened.

Carburising (see chapter 8) is the only effective way to make a hard striking face on wrought iron. Depending on the carburising temperature, a case-hardened coat of 1mm will take in the region of six hours heating to produce. Only the striking surface will have been hardened; the main body will still be soft and subject to the same distorting forces as unhardened wrought iron. There are, however, advantages in not hardening a hammer head. When any deformation takes place, the head can easily be corrected with a few blows from another hammer, and restored to full working condition. A fully-hardened steel hammer-head may have a longer working life, but remedial action would require the services of a skilled blacksmith, and it would take him considerable time to restore any damage. It is therefore quite possible that in some cases hammers were left deliberately unhardened.

Nails

As Angus *et al.* (1962: 957) comment in their paper discussing the find of a massive hoard of nails at the legionary fortress of Inchtuthil (which is described at the beginning of this chapter): 'nails are common finds on all Roman occupation sites, so common in fact that archaeologists rarely illustrate or discuss them'. Nails were used in many different applications, from very large versions for joining heavy timbers in buildings to the small examples used in the hob-nail boots mentioned previously. It has been discussed in the section on disposable weapons the large quantities of such items which would have been required, but nowhere else in the British archaeological record is the scale of the production requirements brought home more clearly than by the Inchtuthil hoard. As Richmond puts it (Angus *et al.* 1962: 956):

> The total number was over 875,000 [nails]. Since the fortress was in process of being built and remained unfinished, it is reasonable to suppose that this large quantity of nails represents the surplus stock destined for use in the buildings that were still to be erected. ... Few discoveries illustrate more vividly than these nails the scale upon which Roman supplies and accessories were manufactured and stockpiled.

There are a number of questions here which need to be considered about the scale of the Roman iron industry: how were the nails made; how long did it take to make them and what level of skill was required, and finally, were the iron nails deliberately carburised to produce stronger (steel) nails?

Manufacture of nails based on the Inchtuthil hoard

The range of nail sizes and types is shown in **77** and **colour plate 28**. With the exception of type F, of which there are comparatively very few (only 28), all the other nails reported from Inchtuthil (and elsewhere e.g. Curle 1911) had square shanks (Type F nails had round shanks forged from the square). Although the types of head style and length varied between group (lengths from 38–370mm were reported: see also **colour plate 28**), the production process was the same. Starting from a bar of suitable length and cross-section, the body and point of the nail is made by heating to bright red heat and hammering the end down to a short square tapering point (**78a, b**).

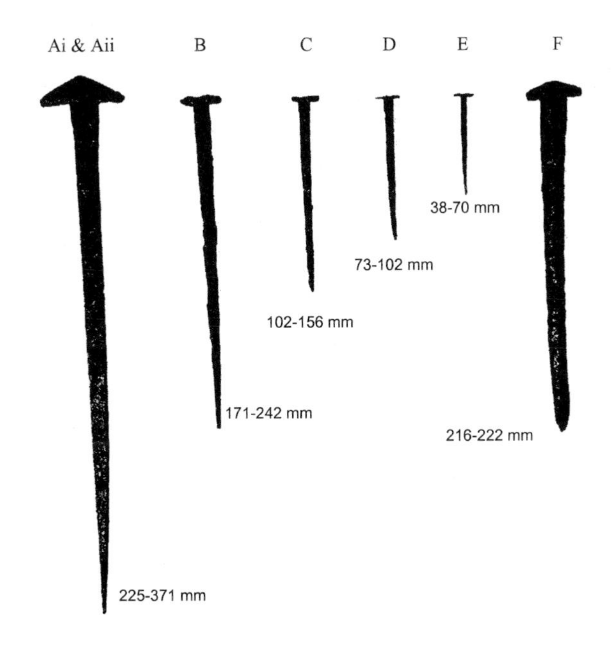

77 *Inchtuthil nail types as classified by Angus* et al. *(1962). Typical range of nail lengths is shown in mm*

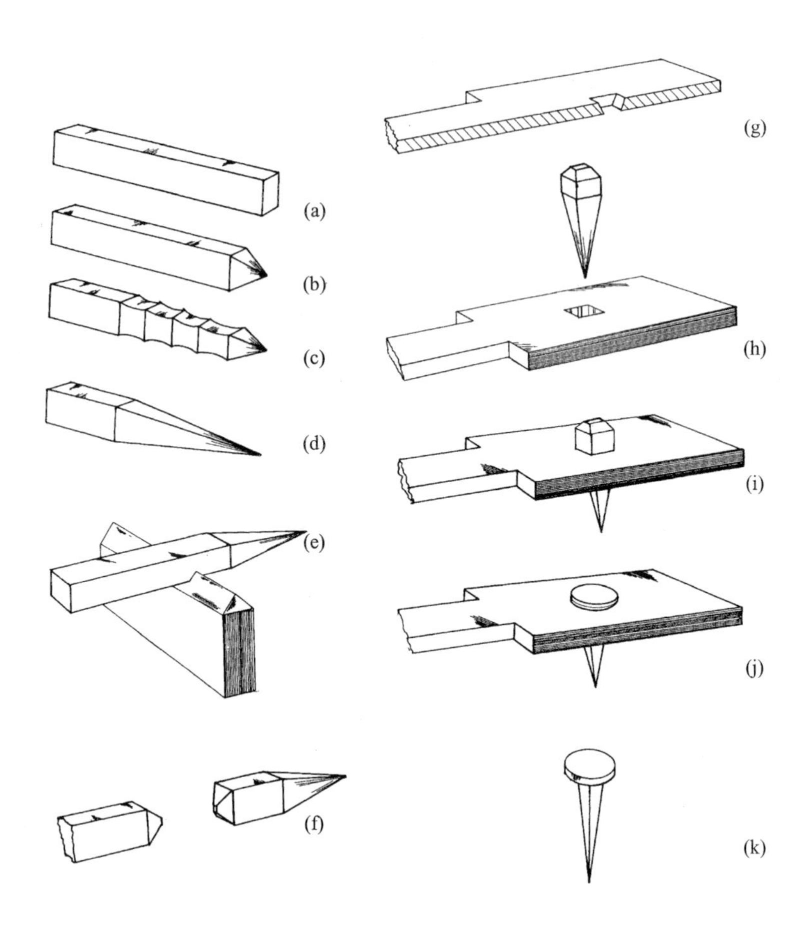

78 *Stages in the manufacture of a nail: (a-d) the bar is forged down to a point; (e, f) cut from the parent bar; (g) section through the heading tool;(h-k) the head is formed*

The main body is formed by heating again to bright red heat and then hammering a long square point using the edge of the anvil and a round faced hammer (**78c**). The sides are flattened on the anvil face with a flat faced hammer (**78d**). The nail is cut off the parent bar using a hot set mounted on the anvil (**78e, f**), and is then ready to have the head put on the body, for which a heading tool is employed.

The heading tool has a tapering hole which is the same size as the body of the nail near the head (**78g**). This tapered hole has to support the nail while the head is being formed. If the nail body is too large it will not fit properly into the heading tool; if it is too small, it will drop through. To form the head on the nail 'blank', the top is locally heated to 1000°C. The blank is then positioned in the heading tool, and the hot end struck with a hammer to form the head and finish the nail (**78h-k**).

The nails found in the Inchtuthil hoard showed a very high level of consistency in their dimensions, especially that of the section of the body (**colour plate 29**). For the type E nails, Angus *et al.* (1962: 957) report that:

> more than 60% fell within the length range 2 Qr -2 Qw inches (57.2-63.5mm) and over 80% had head diameters within the range 7/16-1/2in. (11.1-12.7 mm), while every specimen of this group measured had a shank section of *exactly* [sic.] Qi in. (3.2mm).

As mentioned above, so far as manufacturing is concerned, it is important that the cross-section is as near the correct size as possible so that the head may be put on the nail. It is therefore not so surprising that the shank tolerance is much closer than the other main dimensions. However, this level of conformity does point to some standardisation, presumably in the bar stock and the heading tools – it is difficult to imagine the 760,000 plus type E nails being made using just one heading tool.

Time and skill required to manufacture nails

Sim (1998a: 61ff) reports a number of experiments to investigate the time and level of proficiency required to make nails of the quantity and sizes found in the Inchtuthil hoard. Experiments in teaching nail making (of type E nails) showed that in general the trainees (two women and two children) found forging the shank was a skill which could be learnt fairly quickly, but that heading the nail was a more complicated skill which they had difficulty with. Examination of the nails from Inchtuthil shows that their experience was not unrepresentative! (**colour plates 29** & **30**). It is reasonable to assume that with more practice they could have mastered this too, although a concentric head is not essential to the correct operation of a nail of this size. The larger nails would have required a higher level of competence, and would have been made by semi-skilled or skilled workers. Since considerably more effort would be required to drive in the large nails, it would be important not only that the head was concentric, but that it was big enough to accommodate the *cold working* (flattening) which it would be subject to (see **77** type A).

Table 8 Estimated production times for nails

Nail type	Length (mm)	Number of nails in hoard	Experimental time to make each nail (mins:secs)	Total production time (hours)
Ai	247-371	A(i)+A(ii) = 1344	30:00	672
Aii	225-273			
B	171-242	B+C = 25,088	25:00*	10453
C	102-156			
D	73-102	85,128	04:00	5715
E	38-70	763,840	03:20*	42011
F	216-222	28	30:00*	14

*Estimated time

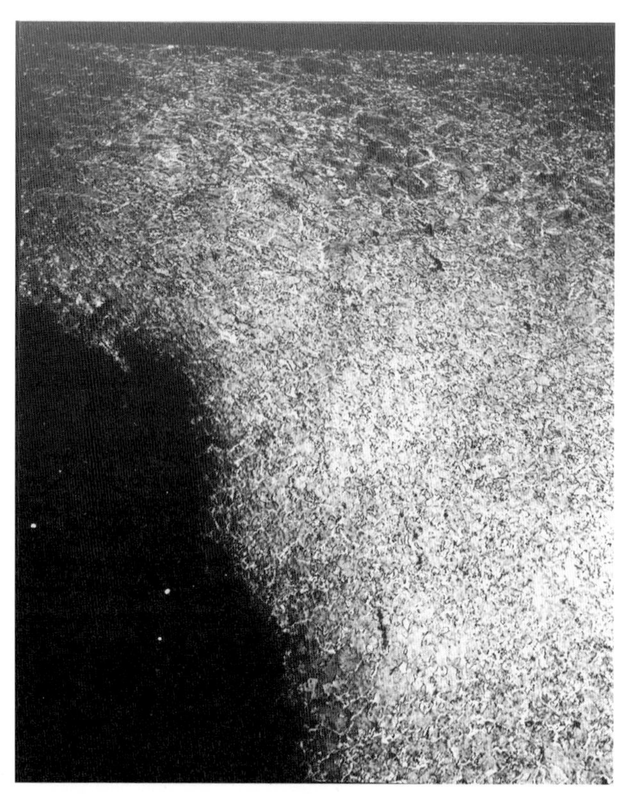

79 *Micrograph showing the carbon content in the area of the head in an Inchtuthil nail*

80 *Micrograph showing the carbon content in the point of an Inchtuthil nail, approximately x 400, polished and etched in 2% nital. The dark band across the middle is a slag inclusion*

Experiments in which the blacksmith was assisted by a striker rather than working on his own found that although the production time for a certain type of nail remained fairly constant, the element of fatigue was significantly reduced, thus making a long working day possible. It is likely that the blacksmith would in practice have had at least one striker and probably an apprentice to help manage the forge.

Table 8 presents the results of the experimental work to determine the time taken to make the various types of nails. Some of these times have been interpolated from other data: it can be seen that the size range of the type B nail overlaps with type A(ii) and the times for B, C and F can be estimated from the times to make A(i) and A(ii). Type E can be estimated from the time to make D. Hence the time taken to have made all the nails (from consolidated bar) found in the hoard amounts to roughly 60,000 hours, or about 20 working years for one person (assuming a working day of ten hours, 312 days a year). This would be a considerable amount of work in a small workshop, but readily achieved by a few blacksmiths working with a team of labourers.

Hardening of nails

In the section of this chapter looking at disposable weapons, it was shown that the Romans did not harden the tips of their projectiles because there was no need to, rather than because they lacked the knowledge to do so.

The nail might be considered as 'disposable' (certainly a consumable), yet its function will benefit considerably from being made of a harder material than wrought iron. In their discussion of the selection of material, Angus *et al.* (1962: 965) present results indicating that the heads of the larger nails, especially types A and B, were of a high carbon content (**79**). Additionally, some of the tips of the nails were of a similar 'steely' condition (**80**). Reference to **81** indicates a local carbon content of about 0.4%C – a medium carbon steel. This would have helped considerably in the operation of driving the nails into the large timbers they were designed for. It is noted that in some nails there are high carbon areas which are completely surrounded by low carbon areas, indicating that the carburisation was a product of the bloomery process in addition to being a result of reheating for forging. It is interesting that the smaller nails have (and need) much less carbon. All of this taken together, as Angus *et al.* (1962: 966) observe, is very suggestive that there was some sort of deliberate grading or selection of material for the manufacture of the different size nails – but it is impossible to be certain.

7

THE USE OF STEEL

An aspect of the Roman iron industry referred to in passing in earlier chapters is the Roman use of steel. Steel is an alloy of iron (ferrite) and a relatively small amount of carbon. There is no precise definition of the level of carbon required in iron for it to be termed steel, but in practice iron may be considered steel when is has a carbon content between 0.1 and 2% (by weight). Figure **81** presents a series of micrographs of steel with differing carbon contents. At low concentrations the carbon tends to collect at the ferrite grain boundaries and forms a structure called pearlite, while at higher carbon levels the ferrite matrix is transformed to all pearlite and cememtite (the term 'steely iron' is sometimes used to describe wrought iron with a low amount of carbon in it). At greater concentrations of carbon – typically 2-5% – the group of cast irons are formed.

The way in which iron was made in the bloomery process meant that it was exposed to a readily available source of carbon – the fuel; and so it is hardly surprising that an iron-carbon alloy occurred. Occurred, or was made? There is no doubt that the Romans produced steel, and it is found in a variety of applications such as ties for building construction (**colour plate 31**), and in the Inchtuthil nails mentioned earlier but the issue of whether they realised that this was what they were doing has been the subject of debate. Pleiner (2000: 137) makes the interesting point that for some applications, especially sheet metal forming and wire drawing, the softer more ductile wrought iron is a better material than steel and so the Romans would have needed to avoid making the latter.

That the Romans appreciated the superior properties of steel for giving an edge for cutting tools cannot be questioned. The metallographic examination mentioned earlier of a moulding plane blade by the authors (Sim and Ridge, 2000), and similar work by others on other artefacts (tools and weapons), has found that the Romans made use of a hardened steel edge welded to a relatively soft but tougher body. Tools such as the pattern-welded sword and axe (items which would be in use for a long time) were given hard steel edges.

Vegetius (*Epitoma Rei Militaris.* IV.8) writing on 'preparing the defence' notes that 'Iron of both tempers and charcoal are kept in the stores for making arms and armour.' So although it can be said that the Romans appreciated the properties of steel and

(a) 0.1%C Ferrite and a small amount of pearlite (dark)

(b) 0.22%C More pearlite present – note finer grain size

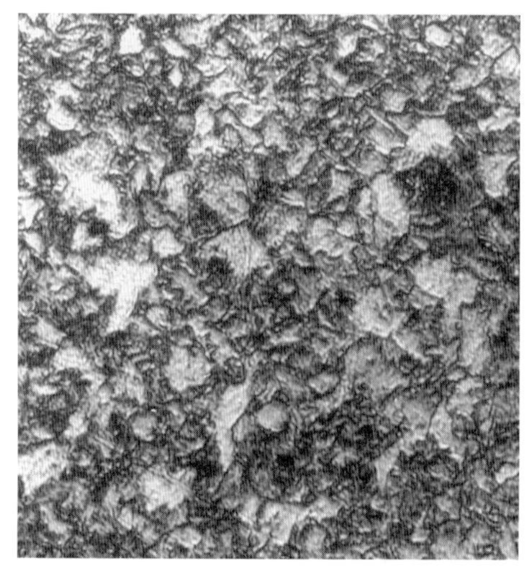

(c) 0.39%C Increased pearlite in the ferrite

81 *Micrographs of normalised steels with differing carbon content, approximately x 400, polished and etched in 2% nital solution*

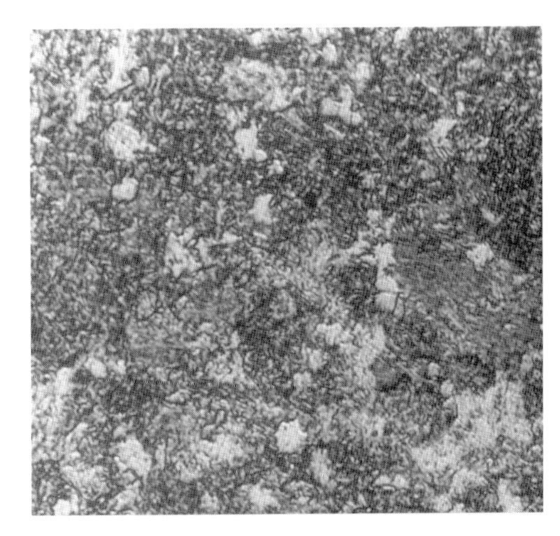

(d) 0.54%C Roughly equal ferrite and pearlite

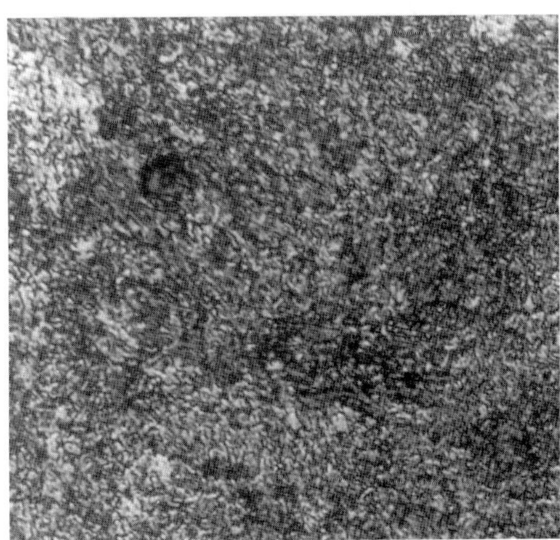

(e) 0.81%C All pearlite

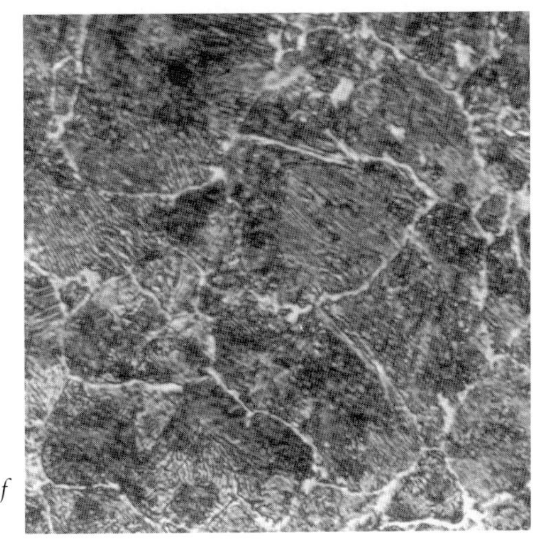

(f) 1.3%C Network of cementite around patches of lamellar pearlite

knew how to harden it, whether they actually thought of it as an alloyed material is impossible to say. While latin had no words to distinguish iron-carbon alloys, the Greek word *stomwma* seems to have been reserved for a high-carbon steel used for the cutting edges of for example quarrying tools. Another word which may have been used to describe steel is adáma/adamas, from which the English word adamant is derived, and which was used to describe the hardest metal, presumably steel, although it possibly refers to diamond. However, the Latin word *ferrum* and the Greek word *sidhro* were applied equally to rigid and sharp-edged weapons, such as swords, and to malleable iron such as the strapping applied to a crane (Burford 1969).

This lack of discrimination may be no accident or looseness on the part of the authors; it is possible that the iron-carbon alloys were described by a single term because they appeared to have been made by a single process, and the variations in hardness and stiffness were thought to be no more a sign of differences in composition than similar variations in bronze caused by beating and annealing, or differences in the strength of timber due to the country of origin. This suggests that the ancients were able to produce a medium-carbon steel directly from the ore, by a process which was to the layman indistinguishable from that by which they made low-carbon wrought iron described above.

Production of steel

There are several methods or routes by which steel could have been produced: cementation (carburisation); directly from the bloom; decarburisation of cast iron; or production in a crucible.

Production of steel by cementation (carburisation)

The cementation process introduces carbon into the wrought iron in a solid state. Wrought iron is packed into containers with a carbon-rich material and heated at around 800-950°C for a prolonged period of several hours or days. Craddock (1995: 252) describes how wrought iron bars 10-20mm thick were held at a temperature of 1050-1100°C for five to seven days to produce the so-called blister steel made in Sheffield from the seventeenth to mid-twentieth centuries. During the heating, the carbon diffuses into the surface of the iron, so forming steel. The depth to which the carbon is absorbed is a function of the temperature and duration of heating. This method appears to be that used to make *stomwma* as described by Aristotle in *Meteorologica* IV.383 (Richmond 1961): cementation followed by homogenisation. This process is still quite widely thought to have been the main steel-making process in antiquity, in spite of the views of Forbes (1956) and Tylecote *et al.* (1971) discussed in the next section.

The cementation method of steeling wrought iron would be much more effective on a thin section. Having said this, it may be very desirable to harden just the outer region of the bar or artefact, in effect *case hardening*, producing a tougher iron core supporting the more brittle hard steel surface.

Maintaining a temperature of 950°C for a period of time (for example, an 8mm thick bar would take 11 hours to convert totally to steel) (**82**), obviously would have some sort of cost implication. The temperature would have been readily attainable (especially where an enclosed hearth was used), but the process would have been time consuming and costly in fuel. It is possible (but pure speculation) that a blacksmith would produce small quantities of steel as and when he needed it. The heat of the forge is more than adequate for the process of carburisation.

Production of steel direct from the bloom

Forbes (1956: 56) states that it was possible to make steel directly in the bloom anywhere that high-quality ore was available. The production of a steel bloom is part of the normal functioning of the bloomery process, if a shaft furnace is stoked with an ore to charcoal ratio of 1.5:1 (Pleiner 2000: 137). As some of the particles of iron form, they will absorb carbon. This in turn lowers their melting point and they become a liquid, dripping down in the furnace to collect in a steely bloom. This has distinct areas of differing carbon content, such as are found in the Japanese Tatara method, where the bloom is broken and sorted into pieces of differing carbon content. These small pieces are then welded into a block which is further processed. In chapter 6 it was shown how breaking the bloom into smaller pieces before welding not only rids the billet of large amounts of slag, but reduces the amount of material lost when forging the bloom into workable iron. It is reasonable to conject therefore that a similar process could have been used to consolidate steely blooms.

The process described here is in one way more economical than the production of a soft low-carbon iron, in that more of the metal from the ore is left in the bloom and less dissolved in the slag (this might make possible the identification of furnaces used for this purpose). Compare for example the very low iron content of 7 out of the 15 slags analysed by Fulford and Allen (1992). On the other hand, the process has the disadvantage that lower operational temperatures prevent the slag from melting, so the bloom contains much slag and even charcoal. Such a heterogeneous mass of a metal, which is in any case not easily hammer-welded, would be even more difficult to consolidate than the iron bloom (unless using the method described above), without losing very substantial amounts of metal by decarburisation. It was presumably that difficulty which deterred the iron-masters of the late middle ages from utilising the direct process, and made them take the longer route via cementation.

Decarburization of cast iron

Just as wrought iron may be made into steel by adding carbon, so cast iron may be turned to steel by removing it. Steel is made from cast iron using a process called *fining* – breaking the brittle cast iron into pieces and heating in a strongly oxidising blast of air to remove the carbon. Once the carbon content has reduced to a suitable level, it may be removed and forged in the usual manner. However, the production of cast iron, whilst not unknown in the Roman period is usually dismissed as an accidental product of the bloomery process, the reason given that the temperatures required (approximately 1600°C) could not be attained. Experimental work by the author however has shown that this temperature could easily be achieved in an enclosed hearth, suggesting that the production of cast iron by the Romans was indeed possible. Mack *et al.* (2000: 95) observe that there is evidence …

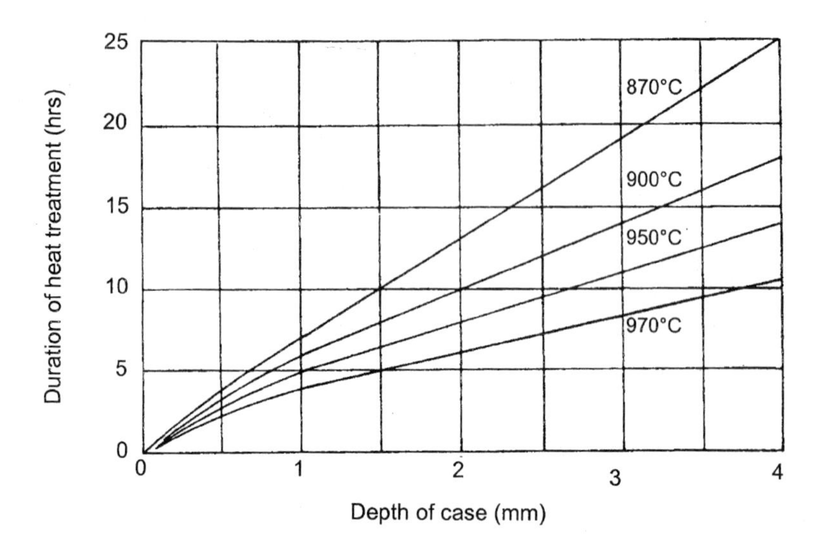

82 *Depth of carburisation of iron as a function of time and temperature.* After Higgins

> . . . that the deliberate decarburisation of bloomery-derived cast iron into high carbon steel may have occurred from the late Roman/early medieval period. Thus the process (described here) may represent a technology that was used at a low level throughout history in many localities until the evolution of the blast furnace in the late medieval period.

Other evidence which points to the use of cast iron in the Roman period is the find of two pillars from the Limeskastell Saalburg, which Krapp (1987: 325) reports 'arouse suspicion of being cast because of their equal opposite angles [symmetry of structure], their plane surfaces and sharp edges'.

Crucible steel

The process involves placing small pieces of wrought iron in a crucible with carbon-rich material such as wood, leaves or fruit skin (rarely charcoal), together with a little slag. The crucibles (which were small in size, holding only a few hundred cubic centimetres) were sealed with clay and packed in batches in furnaces. They were then heated to 1400°C for between one and twenty-four hours. The high carbon presence enabled the steel to melt and become liquid, resulting in a very clean steel, free from slag inclusions. It is not known if the Romans used this technique, but the Seric iron which Pliny mentions in his *Natural History* (XXXIV.145) is thought to be the very high carbon crucible steel that Rome was trading with China possibly via India (where it is also known as *wootz*). This would imply that the Romans had access to steel made in this manner, if not the knowledge to produce it.

Heat treatment of steel

Various heat treatments: hardening, tempering, annealing and normalising can be used on steel in order to alter its properties such as hardness, strength, toughness and ductility. Higgins (1983: 258) writes:

> In all of these processes the steel is heated fairly slowly to some predetermined temperature, and then cooled, and it is the *rate of cooling* which determines the resultant structure of the steel and, hence, the mechanical properties associated with it. The final structure will be *independent* of the rate of heating, provided it has been slow enough for the steel to reach structural equilibrium at its maximum temperature.

For a fuller discussion of the metallurgy of steels the reader is directed to books by Higgins, *Engineering Metallurgy* or Honeycombe, *Steels - microstructures and properties*, both of which have been published in several editions and *Roman Imperial Armour*. Sim and Kaminski 2011.

Hardening

When a piece of steel is heated to a temperature between 723-900°C (the temperature required depends upon the carbon content of the steel), the atoms in the structure become mobile and form different structures (even though at this temperature the steel is not in liquid form). If the steel is then *quenched*, that is cooled rapidly from this state, it is possible to 'freeze' the metallic structure which was present at the elevated temperature, and preserve it at room temperature. The structure so formed is much harder than that which would be obtained if the material had been allowed to cool to room temperature at a slower rate, which would allow the growth of large relatively soft grains of iron and the harder structure of iron and carbon called *pearlite*.

The level of hardness achieved by this process, and the iron-carbon structures formed (*martensite*, *trootsite* and so on), will vary according to the initial temperature, volume of material being treated, speed of cooling, and the temperature and nature of the quenching medium. However, these structures are consistently very much harder than plain wrought iron. The Romans used a variety of liquids for quenching, such as water and oil (Pliny *Natural History* XXXIV.146), urine, blood and vinegar (Healy 1978: 233). Pliny's comment (*Natural History* XXXIV.146) that 'It is the custom to quench smaller iron forgings with oil, for fear that water might harden them and make them brittle' shows an awareness that different material properties are obtained from different quenching fluids.

Tempering

The hard and brittle material produced by quenching has very high internal stresses. In order to lower these and so produce a tougher structure, the steel is tempered by reheating. Plutarch (*Moralia* I, 73c) describes a process which seems to refer to quenching and tempering of steel:' ... just as steel is made compact by cooling, and takes on a temper as the result of having first been relaxed and softened by heat ....

The temperature to which the steel is reheated will affect the level of tempering, but the usual range is between 220-300°C. With experience, the Roman blacksmith would have been able to judge the level of temper from the colour of the oxide film which would appear on the steel: from pale yellow at 220°C through to dark blue at 300°C.

Annealing and normalising

Annealing is a process of softening and relieving stresses in the steel that have been caused as a result of work hardening, that is the severe deformation of the material at low (room) temperature. Processes particularly prone to inducing work hardening are sheet forming or wire drawing. The purpose of annealing is to allow the material to return to its softer, unworked condition, either to allow further working or to restore some of the material toughness. The steel is heated to a temperature between 760-900°C, again dependent upon the carbon content of the steel. After 'soaking' (holding at that temperature) for a time determined by the size of the work piece, the steel is cooled very slowly, by either leaving the steel buried in the ash of the fire (furnace) and allowing it to cool as the fire goes out, or possibly by burying it in a good thermal insulator such as sand. The steel structure thus obtained is very soft and malleable, and suitable for further working without causing cracking or failure. The Romans were familiar with the process of annealing from their experience with copper and bronze, and so it seems likely that they would have employed a similar technique with steel.

Normalising is similar to the annealing process in that it involves heating to the same temperatures, but differs in the method of cooling. Rather than the very slow rate described above, in normalising the steel is removed from the heat and left to cool in still air. This faster cooling rate will produce a stronger steel structure than the annealed steel, but one less hard than the quenched.

Processing of steel

Steel is processed in the forge hearth in the same way as iron; however there is one additional consideration, which is decarburisation (the *loss* of carbon) at very high temperatures. Steel forged in an open hearth without special consideration will easily lose 0.2-0.3% of its carbon content. Because of this problem, a practical limitation on the forging heat for steel is about 780°C (cherry red heat). Operating at a reduced temperature means that less work may be done on the material for each heat, and this in turn will lengthen production time. An additional consideration is that some operations, for example fire-welding, may only be conducted at high temperatures (1100°C); thus the loss of some carbon from the steel in such processes would be unavoidable. Recent work by the author has indicated that the use of an enclosed hearth, rather than the open forge, would have provided significant operational benefits. Not only would the enclosed hearth considerably reduce the effect of decarburisation, but the loss of iron and steel during processing is also dramatically reduced.

The role of the enclosed hearth

The Roman use of the enclosed hearth is depicted in the House of the Vettii (**colour plate 3**) and the blacksmith's forge in the Aquileia Museum (**6**). These sources show relatively small, enclosed box-like structures, both with arched openings and apparently blown by bellows. In both examples, the processes being conducted are associated with forge work rather than smelting operations.

Experimental reconstructions of this type of enclosed hearth were made to investigate the factors of: atmosphere control, temperature control, fuel efficiency, level of oxidisation and decarburisation. These studies found that is it possible to control the hearth atmosphere quite readily, and thus keep both oxidation and decarburisation losses to a minimum (**Table 9**). The atmosphere was controlled by opening the top of the hearth to increase air flow: the 'head' which may be seen on the top of the Vettii hearth is probably a decorated handle for such an opening. It is important when heating the iron (or steel) in the furnace to maintain an oxygen starved (reducing) atmosphere, as this prevents the wasteful oxidisation of the material. However, the lack of oxygen also starves the fire, which will start to go out. Hence an optimum solution was to have a reducing atmosphere when heating the iron and an oxidising atmosphere when the iron was out of the furnace being forged. The benefits for the forging operations investigated were considerable: principal forging process losses were reduced from typically 40% to 11%, whilst for simpler operations the losses were as low as only 1%. The losses involved in fire welding remained more or less constant. Although the experimental work was only undertaken for forging operations, it is a logical conclusion that this type of hearth could be used beneficially for the other iron production operations, especially consolidation of the bloom.

It was found that steel could be forged in an enclosed hearth in a manner that did not significantly remove carbon (as occurs in the traditional open hearth). In the previous section it was reported that without care, the outer layers of steel forged in an open hearth would lose from 0.2-0.3% carbon; similar operations in an enclosed hearth showed no detectable loss of carbon, indicating that steel artefacts can be produced without need for special precautions (reduced forging temperatures).

It should also be noted that as well as reducing considerably the material losses, the fuel consumption was much lower. An open hearth will consume anywhere from 3.5-7kg of charcoal per hour (depending upon the type of operation being conducted), whilst the experimental enclosed hearth consumed from 1.5-3.5kg for the same procedures, a saving of about 50%.

Table 9 Comparison of material weight losses in open hearth and enclosed hearths

Operation	Temperature (°C)	Weight loss	
		Open hearth	Enclosed hearth
Simple forging (bending, cutting)	600–1000	5% to 19%	Maximum 1%
Principal forging (punching, drifting, drawing down, upsetting)	1000–1100	24% to 40%	Maximum 11%
Fire welding	1100–1200	60% to 75%	55% to 75%

These findings offer a significant insight into the Romans' ability to process both iron and steel. The work needs to be extended to include the earlier processing operations such as bloomsmithing to provide a fuller picture, but indicates that the Romans may have been able to process the bloom more efficiently than previously thought possible.

8

MECHANICAL PROCESSING

Until well into the twentieth century most machines were made of wood, which does not survive well in the archaeological record. It is also likely that when a machine was scrapped the large timbers were recycled and the smaller pieces used as fuel. This is the reason why so few remains of ancient machinery survive today. (see Sim and Kaminski 2011). This in turn has given rise to the assumption that the use of machines in the ancient world was restricted to corn mills. There is however strong evidence to suggest that the use of machines was wide spread and that it might have been used in the iron industry.

The use of water power

In chapter 2 it was shown that the Romans were well aware of the power of flowing water, and used the technique of hushing in areas where there was sufficient head of water to remove soil and so on in their mining activities. Healy (1978: 144) describes a 'simple yet effective' washing plant for silver ore which made full use of the energy in water stored at a raised height, and showed how the Romans used funnels to both direct and intensify the pressure of the water (Healy 1978 plates 41-43).

The Romans made use of water wheels as a means of raising the water to drain their mine workings. The system in place at Rio Tinto involved a complex series of wheels in pairs (Davis 1935: 25ff, Healy 1978: 96-100). As Landels (1978: 20) points out, it would have been obvious to a worker finishing a stint of water wheel treading that if he took his feet away, the wheel would slowly reverse, emptying the buckets as it went, and further that a level of force would be required to stop this motion. Equipped with this information, it is then a simple step to see how a 'free' supply of rotational power could be obtained from a running water supply by using a water wheel.

Types of water wheel

The different types of water wheel have been described by various authors (Landels 1978: 17-26, Cotterell and Kamminga, 1992: 42, Lewis 1997 and Watts 2000). The three basic types: vertical axis, and the two divisions of horizontal axis styles – overshot and undershot (**83**).

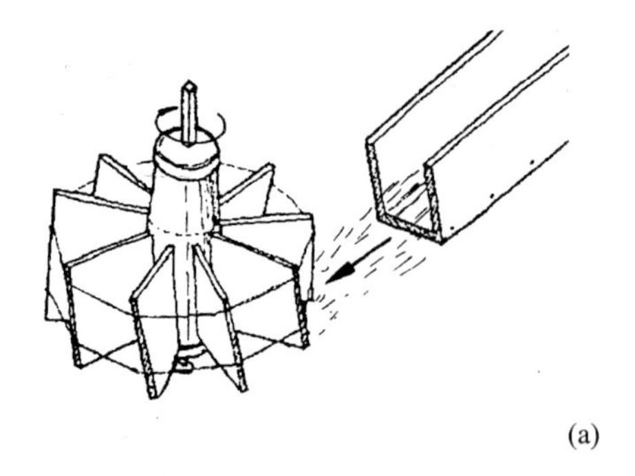

(a)

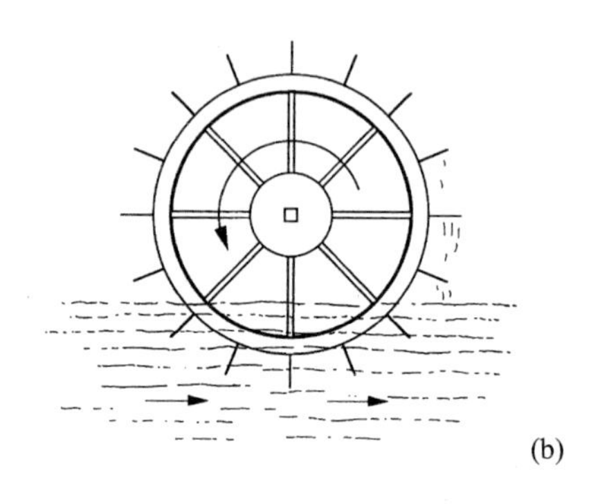

(b)

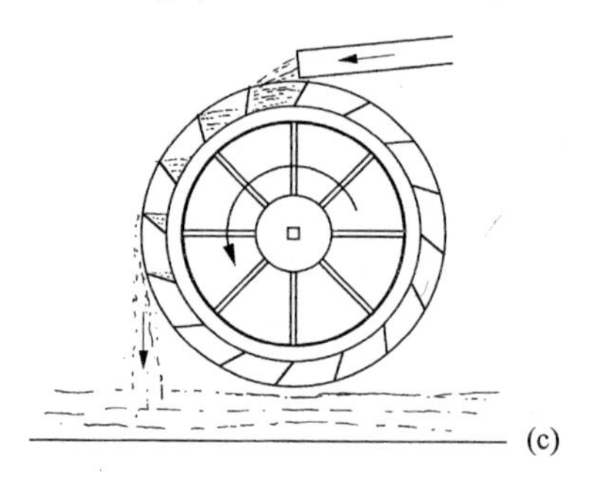

(c)

83 *Types of water wheel:*
(a) vertical axis;
(b) undershot;
(c) overshot.
(a) after Watts 2000: 15;
(b, c) after Landels 1978: fig. 3

In the vertical axis water wheel configuration (**83a**), the water strikes a series of blades which are set at about 30° to the vertical on a central hub. It has been thought that this would have been the first type of wheel used, the other two forms being refinements of it, since the vertical orientation of its shaft makes it most readily adapted to drive (for example) a grain mill (**84**). However, it's effective operation requires a *head* of water of about 3m, a *leat* (channel) to direct the water, and a pit around the wheel to rapidly clear the water so as not to hinder its turning (Landels 1978: 18) ('head' is the distance through which the water is allowed to fall to create kinetic energy to impart to the wheel). These requirements mean that although it was certainly easier to use the vertical output to drive the mill stones, on the whole it would have been simpler to use a pair of gears at the end of a horizontal axis wheel to achieve rotation about the vertical plane (**85**).

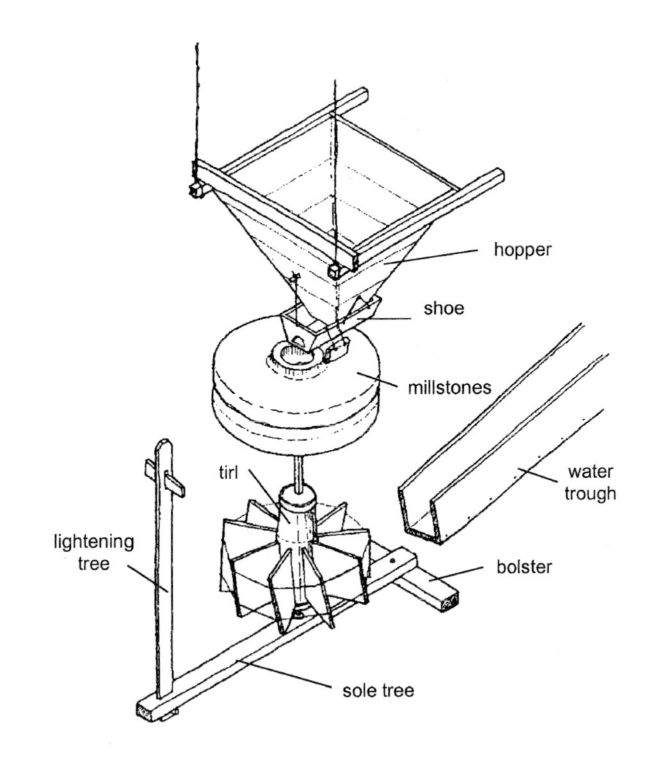

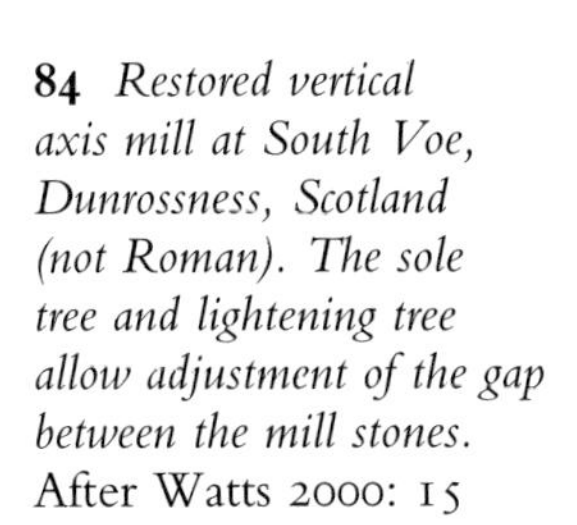

84 *Restored vertical axis mill at South Voe, Dunrossness, Scotland (not Roman). The sole tree and lightening tree allow adjustment of the gap between the mill stones.* After Watts 2000: 15

85 *Simple gear system to change the axis of rotation from horizontal to vertical (supporting structure not shown).* After Landels 1978: fig. 4

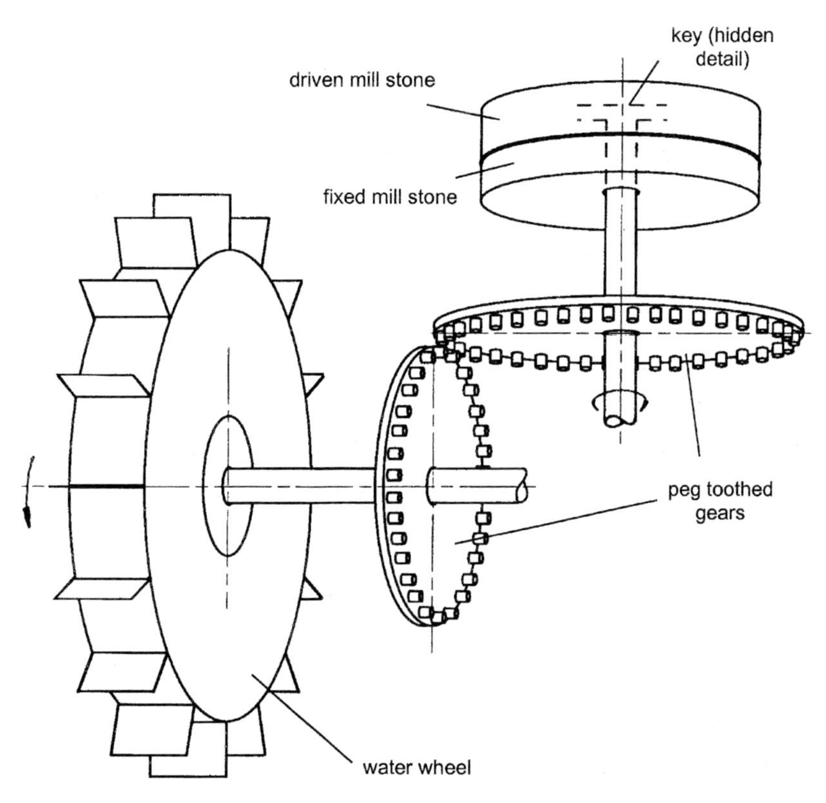

The undershot wheel is the less complex of the two horizontal axis water wheels, in that it requires no head and little by way of surrounding structure (**83b**). The wheel is turned by making use of the kinetic (moving) energy of the stream of water flowing past and impinging on a series of radial vanes. This arrangement has an efficiency of about 22% (Landels 1978: 21).

The overshot water wheel is in appearance the same as the type of wheel mentioned above which would have been used to pump the mine workings and, as its name suggests, makes use of a water flow at the top of the wheel (**83c**). Water is directed via a channel to fill a series of buckets (rather than strike vanes) on the edge of the wheel, which causes it to turn. The wheel makes use primarily of the potential energy of the water (that is the fact that as the water falls it pushes down on the wheel), as well as the kinetic energy (the energy the water has because it is moving). The overshot wheel can achieve a typical efficiency of 65-70%, some three times that of the undershot wheel; however, as Landels (1978: 23) points out, it may easily cost four or five times the capital to build (especially the channel bringing the water in at a raised height), and presumably would only be used where the power from an undershot wheel type was too low for requirements. The first type of wheel clearly mentioned in the classical texts is the horizontal overshot type (including gears), described by Vetruvius in his *De Architectura* (X.5.2), which was written in the first century AD.

It is useful at this stage to consider the power output which might be expected from such systems. Landels (1978: 21) estimates that an undershot wheel operating in a small river (which might be 3.5m wide and 0.1m deep, and have a flow rate of 570 litres/second (l/s) or 125gal./sec.), could generate in theory 2 horse power (hp) and in practice about 0.4 hp, (note that 1 horse power is the equivalent of 745.7W so 0.4hp is about 300W.) A 2.13m (7ft) diameter overshot wheel operating with a lower water flow rate of 140 l/s might produce an actual output of 2-25hp (1500-1860W).

With regard to the gears which Vetruvius mentioned, Cotterell and Kamminga (1992: 96) note that it was not until the seventeenth century that the sophisticated hypocycloid/epicycloid profile of gear teeth in use today was developed. Instead, the Romans had to rely on the rather less efficient pin type wheel. The pins in the gears would either have been fitted radially on the edge of the wheel, and perpendicular to the axis of rotation (**86a**), or about the circumference parallel to the axis (**86b**). These types of gear mesh best if they are of similar diameter, so it follows that they essentially would have been used for changing the axis of rotation rather than any gearing up or down of the output shaft speed.

Archaeological evidence of Roman water wheels

The archaeological evidence of the water wheel systems which the Romans used is scarce. The very nature of the construction materials (essentially wood with some iron fittings) in use in a damp environment means that very little will have survived. Landels (1978: 18) reports:

> A very big installation was built there [Arles in S. France] by the Romans in the late third or early fourth century, and was probably in use for the greater part of 100 years. It contained eight pairs of wheels, each driving mill stones in a mill

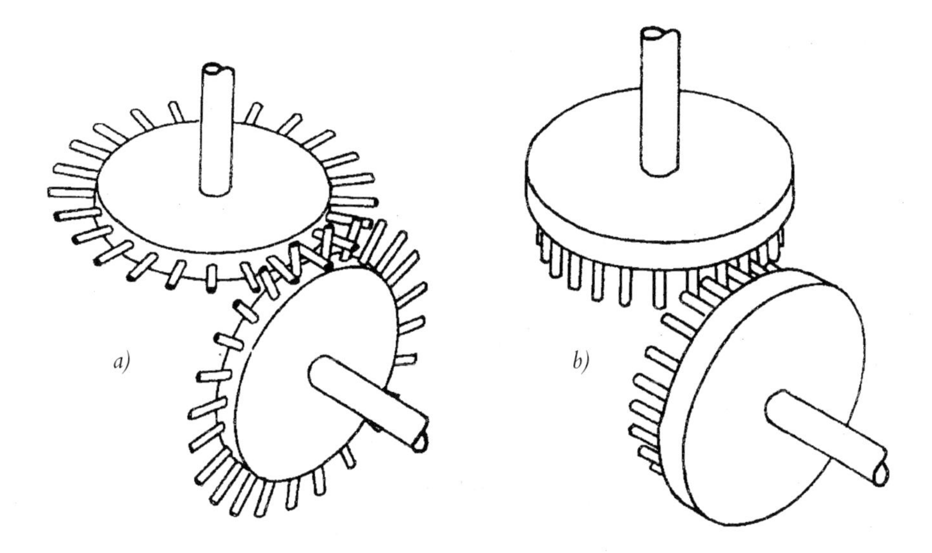

86 *Simple right-angled drives: (a) using pins perpendicular to the axis of the gear; (b) pins parallel to the axis of the gear.* After Cotterell & Kamminga 1992: fig. 4.17

> chamber beside the wheel pit, and its output would have been adequate for not only the 10,000 inhabitants of Arles, but for some area around. The presence of a Roman garrison might account for this. The remains are not very extensive, but the main essentials can be reconstructed from them.

In Britain, Watts (2000: 7) states that water wheel sites have been found at Haltwhistle Burn Head (close to Hadrian's Wall) in Northumberland, nearby Chesters Fort, and further west at Willowford, Cumbria; both places where the wall crosses major rivers (North Tyne and Irthing respectively). Further south evidence has been found at: Ickham, Kent (close to the Little Stour river), a site which was in operation in AD 150, and a bit further upstream a fourth-century site is evident. Watts also comments that:

> Although the number of positively identified Roman water mills in Britain is few, it is likely that power driven mills were more common than once thought. Evidence of milling and baking has been found at many sites, and large granaries, both military and civilian, indicate the importance of corn crops and their processing to the people of Roman Britain and, in particular to the army.

Ore processing

Although it is understood that the Romans used water power for the milling of grain it is however quite probable that the Romans may also have made use of water power in the processing of metal ores. Lewis (1997) suggests that water-powered hammers were used for 'fulling, crushing ore, forging iron and the like'. Watts (2000: 10) comments:

The majority of Roman water-powered sites that have been identified were used for grain milling, but there is evidence to suggest that waterwheels were also used for industrial purposes. The fourth-century site at Ickham, Kent, probably had more than one waterwheel, and in an area adjacent to the corn mill great quantities of metal and numerous artefacts of iron, pewter and copper alloys were discovered. Among the finds were bearing stones and an iron hammer head that showed mechanical wear, which suggests that water power may have been used for metalworking there. Similarly there is a possibility that water power was used to drive ore-crushing hammers or stamps at the Roman gold mine at Dolaucothi in south-west Wales by the end of the first century AD, and further evidence undoubtedly awaits discovery elsewhere.

Ore milling

Consider a typical Roman ore mill (**87**). Healy (1978: 142) states that such a mill would have been operated by four or six slaves pushing on handles, which would have been inserted in the two slots on the edge of the top grinding stone. The ore, which would have already been roasted and broken down, could be further ground using this mill where necessary (as discussed in chapter 4). Healy notes that it is estimated that each mill could process about 4 tonnes of ore in 24 hours.

It is a simple step from what has been discussed above to see how the Romans could have adapted this mill to be driven by water power (**88**). So far as the power requirements are concerned, Cotterell and Kamminga (1992: Table 2.7) give a typical power output of a single person while pushing a capstan as 70W. Thus four to six slaves would indicate a power requirement for the mill under consideration of 280-420W. This range of values encompasses the estimated power from the undershot wheel (300W) but is well below the 1500-1860W which may be provided by the overshot type wheel. Obviously a smaller mill would require less power and the output would similarly be lower. It should be noted that there would be some power loss in the gearing (the level of which is difficult to quantify); nonetheless the power requirements for this example would be well within the capacity of the overshot wheel described.

Ore crushing and stamping

Before the ore could be milled, it was first crushed. This might be performed using an 'edge-runner' *mola olearia* as described by Lewis (1997: 5), in which 'circular stones are made to roll in a tight circle crushing material placed under them' (**89**). As with the mill described above, it would be possible to drive this type of device using the simple pair of gears from a horizontal shaft. It is not known what the power requirements would have been, but it is reasonable to anticipate that they would be similar.

A different device which could have been used for crushing is the ore stamp which is described in detail by Agricola in his *De re Metallica,* book VIII (**90**). The illustration clearly shows an overshot water wheel roughly 3m in diameter powering a four-fold

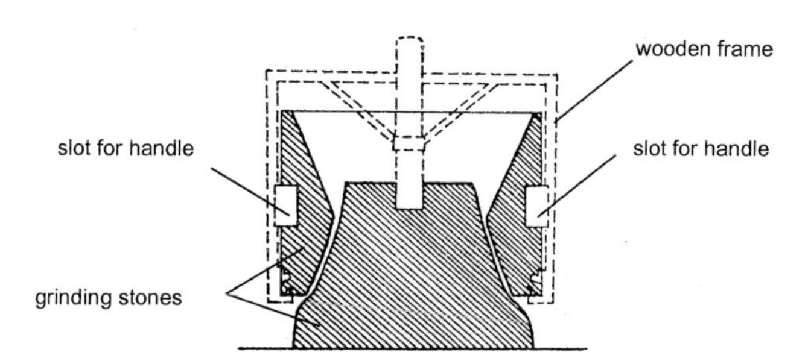

87 *Cross-section of a mill used for ore grinding.* After Healey 1978: fig. 21

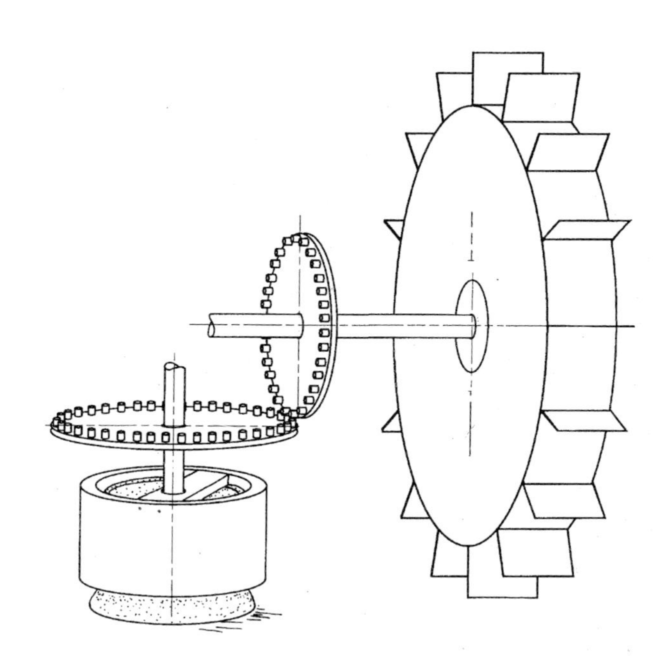

88 *Schematic diagram of a proposed water-powered ore mill (of type shown in* **65***)*

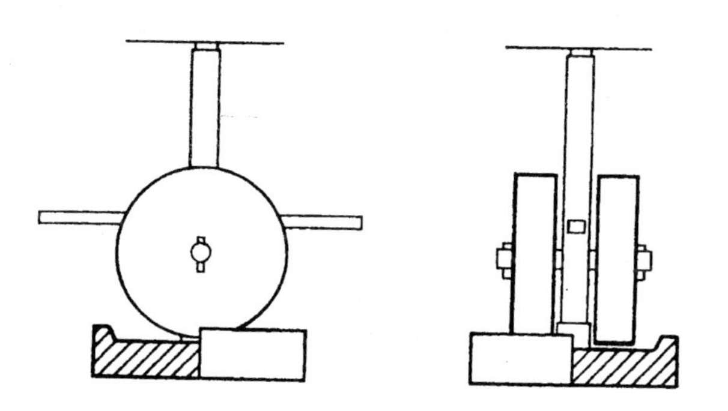

89 *Roman edge runner* mola olearia. After Lewis 1997: fig. 6

90 *An ore stamp from Agricola* De re Metallica *(1556)*

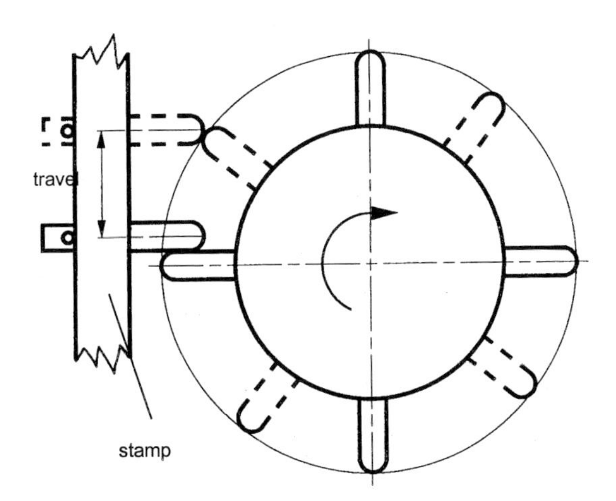

91 *Linear movement from a rotary power source*

stamp. What differentiates this mechanism from that already considered is that it makes use of rotary motion to create a linear movement (i.e. up and down) of the stamps. This is achieved by means of 'teeth' on the stamp which engage on teeth or a 'cam' on the rotary axle, so lifting it until they have turned so far as to no longer engage, thus allowing the stamp to fall (**91**). By spacing the teeth about the circumference of the axle, a balanced system will be achieved and power requirements kept to a minimum. The height to which the stamps rise and fall within each cycle will be governed by the effective length of the teeth: the longer the teeth, the greater the height and, of course, the greater the power requirements.

The evidence suggesting that this mechanism was known to the Romans is found in a series of automata known in antiquity. Lewis (1997: 84-8) describes in detail four examples of Greek automata which make use of the cam to create the linear movement from a rotation as described above. Probably the most well known of these examples is Hero's windmill for blowing an organ, which he describes in his *Pneumatica* (I.43) (**92**).

As an aside, concerning Hero's windmill, Landels (1978: 27) makes the interesting observation: 'The device was clearly a toy, but why did nobody (apparently) see its potential as a power source?' Landels attributes it to the small scale of the device: but it is, as he says, very puzzling.

Trip hammer

In the text cited above, Watts made mention of the use of a hammer, which showed evidence of mechanical wear. Lewis (1997: 6) also draws attention to the use of water-power for operating a trip hammer. He presents a very clear illustration from Spechthart (1488), which shows a forge hammer powered by an undershot water wheel (**93**). As with the ore stamp (this type of hammer could also easily be used for breaking ore), the extent of the motion depends on the configuration of the machine. The distance through which the head is raised and hence the energy with which it strikes the work piece or ore when it falls is determined by the relative distances from the teeth on the water wheel to the pivot point, and from the pivot point to the head (**94**). Along with the weight of

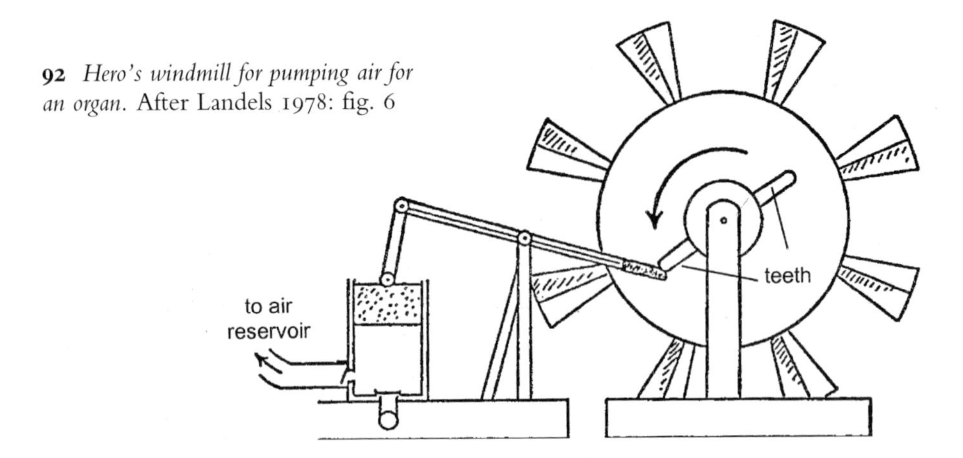

92 *Hero's windmill for pumping air for an organ.* After Landels 1978: fig. 6

the hammer head, these determine the power requirements of the system. To a certain extent, the workman would be able to devise a system which could be powered by the water flow he had available. It is interesting to note the figure shows that even with the less efficient undershot type wheel, a workable system was possible.

Abrasive wheels for finishing artefacts

The experimental work described in chapter 6 which discusses the manufacture of various items of military equipment (**Table 6**) highlights for some items the huge amount of time taken to 'finish' after forging. An extreme example is that of the *gladius*, which takes about 7 hours to forge from a raw billet, and 30 hours to finish. It is not clear whether the finishing of an artefact would have been carried out by the blacksmith, or passed on to another person. The two skills of forging and finishing are quite different, so it would make sense if the blacksmith were free to continue forging other items while a second person undertook the finishing. This distinction has been made in recent times in Sheffield by the two classes of craftsmen who made knives, the 'little mesters' who forged the blades and the cutlers who sharpened and polished them.

Evidence of machines for metal shaping in the Roman period is scant, relying mostly upon interpretation of the traces left on the artefact. Hence it is often assumed that iron artefacts were finished by hand, using hand-held tools such as files, scrapers and abrasive stones. However, this may not be the case. The use of rotary motion from the water-driven mill, (see chapter 6) and the use of the pole lathe (**26**) to turn and possibly finish objects such as *styli*. The pole lathe supplies a reciprocal rotational motion (constant change in both speed and direction), which would not be very appropriate for grinding work. Blagg (1976: 165ff) suggests that the Roman stonemasons used a large rotary (constant turning direction) type lathe for turning stone pillars, arguing his case on three points: evidence of complicated profiles and a strong mathematical precision in its cutting; continuous parallel rilling (grooving) on the face of the stone, and square holes in the top and bottom (which could be used for lathe-mounting as well as column joining dowels) (**95**).

93 *Forge hammer.* After Spechtshart 1488, f.[M7]v, also in Lewis 1997: fig. 7

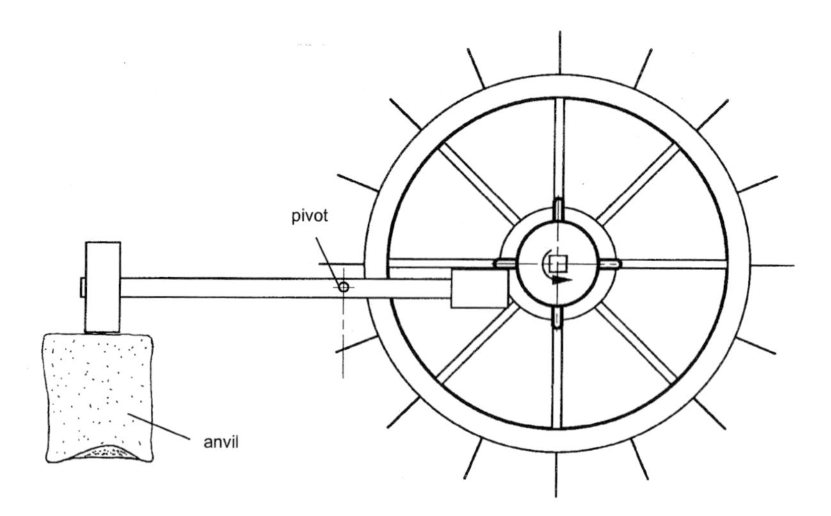

94 *Schematic operation of an undershot water wheel-powered trip hammer (not to scale, surrounding support structure not shown)*

It seems a logical progression that milling stones could also be used to grind and finish iron objects (although it is not suggested there was simultaneous use for food and iron production). Such a grinding stone could be used in two orientations, either with a vertical axis, driven as a mill stone (**85**), or with a horizontal axis, which could be turned directly by a horizontal axis water wheel or even a hand-operated crank. What is particularly interesting to our argument is that the drive mechanism which Blagg (1976: 169) proposes for the lathe would serve equally well as a grinding stone, needing only a rest to aid the operator as he held the work piece against the wheel (**96**). Preliminary experimental work by the author has found that use of a rotating wet stone (in this instance a treadle-operated horizontal axis) could finish a *gladius* in five hours (as compared with the 30 hours mentioned above), an improvement of factor six.

Discussion of the use of water power

The sections above have shown how by simple transfer of the technology of water-powered grain mills which the Romans possessed, a whole range of iron-production activities might have been conducted. These processes include ore breaking or stamping, ore milling and the use of the trip hammer to either break ore or assist in forging work. Davis (1935: 49) and Healy (1978: 194) both mention (and discount as without evidence) the use of water-powered bellows in smelting.

Cleere and Crossley (1985: 72) note in their discussion of the Bardown settlement which is bisected by the river Limden (**2**) that:

> Most of the Roman sites in the Weald have been located through the remains of their slag heaps. These often lie in the beds of small rivers, and this has given rise to the view that the Roman ironmakers were making use of water

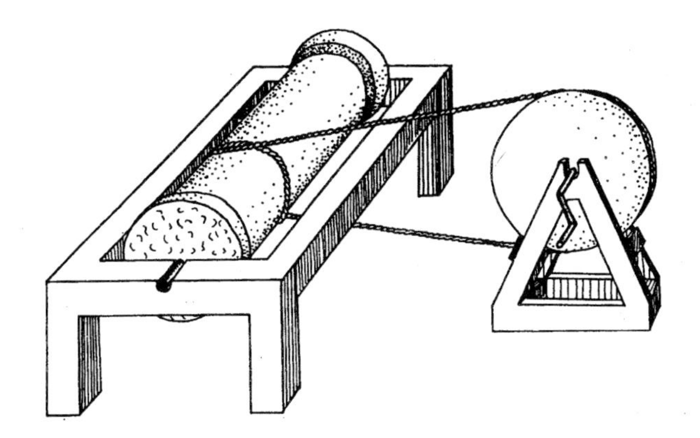

95 *Roman stonemason's lathe.*
After Blagg 1976: 169

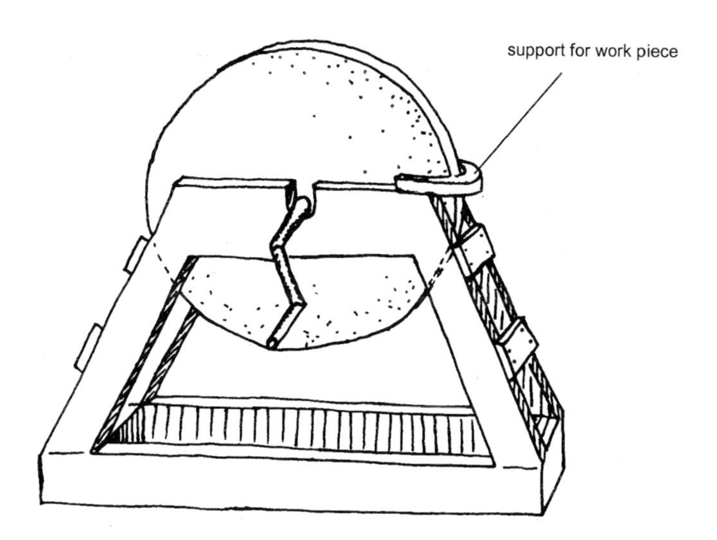

96 *Grinding wheel based on the lathe drive (***95***)*

> power in some form. In fact the relationship between the slag heaps and streams depends upon the fact that these small streams often follow geological faults between the Ashdown Sand and the ore-bearing Wadhurst clay. They cut down through the soft overlying clays in the latter to the harder iron stone deposits.

Whilst this may well be the case for the Bardown site (a 'stream' would be unlikely to provide enough power for an effective water wheel unless a system of damming was employed), the work of Landels (1978), and more recently Lewis (1997), suggests that the proposal of the more extensive Roman use of water power should now be given more attention.

Without more evidence it is dangerous to speculate as to the extent of the use of mechanical tools in the iron industry. It is impossible to know how many Roman iron making sites used any or all of these devices; in many cases the level of production may have been too small to justify the expense, or there may simply have been no suitable supply of water. However, it is argued that where expedient, and where the appropriate water supply (stream/river) was to hand, the Romans could easily have employed this technology to greatly improve their output. It important that one should be alive to the possibilities of the use of mechanical processing (and other techniques) to assist in iron artefact production.

EPILOGUE

I hope that this book has taken the reader inside the Roman iron-making world and shown what a complicated and difficult task it was to transform the iron ore into the finished artefact. I have highlighted the many different skills which were required, and indicated how much material would have been consumed in the process. The experimental work reported suggests that the huge amount of time required to produce so many weapons by accepted methods of production is unrealistic, and that there was a level of technology in existence that is far in advance of the current views. Many areas, such as the use of enclosed hearths for bloomsmithing and aspects of water power, are in need of much more detailed investigation. I have always maintained we should not say 'the Romans didn't have . . . ': instead we should say, 'they may have had, we just haven't found it yet'.

* * * *

It is evening now and our Roman blacksmith has finished his day's work. He has put his tools away and as he makes to leave his workshop he stops in the door and looks out over the hills. He likes this time of the year, when the evenings are long and the western sky turns to a fiery red; he thinks, not for the first time, 'The sky is the colour of my iron when I bring it to life. I can make iron into almost anything, yes, it's amazing stuff, this iron for the Eagles'.

GLOSSARY

Annealing Heating steel to a high temperature (red hot) and holding at this temperature for a time, followed by slow cooling. This renders the steel in the softest possible condition and relieves the stress (see chapter 8).

Anvil Large (usually) iron mass on which the blacksmith conducts forging operations (see chapter 4 and **10**).

Aquilifer A standard bearer (see **25**).

Auxiliaries Specialists in certain types of weapons that were not suitable for the style of fighting the legionaries of the heavy infantry were trained in. Examples include archers and cavalrymen (see **colour plates 15, 21**).

Bar A length of iron forged to a cross-section, (round, square, rectangular etc.), suitable to be forged into artefacts.

Barsmithing The process of forging a bar from a consolidated billet of iron.

Bick The tapered end on an anvil (see **10c**).

Billet A block of purified iron with only a small quantity of slag present.

Blank A section of metal roughly shaped to the form of the finished item.

Bloom A mass of unrefined wrought iron with large quantities of entrapped slag and voids in the structure. The product of the bloomery process.

Bloomsmithing Consolidation of the bloom to a workable billet of iron.

Caligae Roman legionary hob-nail boots.

Carburising See case hardening.

Case hardening A method of hardening the surface of a metal while keeping the interior soft. This is usually accomplished by heating the metal while it is in contact with a carbon rich material, and holding it at this temperature for several hours (see steeling or cementation).

Cast iron Iron containing 2-5% carbon. It is a soft brittle material suitable for casting, but not for forging.

Catapult The Roman army's mechanical artillery, shooting bolts (*catapultae*) or stones (*ballistae*) (see **colour plates 16 and 17**). They derived their power from two torsion rope springs, usually made from animal sinew, which were mounted in frames of wood with metal plating and fittings (iron or bronze). The later improved design of bolt-shooter (*manuballista* and *carroballista*) used all-metal frames.

Cementation (Steeling) A process used for carburising soft iron bars to make steel. The bars are heated for several days in contact with carbon.

Cementite One of the micro-structures of steel (see **81f**).

Cold chisel A chisel for cutting metal that is in the cold condition.

Cold working Deformation experienced by metal at room temperature.

Conductores Assistants of the provincial procurator; men of social standing e.g. *equites* (see chapter 2).

Corvée An obligation to perform gratuitous labour for a *conductor* or provincial *procurator* (see chapter 2).

Cross pien hammer A hammer with one flat face and one rounded face (see chapter 5).

Decarburisation Loss of carbon from steel (see chapter 8).

Direct method Iron produced in the solid state (see chapter 4).

Dolabrae A type of pick axe use by legionaries (see **71**).

Drawing down	The process where the cross-section of a bar is reduced by heating and hammering. The length of the bar increases correspondingly (see chapter 5).
Drifting	A process carried out after punching to bring a hole to an accurate size and shape. The drift is a piece of hard steel forged to a taper (see chapter 5).
Equites	Members of the equestrian rank.
Fabrica	A factory (often for armaments).
Ferrite	Pure iron. Ferrite is the principal constituent of steel.
Finery	Where the first stage of converting cast iron into wrought iron is carried out.
Fining	The process of converting cast iron to steel (see chapter 8).
Flatter	Similar to a hammer, but held and struck with a sledge hammer to smooth out surface irregularities in the bar (see chapter 5).
Flux	Substance mixed with or applied to metal surface to promote fusion.
Fire welding (forge welding)	The process in which two pieces of iron are heated to white heat and hammered together, thus causing them to fuse (see chapter 5).
Forging	Shaping metal by striking with a hammer.
Form tools	Made in pairs that are the reverse shape of the finished product. A blank of hot metal is placed between them and struck with a heavy force, thus forming the desired shape.
Fullering	Metal is placed between two shaped tools that are struck with a hammer; this decreases the cross-section and increases the length (see chapter 5).
Gangue	Unwanted mineral.
Gladius	A Roman legionary sword.
Haematite	Iron oxide ore (Fe_2O_3).

Hardening Steel is heated to a suitable temperature depending on carbon content (870°C for 0.2%C to 760°C for 1.0%C), and is then rapidly cooled by quenching it in water or oil. The resulting hardness will depend on the original carbon content of the steel.

Head Height by which water may fall to provide useful work.

Hot set Blacksmith's chisel used for cutting metal in the hot condition (red heat and above) (see chapter 5).

Immunes Legionary craftsmen exempt from some duties.

Indirect method Production of iron extracted from the ore by heating to melting point (see chapter 4).

Lapping Use of abrasive medium to bring work to finished size (see chapter 5).

Leat Man-made channel to convey water to a water wheel.

Legionary Roman infantry soldier.

Limonite Iron (oxyhydroxide) ore (FeOOH).

Lorica hamata Chain mail (see **20**, **colour plates 15**, **23**, **24**).

Lorica segmentata Laminated (plate) armour (see **21**, **colour plate 22**).

Lorica squamata Scale armour (see **22**).

Mandril, also **mandrel** A metal rod round which other metal items are forged to shape.

Manuballista A type of torsion spring catapult (see **colour plate 16**).

Martinsite A very hard steel microstructure.

Normalising Process for the removal of internal stresses (see chapter 8).

Pearlite A mixture of iron and iron carbide (iron and carbon) (see **81a**).

Pein (also **peen**) **end of a hammer** One face of a hammer head that is shaped to perform a special task, i.e. a ball for making hemispherical indentations in the surface of a piece of metal.

Piled wrought iron — Wrought iron is rolled into strips, then cut into short lengths which are built up into a pile, placed into a furnace called a balling furnace and heated until the strips fuse. At this point it is removed and welded under a power hammer. The quality of the iron is determined by how many times this process is repeated.

Pilum — A javelin with long slender head (see chapter 7 and **20, 21, colour plate 22**).

Plastic condition — When a metal is in its most malleable condition.

Plumbata — A short lead-weighted javelin used at close range, thrown underarm (see chapter 7).

Prefectures — Large areas under the control of a Prefect (see chapter 2).

Procurator — Officer in control of a district who exercised considerable powers of jurisdiction – usually *equites* or freedmen who held the post as part of a civil service career.

Publicani — Members of the *equites* who undertook state contracts.

Punching — A punch is driven through metal to create a hole of the same shape (see also drifting).

Quenching — Rapid cooling of hot steel to produce a hardening effect (see chapter 8).

Roasting — The ore is dried to prepare it for smelting; in the case of iron carbonate roasting reduces it to iron oxide (see chapter 4).

Scorpio — A term for the smallest sizes of bolt-shooter (see p.78) (see **colour plate 16).**

Scutum — A Roman legionary's shield (see **20**).

Set — See hot set.

Siderite — Iron carbonate ore ($FeCO_3$).

Slag — Unwanted waste material – a by-product from the ore during smelting.

Smelting	The process of extracting the iron from the ore (see chapter 4).
Steel	An alloy of pure iron and carbon. Steels containing more than 0.3% carbon can be flame hardened.
Steeling	A process by which wrought iron is converted into steel by packing the iron with carbon in a container and heating it for long periods. The carbon is absorbed into the wrought iron, thus converting it to steel.
Stress raiser	A point in a material where stresses are concentrated and where it will fracture, i.e. at a sharp corner, a sharp change of section, or a slag inclusion.
Striker	An assistant who stands opposite the blacksmith and wields a heavy sledge hammer.
Stylus **(**pl. ***styli*****)**	A writing instrument used for inscribing on wax tablets.
Swaging	Metal is worked to the desired shape by a series of blows from a hammer onto a pair of suitably shaped dies (see chapter 5).
Taxa	A biological category (e.g. species or name).
Tang	The part of a tool or weapon which goes into the haft or handle.
Tempering	Hardened steels are brittle. The brittleness is removed (at the expense of some of the hardness) by heating the steel to between 210–330°C, then quenching it in oil or water.
Trootsite	A hard steel microstructure.
Tuyère	A nozzle for a blast of air.
Upsetting	Metal is heated and forged in such a way that the length decreases and the cross-section increases (see chapter 5).
Vecus	A civilian settlement adjacent to a Roman military camp.
Wrought iron	The end product of the bloomery process. The structure is iron with typically 0.04% carbon and 0.2% slag. It is ductile and malleable.

Appendix

Museums containing Roman metalwork in the United Kingdom

Arbeia Roman Fort and Museum, Baring Street, South Shields, Tyne and Wear, NE33 2BB
Tel: +44 (0)191 456 1396
www.twmuseums.org.uk/arbeia

British Museum, Great Russell Street, London, WC1B 3DG
Tel: +44 (0)207 323 8000
www.britishmuseum.ac.uk

Cambridge University Museum of Archaeology & Anthropology, Downing Street, Cambridge, CB2 3DZ
Tel: +44 (0)1223 337733/333516
www.cumaa.archanth.cam.ac.uk

Chesterholm Museum, Vindolanda Trust, Bardon Mill, Hexham, Northumberland, NE47 7JN
Tel: +44 (0)1434 344277; Fax: +44 (0)1434 344060
www.vindolanda.com

Clayton Collection Museum, Chesters Roman Fort, Chollerford, Humshaugh, Haxham, Northumberland, NE46 4EP
Tel: +44 (0)1434 681379
www.english-heritage.org.uk

Colchester Castle Museum, Castle Park, Colchester, Essex, CO1 1TJ
Tel: +44 (0)1206 282939
www.colchestermuseums.org.uk/castle/castle_index.html

Corinium Museum, Park Street, Cirencester, Gloucester, GL7 2BX
Tel: +44 (0)1285 655611
www.cotswold.gov.uk

Corbridge Roman Site Museum, Corbridge, Northumberland, NE45 5NT
Tel: +44 (0)1434 633168; Fax: +44 (0)1434 632349
www.englishheritage.org.uk

Doncaster Museum and Art Gallery, Chequer Road, Doncaster, DN1 2AE
Tel: +44 (0)1302 734293
www.doncaster.gov.uk

Dorset County Museum, High West Street, Dorchester, Dorset, DT1 1XA
Tel: +44 (0)1305 262735
www.dorset.museum.chara.net

Gloucester City Museum and Art Gallery, Brunswick Road, Gloucester, GL1 1HP
Tel: +44 (0)1452 524131
www.gloucester.gov.uk/citymuseum

Great North Museum: Hancock, Barras Bridge, Newcastle upon Tyne NE2 4PT
Tel: (0)1912 226765
www.twmuseums.org.uk/greatnorthmuseum

Grosvenor Museum, 27 Grosvenor Street, Chester, Cheshire, CH1 2DD
Tel: +44 (0)1244 402008
www.worldserver.pipex.com/chestercc.htmls/museum.htm

Hunterian Museum, The University, Glasgow, G12 8QQ
Tel: +44 (0)141 3304221
www.hunterian.gla.ac.uk

Lincoln City and County Museum, 12 Friar's Lane, Lincoln, LN2 5AL
Tel: +44 (0)1522 530401

The Lunt Roman Fort, Coventry Road, Baginton. Contact: the Herbert Art Gallery and Museum, Jordan Well, Coventry, CV1 5QP
Tel: +44 (0)24 76832565
www.coventrymuseums.org.uk

Museum of London, London Wall, London, EC2Y 5HN
Tel: +44 (0)207 600 3699

National Museum of Scotland, Queens Street, Edinburgh, Scotland,
Tel: +44 (0)131 225 7534
www.nms.ac.uk

Peterborough City Museum and Art Gallery, Priestgate, Peterborough, Cambridgeshire, PE1 1LF
Tel: +44 (0)1733 343329

Roman Baths Museum, Pump Rooms, Stall Street, Bath, BA1 1LZ
Tel: +44 (0)1225 477774
www.romanbaths.co.uk

Roman Legionary Museum, High Street, Caerleon, Gwent, NP6 1AE
Tel: +44 (0)1633 423134; Fax: +44 (0)1633 422869

Rowley's House Museum, Barker Street, Shrewsbury, Shropshire, SY1 1QH
Tel: +44 (0)1743 361196
www.shrewsburymuseums.com

Segedunum Roman Fort, Baths & Museum, Buddle Street, Wallsend NE28 6HR
Tel: +44 (0)1912 369347
www.twmuseums.org.uk/segedunum

Senhouse Roman Museum, The Battery, Sea Brows, Maryport, Cumbria, CA15 6JD
Tel: +44 (0)1900 816168

Somerset County Museum, Taunton Castle, Castle Green, Taunton, Somerset, TA1 4AA
Tel: +44 (0)1823 320200
www.somerset.gov.uk/museums

Trimontium Trust exhibition at the Corn Exchange, The Square, Melrose. Contact: The Trimontium Trust, Cockleroi, Newstead, Melrose, TD6 9DE
Tel: +44 (0)1896 822651; Fax: +44 (0)1896 822522

Tullie House Museum, Castle Street, Carlisle, CA3 8TP
Tel: +44 (0)1228 534781

Verulamium Museum, St Michaels, St Albans, Hertfordshire, AL3 4SW
Tel: +44 (0)1727 819339

Wiltshire Museum, 41 Long Street, Devizes, Wiltshire, SN10 1NS
Tel: +44 (0)1727 751810
www.stalbansmuseums.org.uk

Yorkshire Museum, Museum Gardens, York, YO1 2DR
Tel: +44 (0)1904 551800
www.york.gov.uk

Bibliography

Aiano, A.R. (1975) *The Roman iron and steel industry at the time of the Empire.* MA Dissertation, University of Aberystwyth.

Aiano, A.R. (1977) Romano-British ironworking sites, a Gazetteer. *J. Historical Metallurgy Society* 11/2, 72-82.

Aitchison, L. (1960) *A history of metals.* London: MacDonald and Evans.

Angus, N.S., Brown, G.T. & Cleere, H.F. (1962) The iron nails from the legionary fortress at Inchtuthil, Perthshire. *J. Iron and Steel Inst.* 200, 956-68.

Biek, L. (1963) *Archaeology and the microscope: the scientific examination of archaeological evidence.* London: Butterworth Press.

Bishop, M.C. & Coulston, J.C.N. (1993) *Roman military equipment* London: B.T. Batsford.

Blagg, T.F.C. (1976) Tools and techniques of the Roman stonemason in Britain. *Britannia* 7, 152-72.

Blunden, J. (1975) *The mineral resources of Britain.* London: Hutchinson.

Brailsford, J.W. (1962) *Hod Hill antiquities from Hod Hill in the Durden collection.* London: The trustees of the British Museum.

Brommer, F. (1978) *Hephaistos – der Schmiedegott in der Antiken Kunst.* Mainz an Rhein: Verlag Philipp von Zabern.

Burford, A. (1969) *The temple builders at Epidaurus.* Liverpool.

Bushe - Fox J.P. (1914). Excavations on the site of the Roman Town at Wroxeter Shropshire in 1912. 16. fig 8 no30

Cleere, H.F. (1970) *The Romano-British industrial site at Bardown, Wadhurst.* Chichester: Sussex Archaeological Society, Occasional Paper 1.

Cleere, H.F. (1971) Ironmaking in a Roman furnace. *Britannia.* 2, 203-17.

Cleere, H.F. (1972) The classification of early iron smelting furnaces. *The Antiquaries Journal* 52 (1), 8-23.

Cleere, H.F. (1976) Operating parameters for Roman iron works. *Bulletin of the Institute of Archaeology* 13, 233-46.

Cleere, H.F. & Crossley, D. (1985) *The iron industry of the Weald.* Leicester: Leicester University Press.

Coghlan, H.H. (1977) *Notes on prehistoric and early iron in the Old World*. Oxford: Occasional Papers on Technology No. 8 (2), Oxford: Pitt Rivers Museum.

Connolly, P. (1981) *Greece and Rome at war.* Macdonald & Co (Publishers) Ltd under the Black Cat imprint.

Cotterell, B. & Kamminga, J. (1992) *Mechanics of pre-industrial technology.* Cambridge: Cambridge University Press.

Craddock, P.T. (1995) *Early metal mining and production.* Edinburgh: Edinburgh University Press.

Crew, P. (1991) The experimental production of prehistoric bar iron. *J. Historical Metallurgy Society,* 25/1, 21-36.

Crew, P. (1998) Laxton revisited: a first report on the 1998 excavations. *J. Historical Metallurgy Society,* 32/2, 49-53.

Curle, J. (1911) *A Roman frontier post and its people: the fort of Newstead in the parish of Melrose, Glasgow.* Glasgow: James Maclehouse and Sons.

Davies, O. (1935) *Roman mines in Europe.* Oxford: Oxford University Press.

Drescher, H. (1981) Untersuchung des Riggeflechtes aus Sörup I, Grab K10, in *K. Raddatz, Sörup I,* Otta Bücher NF46 Karl Wacholtz Verlag, Neumünster 186-90.

Engelhard, C. (1866) *Denmark in the early iron age illustrated by the recent discoveries in the peat mosses of Slesvig.* London: Williams and Norgate.

Fletcher, A. (1975) Primitive bloomeries in Mayfield. *Sussex Notes and Queries* 14.9, 173.

Forbes, R.J. (1956) Metallurgy, in *A History of Technology,* ed. C. Singer *et al.* Oxford: Oxford University Press vol. 2, 41-80.

Frere, S.S. & Wilkes, J.J. (1989) *Strageath: excavations within the Roman fort. 1973 to 1986.* London: Society for the Promotion of Roman Studies.

Fulford, M.G. & Allen, J.R.L. (1992) Iron-making at the Chesters villa, Woolaston, Gloucestershire: Survey and Excavation 1987-91. *Britannia.* 23, 159-215.

Fulford, M. Sim, D. and Doig. A, (2004) "In Defence of Rome: the study of Roman Ferrous Armour from Northern Britain. Journal of Archaeological Science, forthcoming.

Fulford, M. Sim, D. and Doig. A, (2004) The production of Roman Ferrous Armour: a metallographic survey of material from Britain, Denmark, and Germany and its implications. Journal of Roman Archaeology, USA. Forth coming.

Gaitzsch, W. (1980) *Eiserne Romische Werkzeuge.* BAR International Series 78. Oxford: British Archaeological Reports.

Gilmore, B.J.J. & Tylecote, R.F. (1986) *The metallography of early ferrous edged tools and edged weapons.* BAR British Series 155. Oxford: British Archeological Reports.

Gordon, J.E. (1968) *The new science of strong materials.* New York: Walker & Co.

Griffiths, W.B. (1995) Experiments with *plumbatae. The Arbeia Journal* 4, 1-12

Hanson-Davies, V. (1989) *The western way of war.* New York: Alfred A. Knopf.

Healy, J.F. (1978) *Mining and metallurgy in the Greek and Roman world.* London: Thames and Hudson.

Higgins, R.A. (1983) *Engineering metallurgy: 1 applied physical metallurgy.* Fifth edition, first edition 1957. London: Hodder and Stoughton.

Honeycombe, R.W.K. (1981) *Steels – microstructures and properties.* Edward Arnold.

Jones, B. & Mattingly, D. (1990) *An atlas of Roman Britain*. London: Blackwell.

Kaminski, J. (1996) *The environmental implications of Romano-British iron production in the Weald*. Ph.D. thesis, University of Reading.

Krapp, H. (1987) Metallurgical aspects concerning two iron blocks of Roman origin. *Radex-Rundschau* 1, 315-30.

Landels, J.G. (1978) *Engineering in the ancient world*. Berkley & Los Angeles: University of California Press.

Lang, J. & Ager, B. (1989) Swords of the Anglo-Saxon and Viking periods in the British Museum: A Radiographic Study, in S.C. Hawkes ed. *Weapons and Warfare in Anglo-Saxon England*. Monograph No. 21. Oxford: Oxford University Committee for Archaeology.

Lewis, M.J.T. (1997) *Millstone and hammer: the origins of water power.* Hull: University of Hull Press.

Mack, I., McDonnell, G., Murphy, S., Andrews, P. & Wardley, K. (2000) Liquid steel in Anglo-Saxon England. *J. Historical Metallurgy Society* 34.2, 87-96.

Mallalieu, H. (1996) (ed) *Antiques Road Show A-Z of Antiques Hunting*, Boxtree Ltd.

Manning, H.W. (1976) *Catalogue of Romano British ironwork in the Museum of Antiquities Newcastle-upon-Tyne*. Newcastle: University of Newcastle Press.

Manning, H.W. (1977) Blacksmith's tools from Waltham Abbey, Essex, in *Aspects of early metallurgy* ed. W.A. Oddy 87-96.

Manning, W.H. (1985) *Catalogue of the Romano-British Iron Tools, Fittings and Weapons in the British Museum*. London: British Museum Publications Ltd.

Marsden, E.W. (1971) *Greek and Roman Artillery. Technical Treatis*. Oxford: Clarendon Press.

Mather, A.S. (1990) *Global forest resources*. London.

Mighall, T. & Chambers, F.M. (1989) The environmental impact of iron-working at Bryn y Castell hillfort, Merioneth. *Archaeology Wales* 29, 17-21.

Millet, M. (1990) *The Romanization of Britain: an essay in archaeological interpretation*. Cambridge: Cambridge University Press.

Ohlaver, H. (1939) *Der Germanische schmied und sein Wekeug.* Leipzig.

Olson, S.D. (1991) Firewood and charcoal in classical Athens. *Hesperia* 60, 411-20.

Pietsch, M. (1984) *Die Romishen Eisenwerkezeuge von Saalburg, Feldburg und Zugmantel*. Saalburg Jahrbuch 39.

Pleiner, R. (1962) *Staré Europské Kováøství* (Early European blacksmithing). Prague: Czechoslovak Academy of Sciences.

Pleiner, R. (2000) *Iron in archaeology – the European bloomery smelters*. Prague: Archeologicky ústav AV ÈR.

Rackham, O. (1983) *Ancient woodland: its history, and uses in England*. London: Edward Arnold.

Richmond, I.A. (1961) Roman Timber Building in Studies, in *Building History* ed. Jope, E.M. London 15-26.

Robertson, A., Scott, M. & Keppie, L. (1975) *Bar Hill: A Roman fort and its finds.* BAR British Series 16. Oxford: British Archaeological Reports.

Sherlock, D. (1979) *Plumbatae* – a note on the method of manufacture, in M.W.C. Hassall, & R.I. Ireland (eds) *De Rebus Bellicis*, BAR int. 63, Oxford: British Archaeological Reports.

Sim, D. (1992) Some misunderstandings concerning the use of blacksmiths tongs. *J. Historical Metallurgy Society* 26, 63-5.

Sim, D.N. (1992). The Manufacture of disposable weapons for the Roman army. J.R.M.E. 3.

Sim, D. (1994) *Beyond the bloom; bloom refining and artefact production in Roman Britain.* PhD Thesis, University of Reading.

Sim, D. (1995) Experiments to examine the manufacturing techniques used to make *plumbatae. The Arbeia Journal* 4, 13-19.

Sim, D. (1997a) Experiments to produce a Roman styli by forging and machining. *Antiquity* 71, 274

Sim, D. (1997b) Roman chain mail: experiments to reproduce the techniques of manufacture. *Britannia* XXVIII, 359-71.

Sim, D. (1998a) *Beyond the Bloom.* BAR International Series 725. Oxford: British Archaeological Reports.

Sim, D. (1998b) The reproduction of a Roman hammer. *Tools and Trades History Society* (TATHS) Newsletter 60, Spring 1998, 17-24.

Sim, D. & Ridge, I.M.L. (2000) Examination of a plane blade from Vindolanda. *J. Historical Metallurgy Society* 34.2, 77-82.

Sim, D. N (2012) *Plumbata: Rome's hail of leaden death.* Kindle Books. London

Spechtshart, H. (1488) *Flores Musicae.* Strasbourg.

Straker, E. (1931) *Wealden iron.* London: Bell & Sons Ltd.

Thomsen, R., Naumann, F.K. & Pliner, R. (1971) *Metallographische Untersuchungen an wikingerzeitlichen Eisenbarren aus Haithabu* Berichte über die Ausgrabunger, in Haithabu, Bericht 5. K. Schietzel (ed.). Neümunster: Karl Wachholz Verlag. 100-109.

Thomsen, E.G. & Thomsen H.H. (1974) Early wire drawing through dies. *Transactions of the ASME: Journal of Engineering for Industry* Nov. Series B. 96 (1), 1216-21.

Thomsen, E.G. & Thomsen H.H. (1976) Drawing solid wires through soft dies in antiquity. *Transactions of the ASME. Journal of Engineering for Industry,* Paper No.75-WA/ Prod-6. 1-5.

Tylecote, R.F. (1976) *A history of metallurgy in the British Isles.* London: The Metals Society.

Tylecote, R.F. (1986) *The prehistory of metallurgy in the British Isles.* Dorking: Alard.

Tylecote, R.F. (1987) *The early history of metallurgy in Europe.* London: Longman.

Tylecote, R.F., Austin, J.N., & Wraith, A.E. (1971) The mechanism of the bloomery process in shaft furnaces. *J. Iron Steel Inst.* 209, 342-63.

Watts, M. (2000) *Water and wind power.* Great Britain: Shire Publications.

Wheeler, R.E.M. (1939) *Report on the excavations at Lydney Park.* Soc. Antiquaries of London, Report no. 9.

Wilkins A. (1995) Reconstructing the *cheiroballistra. Journal of Roman Military Equipment Studies* 6 (1995).

Wilkins A. and Morgan L. (2000) *Scorpio* and *cheiroballistra. JRMES* 11 (2000).

Wilkins A. (2003) *Roman Artillery. Great Britain.* Shire Books.

Wilkins A. and Morgan L. (2012) A suggested reconstruction of Vitruvius' stone-thrower. *JRMES New Series* (forthcoming).

Williams, A.R. (1977) Roman arms and armour: a technical note. *J. Archaeological Science* 1 (4), 77–87.

Zell, M. (1994) *Industry in the countryside: Wealden society in the sixteenth century.* Cambridge: Cambridge University Press.

Index

Page references in **bold** indicate figures and/or relevant text on these pages